Mr Bigstuff and the
Goddess of Charm

Fiona Sax Ledger lives in North London with her daughter.
They have another home and more family in Uganda. She
began her writing career reporting on the performance
of back-hoe loaders and concrete mixers in West Africa.
Mr Bigstuff and the Goddess of Charm is her first book.

FIONA SAX LEDGER

Mr Bigstuff and the Goddess of Charm

PARTIES, CARS, LOVE
& AMBITION
SOUTH OF THE SAHARA

PICADOR

First published 2000 by Picador

This edition published 2001 by Picador
an imprint of Macmillan Publishers Ltd
25 Eccleston Place, London SW1W 9NF
Basingstoke and Oxford
Associated companies throughout the world
www.macmillan.com

ISBN 0 330 37438 9

1 3 5 7 9 8 6 4 2

A CIP catalogue record for this book is available from
the British Library.

Typeset by SetSystems Ltd, Saffron Walden, Essex
Printed and bound in Great Britain by
Mackays of Chatham plc, Chatham, Kent

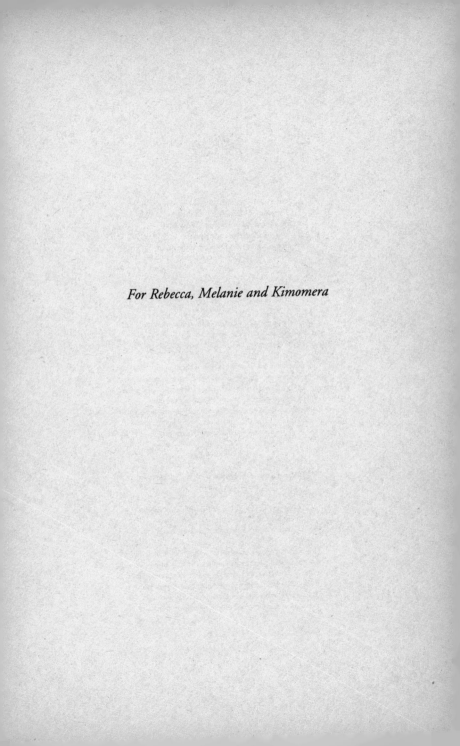

For Rebecca, Melanie and Kimomera

Contents

❧❧❧

Preface

∿∿

This is a book of encounters which take place in parlours, shops and offices, hotel bedrooms and government corridors. They date from the last ten years of the cold war to the present. During this time, I have worked both on my own account and for the African Service of the BBC World Service. Sometimes I make radio documentaries, sometimes I direct plays, sometimes I teach people how to record sound. The people I meet, although occasionally angry and frustrated, are, on the whole, winning through. There are few lions, hippos, refugee camps or hungry people. This is a book of heroes and villains, pen-pushers and artists. They come from a continent which, in western eyes, is distinguished by its tyrants, victims and disasters. The view is not from a light aircraft, scanning the land for smoking fires, explosions and devastation. The view is from the ground; of course it's my view and as biased as the next person's, but it's close up.

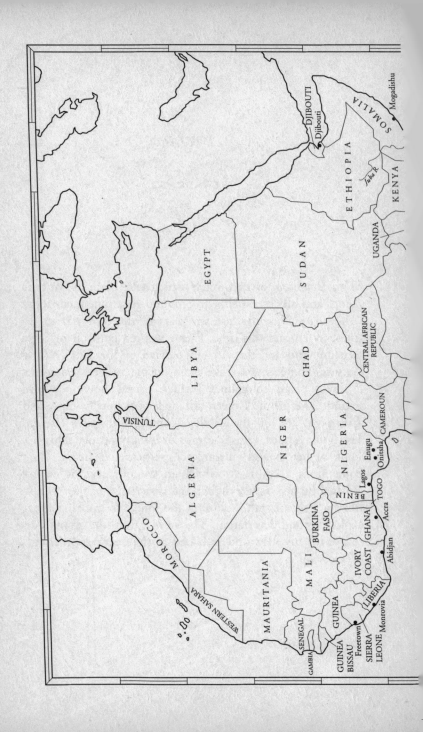

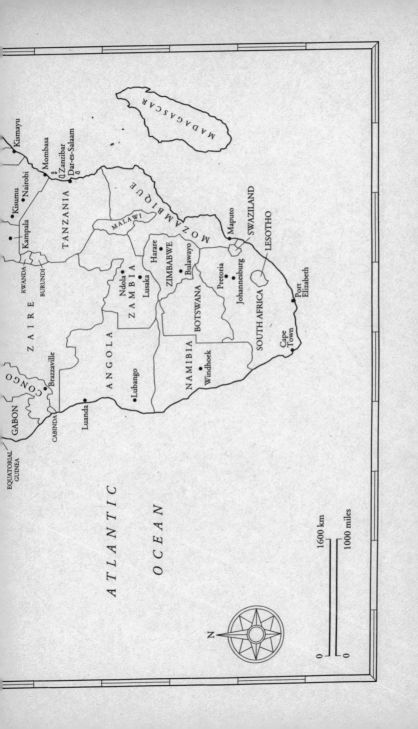

ONE

Whose Party Is It Anyway?

~∘∾∘~

COLONIAL RELICS

It is October 1980. Kaduna, Northern Nigeria, almost twenty years to the day after independence. But the scent of colonialism still hangs heavy in the air. The United Africa Company (UAC) guest house has not changed much since colonial rule, I imagine. The same tables, chairs, beds and mosquito nets; in nearby buildings are many of the same offices which existed before independence, with the same typewriters, invoice pads and revolving date stamps; and there are photographic studios still standing by to capture the public and personal achievements of municipal life. Inside the guest house all is orderly and quiet. My fellow guest is an accountant from England; he has just been made redundant. The textile mills of UAC are grinding to a halt, unable to compete with the Far East and Holland. As Philip, the accountant, has pointed out, the figures just don't add up and with that final act of reckoning he has done himself out of a job. He folds his heavily starched and ironed napkin for the last time – it'll be serviettes back home or nothing at all. He has been in Nigeria seven years – all his working life, and he doesn't know what to do next. He is gloomy and reserved. I would like to say to him, 'Cheer up, Philip, you'll find a job, a fiancée, a house with a proper garage door and peace of mind in the home counties. This will all seem a dream quite soon. You'll have a Nigerian successor, who'll be bullied and bribed. He'll get frustrated like you, but he'll relish the position more than you, and he'll never be homesick.' I can't say any of that because Philip is not companionable and would only be embarrassed if I tried to talk to him with any degree of intimacy.

We have just finished a meal of lamb chop served with Bisto gravy and overcooked vegetables; I imagine it comes straight from a between-the-wars edition of Mrs Beeton – the section on winter menus, p.1576, perhaps? But that's enough bad English cooking, now I want to eat a pawpaw; I've never eaten pawpaw before.

'I'd love a slice of pawpaw.' The old African steward limps towards me in starched white jacket, and inclines his head to hear better. It is so quiet that my voice can hardly cut through the stillness. 'Pawpaw, please.'

The old steward, who is also called Philip, frowns, fierce and disgusted; he enunciates with hard, old-fashioned vowels. 'There is treacle tart and custard, Madame.' (The French pronunciation is always used in Nigeria.) Outside, beyond the trees, the blue sky shimmers with heat.

Philip the accountant unfolds his napkin. 'I think I might be tempted by that.'

But it's not African, I think, though I daren't say it aloud. I want something African. But the steward makes it plain he won't be crossed with requests for humdrum African fruits. Treacle tart and custard it is.

We eat our pudding in silence. It would take an earth-quake to make Philip the accountant and me chum up, or even me and Philip the steward. An imam calls to prayer in the distance. I pity the steward for being such a colonial relic. He despises me for not being a proper Madame. Philip the accountant is wondering if he should buy some souvenirs

2

for his mum and dad – carvings and whatnot. They'll expect that, him having been in Africa; duty free won't do at all.

MAN THE GATES, THE PRESIDENT IS COMING

From north to east. Enugu. Poor neglected Enugu, punished along with the rest of the east for the Biafran War. But now things are beginning to look up in the east; while the mighty United Africa Company and their parent company, Unilever, are shifting from production to retail in the north, over in the east the Germans are setting up shop with a brand new Daimler-Benz factory. And the President of Nigeria is coming to the opening ceremony. This isn't just an example of German industrial might, this spells forgiveness for the Biafran War. The President is coming. The first Nigerian President to come to this region since the end of the war. And of course, the Germans are planning for it to be a perfect occasion. Everything is anticipated. Nothing will be left to chance. There's the Daimler-Benz security staff, there's the local police. There are even soldiers. But nobody told the Germans that in Nigeria it is the gods who decide who succeeds and who fails; total control can never be achieved.

The high point of the ceremony is supposed to be the appearance of the first Daimler-Benz truck ever manufactured in Nigeria, the first one off the assembly line, that is. But deadlines have been missed – crucial spare parts went missing at the port and never resurfaced – so a truck has to be flown in from Germany.

'You will not write that in your magazine,' commands one of the German managers. 'We want this occasion to be very fine, so you help us, ja?' whispers his colleague, urgent and lecherous.

A vast buffet has been laid out for the presidential entourage and the VIP guests. We wait and wait. As the

3

Germans grow more tense, the Nigerian security staff become more relaxed; policemen wander around hand in hand, quietly chatting. The firm's own security guards are more wary, but lean elegantly against the wall surveying the scene. Outside, energy levels are high; people are beginning to gather along the perimeter fence and gates, full of curiosity and yearning for the good things they know are inside. The Germans are getting a little more nervous. 'Hermann, please activate the guards,' calls the managing director. Hermann begins to harangue the guards; they listen, patient, solemn and gentle in their new uniform. The perimeter fence is beginning to bulge now in places, and people are scaling the gate. Every time someone reaches the top a security guard climbs up from the other side and pushes him down. The President is an hour and a half late. But suddenly the news ripples through: the President is coming. Yes, he really is coming. No, false alarm. The President is not coming. Not just yet. One young man has successfully climbed over the gate and is now being pushed back over it again, his legs ranging in all directions. One truth is evident, and it's a truth which nobody wants to confront: when the President comes through the gate, half of Enugu will come in with him.

A whine of outriders' sirens gets closer and closer. And despite viciously lashing out at the people surging forward, the guards are powerless to stop the rush for the gate, which has to be opened to let the entourage through. The car finally noses its way in, and that's it, the floodgates are open; over a hundred men, women and children pour through, braving a rain of blows from batons, whips and sticks. But the President is safe. The outriders provide an inner ring and he is hustled out of his car and into the main ceremony room without so much as the hem of his gown being tugged. He is now ready to salute the first Nigerian-made Daimler-

Benz truck to come off a Nigerian assembly line. Or rather the first Daimler-Benz truck assembled in Stuttgart, masquerading as a Daimler-Benz truck assembled in Nigeria, to come off the assembly line. The ceremonial room is sealed off by a mixture of presidential guards, Daimler-Benz guards and local policemen, each jostling to show their efficiency. Through a gap in their ranks I peep into the neighbouring room, where the buffet is laid out ... but not for long. Large ladies are taking off their headscarves and sweeping egg florentine, vol-au-vents and smoked salmon off the table and into their headgear. Small boys are piling rice into their T-shirts. Bigger boys are picking up piles of plates and carrying them out. Everyone works silently and methodically, with only the occasional bad-tempered jostle.

When the speeches and clapping are finally over the Germans lead the way proudly to the buffet room. The intruders have all gone – and so has all the food. The President pretends nothing has happened and gazes ahead vaguely, benign and polite. The Germans begin to shout at one another.

Kidnapped!

'Ah, so you need a lift, Ledger, to the airport?' says the old chief.

'Yes, please.' I have run out of naira notes again, and traveller's cheques are difficult to cash.

'We can do that.'

'Oh thank you, thank you.'

He has told me his life story, from selling matches on the streets of Enugu as a small boy to become a big businessman/trader; and now chairman of several large companies. He is a knight of the Order of St John.

'You must wait.'

I wait. To be dependent on the kindness of strangers has advantages and disadvantages. You'll probably never see them again, and they'll save you money. But you are at their mercy for the duration.

We set off to make the hundred-mile journey from Onitsha to Enugu. The chief pats my thigh. I cough. Another ten miles and he puts his arm round me. I am seized with embarrassment. I wriggle. He lets go and smiles serenely. We suddenly turn off the main road. Is it even worth asking where we are going? Bump, bump, bump, bump. Small children gaily skip after the car. We walk through a village and enter a compound. He can see I am doubtful. 'Come,' he gestures encouragingly. We visit a hut. Inside is a very old woman, shrivelled and bony. 'This is my mother.' I shake hands. She makes a sound, half sigh, half greeting. We go. Back in the car, the wrestling resumes. 'But now you have met my mother,' he says. An arm slides over my shoulder and old slim fingers search for the crest of my breast. I lurch forward, asking brightly, 'How much further to the airport?'

'Seventy miles.'

'When will we get there?'

'Tomorrow.'

'Tomorrow? But I want to catch a plane today.'

'I will take you tomorrow. You will stay in my guest house tonight.' The old chief looks sullen; he gazes out of the window. He doesn't mind a degree of skittishness, but he is beginning to get irritated, tired of being checked by me all the time. He is wearing a rather magnificent gown of broderie anglaise. And out of the vortex of anxiety and homesickness that has suddenly gripped me, a memory forms: my sister and I, at the dressmaker's, being fitted for summer dresses in broderie anglaise. It occurs to me for the first time that it's a very labour-intensive material: every little hole – and there are thousands of them – is embroidered. It certainly is a material fit for powerful Igbo chiefs, and perhaps even nicely brought up little English girls.

As swiftly as a first-night curtain, the sun falls below the horizon and night swallows us up. When the car stops outside his guest house, it is perfectly dark; a roar of crickets ebbs and flows from the shrubs and trees. I am tired.

Up the steps we go into a simply arranged room, with squidgy, Italian furniture and a big chandelier to mark status. He directs a steward to put my luggage and his luggage into one of the bedrooms. Now's a chance to make a non-verbal point. I retrieve my suitcase and lug it into a separate room. The old chief appears not to notice.

'First we break kola nuts as welcome.' (He realizes I am ignorant of the custom.)

He hands me a piece. For some reason I imagine it will be quite delicious. I crunch with my teeth. Yeech! My taste buds refuse to be educated. The kola is bitter; so bitter, it shrivels the inside of my mouth. I do my best. Munch, munch. There's salvation in sight, courtesy of the chief again.

'Let us drink champagne.'

A bottle of warm champagne is produced. I drink. I am thirsty, and desperate to get rid of the kola. The chief barks out more orders. From the corner of my eye I see my suitcase being removed from the second bedroom back into the first bedroom. The chief removes his top, revealing a huge, almost perfectly spherical expanse of belly.

I am suffused with embarrassment again, and for some reason think he might consider a plea for modesty.

'Don't you think you ought to put your top back on?'

'I can do what I like in my own home,' he says grimly. And more kindly, 'The champagne is good, you like it?'

'Oh yes.' I am anxious for us to agree on something.

He stretches. 'Now I shower and change, then I go for dinner with the President.'

I resolve not to wash. A dirty protest might keep him at bay. He returns from the bathroom, washed and groomed. He is wearing a pale blue damask gown, splendid and Henrician to a European's eyes, its massive shoulder wings and folds offset by a symmetrical chest panel heavily encrusted with silver embroidery.

'Goodbye, Ledger. I will see you at eleven p.m.'

'Goodbye, sir.' My heart is suddenly light. Of course, now he is going and I can escape, although where to is another matter. Perhaps I could find a hotel that would accept traveller's cheques? As he passes the threshold he calls to the two servants and issues instructions. Then he shouts for the driver and leaves. The two servants visit one room after another, locking the shutters of the windows as they go. They finally step out of the sitting room on to the porch outside, and with a brief backward glance in my direction – I am sitting anxiously on the oatmeal and leather sofa – they close the door, locking it behind them. My heart is heavy. I am a prisoner.

The chief is splendid, but old, and huge. I am just a wee lassie, with a nice boy at home who organizes long walks with an ordnance survey map, and makes me up compilation tapes of Tamla Motown greatest hits.

I finger my copy of *The Game of Love* by J. Abiakam (copyright reserved), newly purchased after some formidable haggling in Onitsha market. It is a useful compendium of advice, strategies and letter-outlines for dealing with that most vexatious of topics: relations between man and woman. I read a letter from Beatrice to her over-attentive suitor. If only Beatrice Dike could do the talking for me. She deals with her admirer, Eddy, so eloquently:

Dear Eddy Maduako,

I acknowledge the receipt of your letter dated the 4th April 1965, the contents were clearly understood. I will like to tell you some of my likes and dislikes. I don't like to read letters full up with immoral words. Don't address me 'My dear Sweet Heart', just write 'Dear Beatrice', it is okay.

Another thing is this, do not be writing to me very frequently. One letter in six months or in nine months is alright. I do not want anything to disturb my studies, and I am not interested in reading or writing letters always.

Eddy, I must be open to you. If you are trying to befriend me in a sinful way it will not be possible. This is the sole objectives of so many boys, which I am opposed to. I would like to befriend you on condition that you will always respect and keep the laws of God at all times.

My mother is educated and my father is a Ph.D. holder and they are good Christians. I want to follow their good style of life.

I will like to close till you reply. Be studious to make the next Christmas feast a joyous one. Convey my cordial salute to your friends and your well wishers. Wishing you the best of the season.

I am
Your dear
Beatrice Dike

Sweet Beatrice, she's got the right idea. But would she, I wonder, consider *fighting* for her honour? It isn't something I've ever had to resort to in my life. I do have a Swiss penknife, and I do have hairspray. But I really don't want to shed any blood.

I pace up and down, cursing the silly, winsome ways I adopted when I first met him, anxious as I was for an interview; if only I'd been more like a chap – hard, grim, forceful. I turn on the television. Wobbly camerawork pans across a great banqueting hall, full of men in huge gowns and ladies with head-ties as large as laundry baskets. The camera zooms in jerkily to settle on the face of the President. He is picking at his food, and as usual has a vague and slightly myopic expression on his face. The camera hops away from him, and lands on a panel of embroidery glinting in the television lights; curious, the camera crawls up the panel to reveal . . . the old chief; he is tucking into a huge pile of something with enthusiasm. I wish he could stay there behind the screen, in the box.

Eleven thirty p.m. A car draws up, spraying gravel. I am lying on the sofa with a towel stretched across my body. My suitcase is next to the sofa. This is it. The key turns in the lock. I pray to be good for the rest of my life, if only I don't have to . . . I close my eyes as the door opens. Footsteps draw near.

'What is this, Ledger? Why are you on the sofa? This is no good. You are my guest.'

I open one eye and then another. The old chief actually looks concerned. I start babbling, 'Well I just don't want to go to bed with you. I'm engaged, and . . . and I may be expecting a baby . . . and my fiancée would kill me.'

'Come, you share the bed with me, no sex. We talk.'

'Oh, all right then.'

I trot after him.

'Feel my manhood – it is big, but I can control myself.' He takes my hand; yes, there's no disputing the size and hardness of his manhood. As long as it stays where it is, I can live with it.

And so it does. The old chief is as good as his word. He puts on pyjamas, I keep my dress on. We spend the night together in his bed, with a fine Onitsha moon shining through an unshuttered window, talking about life, death, sin, the devil and the world.

MAKE WAY, MAKE WAY

Last day in Nigeria. Lagos. The Mainland Hotel, Ebutta Meta. I am sitting on my candlewick bedspread sorting out my business cards. I think I have enough information to write at least two articles for the mag: one on vehicle assembly in Nigeria, another on the best generator for a tropical site. There's a cursory knock at the door, and a porter barges in carrying expensive luggage. He's followed by a cheery Oga in full gown and hat.

'Good morning. Now this looks interesting.' He picks up the magazine I work for. 'These back-hoe loaders can really do the job. Do you sell them?'

'No, I work on the magazine.' By now more luggage is pouring in, and a perfectly formed young woman in a grey silk-jersey wraparound dress walks in lazily, on very high heels. Time now, I think, to state the obvious.

'Excuse me, but this is my room.'

'It is my room,' says the Oga crisply.

'No, it's mine. Hey!' The porter is now removing my luggage. 'Put that back.'

'Im no Madame's room. Madame no have room,' says the porter looking straight ahead. I follow him out of the room to get my luggage.

The young woman smirks and closes the door behind me.

Down in reception I demand an explanation, as they say.

'There is nothing we can do, Madame. It was a mistake. You have no booking.'

'I made the mistake – I forgot to bribe you when I booked the room, that was my mistake.' The man at reception turns away, appalled at the gross tactlessness of my remark. There's only one thing left to do now. I start to cry. The man at reception looks alarmed.

11

'Please, Madame, Lagos is a very big city. You will find another hotel.'

'But I don't want to move.' I begin to sob loudly. Guests turn to look. I provide an interesting spectacle. If Europeans had any one admirable quality – and that was debatable in post-colonial Africa – it was self-restraint, and stoicism in the face of adversity. I was letting the side down, and very noisily.

'Please, Madame, come into my office.' It was the Lebanese manager.

I begin to howl.

'Madame, we find you a room. It will be small and the air-conditioner – it's not working so well. Samuel, take Madame to room number thirteen.'

I nearly decline the offer but I am too tired, too tired to care about the green and grey slime oozing from the clanking air-conditioner and making streaks on the wall, too tired to care about the sagging bed and the unlucky number. This was a room for me to rest my weary head in, and that was what I did.

That night I dream of wet streets in London, of autumn leaves falling from those big town trees, brushing against my face, my arms, tickling them; in my sleep, I brush them away, again and again, but the leaves keep coming. The next morning I try to wake up, but my eyes see only a thread of light. My face feels thick, my hands are like paws. I squint at them: they have become paws – puffy paws, riddled with red bites. I have been bitten by a swarm of mosquitoes in the night. I inspect the window; there is a huge rent in the netting. I bet net-maintenance was more efficient under colonial rule.

DOWN WITH COLONIALISM

God bless our valiant mosquitoes
Which chased away our foes;
And saved our land from pirates' hand
Gave Africa a noble stand
To battle with our foes.

God bless those little tiny wings
With venom in their stings,
Which made our land the Whiteman's grave.
Our heritage from pirates save
With Africans as Kings.

God blew their little thready legs,
That gave the wings their treat,
To beat the pirates with their bags
Which made them look like human hags,
When bidding their retreat.

We thank them for the infectious bites
Which made the invaders mad;
The fever which each bite ignites
Were all protections of our rights
For which we're jolly glad.

Praise God from whom all blessings flow
And bless our mosquitoes
Praise those insects here below
Which chased the invaders down below
With itchings on their toes.

(An ode to the valiant mosquitoes
of West Africa by Sierra Leonean
radical I.T.A. Wallace Johnson, 1961)

. . . generally speaking, it is the detribalised native who responds best to communism, as he misses the narrow confines of tribal life and a leader on whom to bestow loyalty.
(Notes on the Aims, Strategy and Procedure of the Communists in Africa, 1.5.56, UK brief no. 31 (secret) Foreign & Colonial Office)

I.T.A. Wallace Johnson was one of those detribalized natives, a Krio of Sierra Leone, descended from freed slaves who returned to West Africa in the late eighteenth and early nineteenth century. He was not a communist but he visited the Soviet Union in the 1930s. He was a radical socialist, who believed that Sierra Leone should be independent. He was a great friend of the Jamaican socialist and one-time communist George Padmore, who sat briefly on Stalin's Central Committee before daring to quarrel with the great moustache. These were the men who planted the seeds of nationalism in Sierra Leone. I.T.A. Wallace Johnson died in the 1970s. By 1989 there were few left of his generation. Among the survivors was a man called Marcus Grant. I sent word that I wanted to meet him, and I received the reply that he would speak to me.

It is two o'clock and I am sitting on the edge of an old brown velveteen sofa. I have just swallowed my anti-malaria pill with the help of a bottle of warm Fanta. The floor is wooden, the symmetry of the floorboards broken up by neatly positioned hook carpets, and where the ceiling and wall meet is an overlay of intricate fretwork. There is a porch too. The design is American colonial. All around there are photos of African ladies in bustles holding fans, and gentlemen wearing thick, scratchy-looking, three-piece suits, their hair combed into obedient side partings with lavish helpings of pomade. This was new to me – Africans dressed as Europeans.

In Britain, black people from long ago are supposed to be exotically dressed, or maybe in chains. I wonder if the parents of the people in the photos started out in chains, or perhaps they were just born in servitude. They must have made some southern families rich on cotton, working for nothing. But despite the wretchedness of slavery, when they crossed the ocean to return to the continent of their ancestors, they brought with them the dress of their masters, and American plantation habits. Since their trip had been facilitated by British philanthropists they cultivated a sense of loyalty to the British Empire. The Krio believed as fervently as any European that the natives inland needed educating and converting.

It is now two fifteen p.m. The velveteen prickles and I am sweaty. I am still waiting. The owner of the house is old and having a nap. He was once a firebrand, a scourge of the colonial rulers. He is Krio, but not so grand that he wanted to hang on to an old order of waxed moustaches and servants in uniform. He grew up in the twenties and thirties, when well-to-do Krios would spend their weekends at the pleasure gardens known as Horton's Maze, larking in the swimming pool, refreshing themselves in the tea garden, entertained at the bandstand, climbing the lovers' lane and of course getting lost in the maze. This was a time when fine Krio ladies enjoyed hobnobbing with the British colonial authorities, and having themselves carried around Freetown in hammocks and sedan chairs by Africans from the hinterland dressed in elaborate uniform with epaulettes and fez hats; and Marcus Grant thought that was wrong. He believed the old order needed to be changed.

And perhaps the grander Krio ladies themselves were getting fed up with the younger generation of colonial ruler. The new man was keen, perhaps a little brutalized by the war; at any rate he wanted to tidy up the rules of the game, clarify the rights of Africans or rather the lack of them. 'Africans, know your limits,' seemed to be the rationale. And so a kind of meanness and racial intolerance began to bite hard after the First World War. Meanwhile, quinine became more widespread as a means of protecting yourself against malaria. Young clerical workers from Dorking could be safely dispatched to Calabar, blighting the chances of local people being promoted. And more and more Europeans took to driving cars, so cocooning themselves from the hardships and joys of the people they governed.

> **Sierra Leone Weekly News, 5 *December 1936***
> *The times are changing. If it had only been in the days of Sir Frederick Cardew, Sir Charles King-Harman, and the matter of fact Governor Sir Leslie Probyn, when our mothers used to stop their hammocks, when they were passing either at Krootown Road, Pademba Road, Kissy Road, Rouah Bay Road, or Water Street, to pour out their minds to these Empire builders in connection with how things were going on, and the ready listening that was always accorded them gladdened their hearts, and the result was always good. But now, who can stop a motor car? In fact very few people have a chance to know their governor.*

Two forty-five p.m. I am still waiting. The owner is still napping, his young wife informs me. Marcus Grant's father was a carpenter and built the house we sit in. It is a good deal more beautiful than the modern architecture of Freetown. I have just come from the Bintumani Hotel, a temple to poor craftsmanship, although classed as a four-star establishment. Mustiness is fermented by ill-fitted carpets, the rooms lit by pointlessly elaborate chandeliers.

This morning it was the venue for a meeting between the President and his French friends. When Marcus Grant was a boy, the French were confined to textbooks; now they own 90 per cent of the tourist business. A transcontinental truck rally came to an end today. The Bintumani Hotel was holding a reception for this French PR exercise, which mixed derring-do with carelessly scattered medical aid. President Momoh made a speech.

He was in full military uniform but, unlike most military men, he relished the business of after-dinner speaking. Whether he wrote the speech itself, I cannot say, but he certainly enjoyed delivering it. 'Participants in the Sud Objective rally, ladies and gentlemen. I would have loved to speak in French, but since most of you here do not understand that language I will say my speech in English. Let me welcome you in this first Sud Objective rally.' The crowd responds to this opening flourish with faint clapping. 'We in Freetown have everything to make you relax: the warm Atlantic Ocean, and wonderful beaches . . . the rest of the entertainment you have to discover for yourselves.' A couple of dirty laughs ring out. The President pauses, pleased that the lewd innuendo has been picked up. Then a more sanctimonious tone is adopted. 'I want to especially thank the organizers of the rally. The villages which you must have seen in fleeting moments have to be provided for, in the long run, with electricity and water. And those rugged roads will have to be properly constructed . . .' Momoh talks as though he is leading an expedition to some newly discovered kingdom. He concludes, 'It is therefore my sincere hope that, as dramatic as their entrance into Sierra Leone has been, the participants will be able to remember us and give what little they have to help us in our development endeavours. Education, tourism – you name it – the people of France are playing a very useful role. In the past decade the French government has placed considerable effort in the development of tourism. Let us hope this will continue.'

My legs are aching from standing for so long. I survey the scene: the French listening politely, all the while dreaming of the profits to be made. And I wonder at their genial host. Has the man no pride? No shame? Where is his sense of duty? Does he think the business of government is done *for you* by foreigners? They say he is kind-hearted, another way of calling him a fool; they say he is controlled by a coterie of wily old-time politicians; he is said to be tender-hearted with the fairer sex – easily manipulated. The British High Commission is awash with visa applications for young girls who have persuaded the President to pay for them to do secretarial courses, business administration diplomas. I meet a careworn lawyer who says he has just drawn up the title deeds of a substantial property in Freetown in the name of one of the President's young lovers. 'And to think only last year she was my third-year pupil,' he remarks bitterly.

It is now almost four p.m. Saidu Momoh, formerly a professional soldier, before that a trainee priest and now the President of Sierra Leone, has become rich and fat. Marcus Grant, who struggled for independence, is now skinny, old and poor.

Finally Marcus Grant walks into the room, slow, dignified, like a man used to making entrances in front of big crowds. I am not sure how much he wants to be interviewed. He probably has mixed feelings about Europeans. He is of that generation who experienced them both as benefactors and as oppressors. He takes his time and starts by presenting me with his credentials. 'The British taught me, em-eh, trades unionism – I've been to Nottingham, I've been to France. I set up the, em-eh, Youth League with I.T.A. Wallace Johnson.' His voice is clipped and punctuated regularly with a mannered hesitation, 'em-eh'. I subsequently heard it among others of his generation of educated English-speaking Sierra Leoneans. 'Em-eh, we wanted to improve the conditions of the country. But then there was a policy of divide and rule. Intimidations and threats.'

'By whom?' I ask politely, too confused and charmed by

his manner and his house to comprehend the bitterness the past throws up.

'By the British government, by the British.' His voice is sharp and high with indignation.

'But Pa Grant, what do you think of politics today?'

He closes his eyes, lifts his eyebrows, leans back, then leans forward and looks me straight in the eye. I bet he's going to say something interesting. I twiddle the button of my recording level in anticipation.

'I would advise you to call me Mr Grant.' The genteel wording gives edge to the rebuke.

My cheeks become hot, my voice falters.

'Oh, I'm . . . I'm sorry.'

But everyone else had called him that. 'Go and talk to Pa Grant,' they said, 'if you're interested in the old anti-colonial types. Pa Grant's a great talker. He knew I.T.A. Wallace Johnson.' And it has to be said that I really liked the idea of him being called *Pa* Grant. It was like America (I'd never been to America). Perhaps Pa Grant sat on the porch singing the blues, and ate hominy grits. I knew his grandparents or great-grandparents would have been slaves in America. Perhaps he could sing some Negro spirituals. Now I'd made the 'Pa' mistake I'd never have the courage to ask him to sing for me. But he hasn't told me to go away yet, so I'll try for something a bit safer. I ask him about his early life. And he tells me why his plans to become a carpenter, like his father, were never realized. 'Unfortunately I became, em-eh, height conscious and could not complete, so I diverted from carpentry and after school I became a clerk with the late Claude Wright.'

'May I ask how old you are?' Sailing close to the wind again.

'One of the things my father told me is never to disclose my age. But I've seen quite a lot.'

He must be at least eighty-five. But it was his youth that made him remarkable. His youthful activism had no precedent. It was aimed at a cabal of old men who believed they would be the elite for ever, propped up by a 'special' friendship with Britain. Eat your heart out, Valentine Strasser and Johnny Koroma; young men were kicking up hell long before your parents were born, and they had nicer table manners. We get on to the subject of the fabled I.T.A. Wallace Johnson. Earlier in the week I had met I.T.A.'s son. Now in his sixties, his entire career was made on the coat tails of his father. He's been the guest of every ruling communist party in the world. But his views on politics are incoherent and foolish; as you would expect from a person who has never been made to think. I mention this meeting to Marcus. He wrinkles his nose, but retains a dignified silence. So much for the son, but the father is a different kettle of fish. 'Wallace Johnson was a stern, meaningful, forceful and determined man. On his return to Sierra Leone it was thought he should join older ones and follow their advice, but he was more forceful.' Mr Grant pauses and completes the picture. 'Em-eh, he was very humorous. In politics you have to be humorous. As soon as he entered a meeting they hailed him.'

I remind him that the newspaper commentaries of the day accused the West African Youth League on the eve of the Second World War of being unpatriotic because it was attacking the British. He's sensitive to the accusation of anti-patriotism, despite his loathing of British colonial rule.

'Well, we have been used to the old slavish ways from one section of life. The newspaper was just creating trouble for us, until we could convert more people.'

I ask him what he thinks of communism now. He sits up straight and looks indignant.

'But I am not a communist – no, no, no. To be candid I

just don't like some of its administration, the way people have to live under communism. But let me come out plainly. During my tour when we were forming the International Confederation of Free Trades Unions in 1949, I was approached to be a communist agent with a lot of money. One fellow had been made a communist in Nigeria, and I was available here in Sierra Leone, but I was not available to them.' At this Mr Grant laughs triumphantly.

But whatever his views on communism, Mr Grant was not averse to a bit of class struggle. In 1955 he organized the first general strike in Sierra Leone, and his memory of it is detailed and clear.

'Our picketing was lawful of course. But those others killed 154 people, looting and rioting. It was not us. Em-eh, we were properly organized, we informed police, we informed our pickets. Later we got what we wanted.'

He is heartened by the reminiscence.

'By jove, the strike started with only one or two unions, but affected the whole country. Em-eh, it happened 9 February 1955. The whole country was panicked. It lasted three days. Em-eh, I don't like strike, but it's the workers' weapon. Up today it changed the atmosphere. It changed the mind of the people.'

And today? It seems almost cruel to ask, but how is Mr Grant's life in Sierra Leone today?

'Em-eh, a bag of rice was 9 leones then. It is 1,500 leones now.'

His voice becomes slow and emphatic.

'Why should I like politics now? The workers should have food to eat and live in peace and harmony.'

He gazes gloomily out of the window, and then regains momentum; a vision of how things *should* be lights up his face.

'Nothing will change until we get two things right. One:

change of our currency, we want currency with international recognition; secondly, we want the return of our old train system, because goods are perishing. After that we want priorities. Health is first. Agriculture, education, we want those priorities. God will hear me. In him I will put my faith and trust.'

I thank Marcus Grant for the audience and pay him in kind, with a bag of rice.

DIAMONDS AND BOOKS

There was a time when John Lewis took Freetown orders for ladies' summer dresses without hesitation, cash on delivery. But the payments got slower and slower and then vanished. Everyone was owing everyone, and the one sure banker, the diamonds – the only source of foreign exchange in an economy with a non-convertible currency – were haemorrhaging out of the country undocumented. The money they earned stayed outside too. Successive governments took their cut – organized by a cartel of Lebanese (Muslim and Christian), French and Israeli businessmen. In truth Sierra Leone became a fiefdom of the Middle East, its wealth feeding the diamond-cutting centres of Tel Aviv and the banks of Switzerland. Not so surprising then that by the mid 1990s young men up-country took to wearing wigs and masks, first desperate, then cruel. After all, there's no satisfaction in watching others take all the cake, along with the recipe and the ingredients.

'Don't try and cover that diamond story. You'll get a bullet in your head if you do,' advised a friendly Lebanese businessman who made his money out of video rentals, not diamonds. Yes, the biggest stories never get told, I thought, at once wistful and cowardly.

Not only was Sierra Leone rich – it had academic standing

too. Fourah Bay College in Freetown was the oldest university in sub-Saharan Africa. Founded in the middle of the nineteenth century, it was the envy of West Africa. It has a collection of old newspapers going back to the 1880s, reflecting its glorious past. High on a hill overlooking Freetown and the bay, its position, above the worst of the malarial areas, firmly allies it with the elite. This is where the Europeans used to live.

Yes, once Fourah Bay College was the principal seat of learning in all of Africa. Back in the 1930s the man who went to Fourah Bay College was a man of superior knowledge, leaving others far behind. He might be Nigerian, or even a Gold Coaster. No Ghanaians go to Fourah Bay College these days. The students are all home grown. They hang around, half desultory, half conspiratorial. I feel I could be one of them, on the way to a lecture, with an essay due. They don't see it that way; they look at me with unsmiling, immobile faces as I breathlessly ask where the library is. Inside the air is heavy with weariness and what seems to be boredom, but could equally be hunger (given the price of rice) or thirst. There's a smell of carbon paper and old books, of heat on the printed page.

'Please can I work in the stack?'

A librarian looks at me as if I'd proposed carving my name on her desk. There is silence. I probably need a memo of authorization from the Ministry of Education, along with a letter of permission from the Chancellor. Then to my surprise she gets to her feet. Resentful, irritated but sensible of her duty, despite the fairy salary that she is paid, she opens the door leading downstairs and takes me to the microfiche room. It's almost a cellar with high windows on one side. There's a microfiche in one corner; in another is a pile of books. Not any old pile, this pile cascades down, almost from ceiling height – a sort of frozen book waterfall.

Pull one out and there would be an avalanche. I make a few surprised sounds, hoping to engage my guide in conversation; I cock my head sideways trying to make out the titles. There's all sorts: Shakespeare's *Richard II*, *History of Nigeria* by Sir Alan Burns, *The Lives of Kings and Queens of England* by Antonia Fraser . . .

The librarian will have none of it and leaves me to my one-sided conversation.

'Goodness me, someone ought to sort these out. There's some quite good stuff here. A big resource, if only somebody could get it organized. I bet there's students up there looking for just these very books, and can't find them. I suppose nobody wants to take the initiative . . .'

The microfiche machine is waiting for me. I stop gawping at the books and concentrate on trying to get the machine to work. There are plenty of old newspapers in these microfiche films that I want to look at. Plenty. If only I could get the machine to work. I can't. I go upstairs and ask the librarian for help. There is a pause again. She gets to her feet and sashays wearily to a door leading down to the stack. She can't make it work. I can't make it work. This is what independence is about – having a bunch of things you never asked for and can't work. The librarian leaves me to have another go. I fail.

'Terribly sorry to disturb you again, but could you show me the way to the room that has the newspapers in bound volumes?' She is too fed up even to waste her breath on sighing. She noiselessly gets up and we go to another room. She gestures and leaves. Everything is very tidy here. I choose from the shelf. A pleasurable sensation sweeps over me – *Sierra Leone Weekly News* 1893; nobody realizes (i.e. I didn't until now) just how ancient the craft of journalism is on the humid shores of West Africa ('Bight of Benin, Bight of Benin, two men come out, twelve went in'). I open the volume ready for some authentic time travel. But as I do so the paper inside crumbles, reduced to the consistency of yellow dandruff; the past is disintegrating before my eyes. I clamp the volume shut guiltily, half hoping that this will reverse the process. But the sudden motion causes even more damage, creating great puffs of dust. What have I done? I shouldn't have looked. Now I've destroyed it. But then what's the point of history if you can't get at it, or look at it? Trapped between covers, or reduced to dust – either way it doesn't exist. The dust dances in the sunlight, then finally settles; a sense of defeat descends. Perhaps I should be talking to live politicians instead of reading about long dead ones? Whatever I do, I dare not enlist the help of the librarian again. I must use my own initiative.

I select a more robust volume which agrees to reveal its fading charms without disintegrating in the process. I settle down for a good read, and find myself comforted by the domestic detail of another age. In the *Daily Mail*, 4 December 1936, I come across instances of marital friction, from the bed and the breakfast table, which would be as irritating in Reigate as in Freetown:

What have Sierra Leonean wives to say of their husbands?

My husband will invariably, on settling himself for the habitual half hour's read, balance the pillow on top of his head for a full minute before sliding it to a comfortable position at his back. I have trained myself to look the other way.

When my husband has finished a boiled egg, he always reverses the shell in the egg-cup, making the egg appear untouched. This childish habit never fails to annoy me.

A PLACE ON THE WAY TO SOMEWHERE ELSE

Lusaka University is positively red-brick compared to Fourah Bay College. It's in keeping with the country. Lusaka, the capital of Zambia, has a provincial air about it, part suburban, part home counties; the cafés sell steak and chips (big steaks, mind you) and the street traders are meek. Nobody in town wears traditional clothes. There's no noble mingling of European and African ways over the centuries. Zambia, or northern Rhodesia as it was known, existed for one reason only: the copper. Most towns in Zambia are just ribbons of houses built along roadsides on the way to somewhere else, and usually that somewhere else is a copper mine. Europeans didn't come here to trade or exchange philosophical insights, although conversion to Christianity was a mission; most came to mine, a few to farm. And as in every country where Europeans have owned land, they impose their will on all around, and it seems as though the life force has been sucked out of the place, the natural order – power and position – destroyed. Out of town is different, I am sure, but I stick to towns.

Sometimes, of course, the lure of the open spaces gets the better of me. I inquire about riding and am directed to the Lusaka Gymkhana Club. A little bit of England, as they say, except the owners of the horses (many of them children) are horribly spoilt. Here, every horse and every child has its groom or 'boy' to do the hard work, whereas in the English shires grooming and tacking your horse is the price you pay for the pleasure of riding. I wonder if the grooms here like horses. I never saw any of them ride. If an animal isn't part of your culture it can be an indignity to be cooped up with it all day, touching it, at the mercy of its moods. The horses here don't thrive as well as in Europe – life expectancy is eighteen years, although they do better in tropical Ghana,

26

and very well in the high altitude of Lesotho. The woman who runs the stables is delighted that I want a ride. She dresses for a chilly autumn day in the shires: jodhpurs, sleeveless puffa jacket. Her face is sunburnt and keen. She does her best to nurture the spirit of England on the lateritic soil of Zambia. I am given a monstrous seventeen-hand mare, sweaty and irritable.

'Last time I was in England I bought all the boys woolly caps from M & S. They're nothing much, but the boys love them.'

I look around: yes, the boys are wearing their hats. I am taken out with two expatriate wives by the sort of man who might call a young girl a *filly*, and whose social status has swollen in the Zambian heat. I don't take in much about my fellow riders, all effort concentrated on convincing my horse I'm in charge.

'All right for a gallop?'

Not quite all right for a gallop; I'm unfit, it's hot and the horse would like to get rid of me. The question is rhetorical. Before I have time to reply we're off at a furious and relentless pace, oscillating between gallop and canter. Our leader seems to be amused by my terror and exhaustion. But I survive. Getting off and breathing in the delicious smell of horse's body, I reflect on the business of riding. The horses are generally nicer than the people who ride them.

There are no tsetse flies in Zambia; there are mosquitoes, but not enough to seriously inconvenience the Europeans. The last time Zambia was exciting was during the liberation war in Zimbabwe. ZAPU had its bases here and the place was regularly bombed by the Rhodesian Air Force. Journalists thronged into Lusaka to cover the story. Now it is sleepy. 'You neglect us, you journalists, now there is no war,' says a teacher buying his third bottle of beer at the Lusaka Theatre Club. 'You are only interested in death and destruction.' He has a point. But there's a further point to consider: Zambia is a bit boring.

The Theatre Club, despite the promise of its name, is sunk in inertia. Once resounding to the dialogue of Douglas-Home drawing-room comedies, it is now largely a bar for black Zambian intellectuals and a few white Zambian rednecks, who sit obstinately in a corner cursing into their beer. Occasionally the drinkers, whatever their identity, will hold their beer bottles to the light to examine them for floaters – small particles of organic matter left in the beer, on account of the pasteurizer at the brewery having broken down. There is a truce between Africans and Europeans, but the barrier is there. At Christmas time tempers rise. The few Europeans left on the Theatre Club committee are then driven by some primeval, seasonal instinct to put on all-white productions of *Snow White and the Seven Dwarfs* or *Peter Pan* – well, for the kiddies' sake (Africans welcome, of course).

Zambia is not the place for Michael. 'Man, they got no energy here, no discipline,' he muses, sipping his orange juice. Michael is a former Black Panther who now lives in Lusaka, earning a living teaching basketball. 'I may go to Zimbabwe. Looks like there's more to it than here.' Michael once conferred radical chic on cocktail parties held by American liberals in New York in the 1960s. Now he's taken on the role of expatriate trainer.

The Zambian government is happy to host Michael and his dissident past because the President likes to foster the idea that Zambia is radical, and even had a liberation struggle. Not everyone is convinced. 'My dear little English girl,' says an ANC man as handsome as hell, 'they never had a revolution, they never had a struggle. Just boys chucking a few stones at the governor's car. Their independence was handed to them on a plate by the British.' I swoon at his style and want to devote myself to his struggle for the rest of my born days. But my mission is to talk to the chief stone chucker.

The chief stone chucker loves to be interviewed. Like most heads of state in Africa he loves the foreign journalists more than his own boys and girls. The price I pay for this interview is hours and hours of waiting. Even the chief stone chucker doesn't want to make himself cheap. I tire of sitting on the old candlewick bedspread, gazing at the phone. It's off to the swimming pool. The nice man at reception can track me down if I'm summoned. I am nervous. So what if he didn't fight a guerrilla war; he's the President. He actually didn't chuck any stones, although he was imprisoned for political agitation by the British in 1959. He is far too nice to scratch the paintwork of a colonial Bentley. But, they say, he has never been averse to turning a blind eye to the yobbery of his supporters, if it improved his position. Kind, blind – whatever ... I'm now feeling nervous about interviewing him. Suppose the apparatus packs up? Print journalists have no idea how lucky they are. Lose a notebook and you've got your memory, lose your memory and you can always make it up. But us radio types are at the mercy of batteries, pinch wheels, electro-magnetic tape being sufficiently electro-magnetic, flawed mini-discs, recording levels, headphones – it is a nightmare. On and on I swim, up and down. There's someone doing the same thing, up and down. We cross mid pool, he keeps looking straight ahead. Very familiar, terribly familiar. I know where I last saw that face: walrus moustache, impassive expression – faintly arrogant, faintly cruel. Yes, on a double-page spread in the *News of the World*. Who else but Lord Lucan? The words form themselves in my brain: 'You are Lord Lucan and I claim my £5.' Only I don't say it because I am far too worried about the interview. Oh God, the interview, the interview ... Hang on, have I gone mad? Lord Lucan? It can't be, not in Zambia

29

– why would anyone like Lord Lucan want to go to Zambia? It's the most dreary . . . Precisely. If you'd just accidentally knocked off your nanny, Zambia is the last place anyone would look for you.

'The President will see you now.' Right, get everything in order: cassettes, batteries, questions. The interesting thing about State House is that it's still the only bit of Zambia in pristine condition. This proves my theory that if you really want something done you can get it done anywhere in the world. Kenneth Kaunda really wants it looking like it did under colonial rule and it does: flawless white neo-classical columns, wooden panelling, polished brass. Maybe the red carpet is a little worn, but that's more than made up for by the peacocks strutting about the grounds. The rest of Lusaka is faded and temporary-looking.

I walk into the President's office. He is sitting there, very polite, nice really. He offers tea and pours it. How charming: a President being 'mother'. I am in his thrall, almost. He has worked hard on his image. He is very fond of proclaiming his admiration for Queen Elizabeth II, and is ostentatiously Christian. So he's allowed to get away with being a bit of a socialist. The western press has always been entranced by his willingness to weep in public, accompanied by a good deal of dabbing with a white handkerchief. He has his handkerchief with him even now. His assistants are probably less nice than he is, but will make the effort to appear polite because he is there. Two other machines are recording the interview, one from his press office and one from the national newspaper which is graciously allowed to share an audience alongside me. I've come because of the election. It's presidential as well as parliamentary, although there's only one presidential candidate: K.K. He has the sin of pride which comes with wanting to be truly humble.

'I had some very strange dreams when I was young. One

is that I saw in my dream that there were five bundles of grass and they were being carried by evangelists – people who worked with my late father. I had my own bundle. We came to a certain point and we put our bundles down, and all the other bundles fell down and began clapping, more or less clapping hands for my bundle. And when I woke up the next day I told my mother and she was very angry with me. She said, "Joseph, you dreamer, you think your brother and sister and myself are burdens for you?"'

Kenneth Kaunda (also known to his mother as Joseph, and to the people as K.K.) is not wearing his coloured coat. Today it's a safari suit with cravat. Kenneth Kaunda likes to see himself as top boy.

And he achieves that by a sort of passion and commitment to the business of power which has nothing to do with homework, least of all homework of the economic kind. In a rather desperate attempt to revive the flagging economy, Kaunda has succumbed to the siren call of early 80s Thatcherism and declared that Tiny Rowland and his Lonrho company would be welcome in Zambia, yet he wants to be seen as a socialist.

'First of all I am what you might even call a die-hard socialist. This is at the heart of humanism. We all need capital to develop in one form or another.' The words flow effortlessly. 'The capital that comes through state enterprise can be utilized for the good of the many. Some capital can be utilized for the good of the few.'

At the moment the shops in Zambia are full of South African goods despite Zambia being a party to trade sanctions. This is to soften people up for the elections. Who does the negotiating with South Africa to stock up the shops and market stalls is a mystery. Some dodgy expatriate in a blazer probably. The President makes it clear that officially South Africa is untouchable.

'In South Africa big investment is being used to exploit the black man. That type of exploitation is not acceptable to us. So we think in terms of industrial participatory democracy.'

He has a strange way of talking, snatching at words and phrases jerkily but with hard precision. He says 'participatory democracy' very fast so it sounds like 'treemocracy'. I ask him to repeat the phrase because I can't understand what he's said; he does so affably enough, but I still don't get it. Back home, a kind, older colleague deciphers what turns out to be his catchphrase of the moment.

He goes on with his vague denunciation of bosses and leaders.

'We want to create conditions so that the capital will not be controlled by the few against the many, but by the many for the many.'

I try to pin him down. Where does capitalism start getting distasteful? Is it a question of scale? Would the man with a small shop get his backing, or be vilified in line with article 16 of the constitution, which urges people to struggle against capitalism and construct socialism?

'If Mr. X has got a shop started and he is employing himself there and probably his sons and so on, they are exploiting no one and the party welcomes this very much indeed. It's when they start employing some other people and paying them a minimal wage, while keeping the profits to themselves – that is when the party moves in and says you're wrong here.'

He has a cosy turn of phrase, as though explaining economics to a six-year-old. A dash of religiosity is thrown in to stiffen the strength of his argument.

'Your brain must be used in the interest of the people as a whole, because God made it.'

President Kaunda's grasp of the relationship between

economics and human psychology, I think irritably, is pathetic. But then he's been encouraged to think like this by the UN and the western left, both secure in the delusion that money is like air – it just needs to be distributed by a benign central being and all will be harmony; secure in the knowledge that, in their neck of the woods, the economy's ticking over nicely, providing enough wealth and jobs to keep coups and revolutions at bay.

There's another problem about Kaunda: saintly he may be, but he cannot delegate, he cannot let others have a stab at the problem too. Not a single educated man has survived for much more than a year in his inner cabal. Kaunda is an old-fashioned African leader – in his view the business of ruling is not about transformation, it is about affirmation of power. And he loves it. Zambia was declared a one-party state in 1972. The business of the election makes him swell with humility.

'I have always accepted what the people of Zambia say. And as long as they want me to remain in this post, and as long as, God willing, I am in good health, I shall continue to offer my services. I have always been fascinated by the word power.'

The previous month party heavies had gone round the market demanding to see the membership cards of the stallholders, threatening to chuck out those who could not produce them.

But Kaunda maintains that God is on his side.

'I like to believe that the people of Zambia, like all other people on earth, belong to God, and those of us who are asked by our fellow men and entrusted to our fellow men ought to know that it's only through him, our Creator, that we can have what we have.'

Of course, this is the divine right of kings rekindled and so I suppose it's only fitting that this election has only one presidential candidate, Kenneth Kaunda. His symbol is the eagle. If you want to vote 'no', you put your cross by a deeply mournful frog. I met people who said it's not worth voting. But for Kaunda voting is ritual affirmation of the end of colonial rule.

'It *is* worth voting, because if you say you don't vote you are depriving yourself of the basic reason why we fought for independence.' He is so confident, I think, as he expands on his theme: 'Whoever we put in is doing some good work, we vote for him, and if he isn't doing good work, the constitution says you have the right not to vote for him. And of course, if we have more "no" votes, the fellow falls out and we find another one.'

Kaunda has a trick of disassociating himself from himself – he wants to be party and president, ruler and ruled, elected and voter. And he has convinced himself that he can be all things at once, but it makes debate difficult. I have gone through the looking glass. I am thirsty, and have been offered a biscuit.

I am also getting worse and worse at interviewing him. His niceness is snaking round me, stifling every critical impulse in my brain.

'Has your philosophy of humanism stood the test of time?' I find myself asking him sycophantically. It would have made more sense to ask if it had stood the test of logic, since nobody really knew what it was about, but everyone pretended they did. Western left-wingers with an interest in Africa and a hatred of the right were thrilled by this philosopher king.

'I am very happy this philosophy has been under-stood . . .' He has become misty-eyed, enjoying the sensation of drifting in the intellectually abstract. '. . . has been accepted, is being implemented – albeit too slowly – and being implemented in a practical manner. We have very serious problems. You reminded me of a question which I used to be asked by an English friend of mine, editor in chief of the *Daily Mail* here. His name was Dolphus. He used to say to me, "Mr President, this is a very good philosophy, but what's going to happen once you die? Will this carry on?" I told him I thought it would stand the test of time, as I'm glad it's beginning to do.'

Humanism is one of eleven prescribed topics that the parliamentary candidates are allowed to discuss. In the official list it is described in brackets as 'Love for one another'. Other topics on the list are:

Development since Independence
Need for Self-reliance
Need for Unity
Meaning of 'One Zambia, One Nation' (KK's rallying cry)
Economic Recession in the World and how it Affects Zambia
Meaning of KK's song 'Tiyende Pamodzi'
Meaning of Zambia's Emblem
How to Combat Crime
Problems in Parliamentary Democracy
Other Subjects Related to the Party.

Rules:
No candidates can organize meetings (this is the job of the district committee).
There is to be no door-to-door canvassing.
All meetings shall be open to public and press.
No jeering or cheering.

Attention has been paid to preparing voters on what to do. I go to a mock election held in a small communal hall. It is poorly attended. A tall, earnest, young party functionary is providing the tutorial. He is particularly excited that I am there.

He hands out the ballot slips exhorting the voters to think about the unity of the nation and the need to build a new future. 'Now you can see we have here the eagle – the mighty strong eagle – if you put your cross here you will be voting for stability, continuity. If you put your cross against the frog you will be voting "no" to that. Now I want you all to show Miss Ledger how well you can vote.' Forty-three people apply themselves to distinguishing between the mighty eagle and the sad frog. He collects the results and examines them. 'Very good – forty-one voted correctly. But what is this?' He holds up a ballot slip with a cross right in the box where the eagle symbol is, not in the box next to it as prescribed. 'Who did that?' There is laughter. A woman puts her hand up. She isn't laughing; she looks sad. 'You have put your cross in the same box as the eagle. There is no room – look, you have a box specially for your cross next to it.' He picks out another slip, brows furrowed. 'I have a "no" vote here.'

'Oh that's interesting – democracy in action,' I offer.

His tone changes from reprimanding to eagerly concilia-tory: 'Not that it's wrong to vote no . . . there is, of course, a choice, but maybe this voter got too excited . . . or didn't understand. Now who did that?' There is sullen silence. The man will not give up. 'I think there was a confused person here – what they meant was "no change", a vote to stay with Kaunda. Yes, it's a "no change" vote on this ballot, and the cross was put in the "no" box by mistake.'

The parliamentary candidates are just as well drilled. It seems their job is to act as some sort of Greek chorus confirming Kenneth Kaunda's right to rule. The Roma constituency, just outside Lusaka, has three candidates. Today they are presenting themselves to the voters. They start by singing the National Anthem, and then everyone is encouraged to vote for Kaunda.

The first candidate is Julius Banda. He looks a little worried. He doesn't want to be standing in this ward – he claims his mates are in another ward. People chant his name, it's hard to tell whether mocking, admiring or maybe just for the hell of it: 'Joolli, Joolli, Joolli.' He limbers up with the usual old call-and-response routine:

'One nation, one Zambia, one leader – and that leader?'

'Dr Kaunda – vote yes!'

'That leader?'

'Dr Kaunda – vote yes!'

'That leader?'

'Dr Kaunda – vote yes!'

And for the sake of variety:

'27 October?'

'Vote yes!'

The candidate has been instructed by the moderator to talk about the problems of the constituency, but since he does not appear to know anything about the constituency he sticks to the tried and tested: the admirable qualities of the President.

The moderator bangs the table, and Joolli is cautioned to stick to the subject; he says he'd be better at talking about problems in the constituency if they elected him as MP.

And on this theme he then romps recklessly through his prescribed twenty minutes to a mixed reception. The moderator takes up the 'one nation one Zambia' theme before introducing candidate number two – the outgoing MP, another Banda, this time Dingiswayo Banda. His nickname is 'Dictionary'. The voices of the crowd take on that curious bellowing quality, reminiscent of British MPs in full debate. Words are hit hard and then allowed to die away. 'Dee, Dee, Dic-tionary' they chorus.

Mr Banda breaks into a song in praise of Kaunda. He addresses his audience. 'Mr Chairman, comrade trustee, visiting councillors.' He pauses to make a fair imitation of a cockerel, for cockerel is the meaning of his name. He points out that the cockerel is his symbol, and Kaunda's is the eagle – the two belong to the same family.

He then screams in English, quickly gathering rhythmic momentum:

'Unless you can get organized at the section level, unless you can get organized at the branch level, . . . district level, provincial level . . .' The thigh bone's connected to the knee bone, the knee bone's connected to the shin bone . . . And for a finale: 'Your salvation is in the United Independence Party.' His voice is getting hoarse. Everyone is very excited.

Suddenly his twenty minutes are up, but he has ended on a high note.

Candidate number three: Yona Phiri. He is the cockerel's serious rival. He senses the excitement in the crowd as he appears, and leaps on to the table. People are fairly evenly divided into cockerel supporters and Phiri's supporters, and have grouped themselves accordingly. A shower of flower petals is thrown over Mr Phiri and he does a jig on the small, rickety table.

'Branch and section leaders, ladies and gentlemen. This afternoon we have been able to come here, freely leaving our girlfriends as we can under KK's leadership.'

He's misjudged the prudery of the people on sexual matters. There's a great roar from the crowd of 'Shame, shame.'

Supporters of Dee, Dee, Dictionary insult Mr Phiri, and are then thrown out. The anger is dissipated by some KK chanting. Then Mr Phiri is off again, this time singing the praises of himself. Someone in the crowd complains that he is talking 'unsensible things'. Undeterred, Mr Phiri puts a piece of cloth round his waist and wiggles his hips. 'He's very hopeless,' says a large elderly woman turning her head in disgust. Someone produces a drum and begins to play it. Mr Phiri catches the rhythm. His table begins to sag. But Mr Phiri is on a roll and cannot stop himself. He is singing, dancing, chanting. His male supporters are all behind him, and he is enjoying himself. A woman calls out, 'You frog, we don't want to hear your words any more.' Her view is endorsed by other women. Mr Phiri laughs defiantly, wildly. The table slowly collapses and Mr Phiri disappears from view. As though to spare him embarrassment, the moderator announces his time is up.

Kenneth Kaunda didn't like clever men. He created a party to give the disadvantaged, the uneducated a chance to control the country, but it was a party which was jealous and fearful of the educated class, the professionals. Some of them were, it is true, happily corrupt. Others were knowledgeable, gifted and . . . yes, probably corrupt too. Once excluded from power, they took to mulling things over in their favourite meeting place, the Flying Club. And that all went to prove to Kaunda what a snooty, conspiratorial bunch they were. By 1983 he had them tied up in knots in one of the most Byzantine treason cases the continent has ever known.

I only ever knew one person who understood it, a South African journalist who as a child had escaped fascism in Europe, only to see cruel injustice replicated in South Africa; she left the empire of apartheid and put her heart into the newly independent countries of Africa. And when things went wrong, when the dreams turned to dust and bickering, it hurt her. But being clever she wanted to make sense of it all, particularly this treason case. Like the Ancient Mariner, her knowledge became a burden, and she was anxious to share it with anyone who would listen; but the moment she started up with her monstrous train of facts and dates, her audience would find their heads spinning. Then excuses would be made, pressing appointments would suddenly be remembered. Soon enough someone else would innocently ask her to explain the treason case in Zambia, and she would oblige, unloading once more her burden of names, family blood-ties, long-running feuds, land-ownership, and secret rendezvous. She left Zambia in the end for the less stagnant waters of newly independent Zimbabwe, and now I believe has returned to the new South Africa; I hope she is not disappointed.

In truth I think Kaunda began to find Zambia boring. He took to tangling himself up in everyone's affairs in southern Africa, relishing his role as honest broker, particularly on behalf of Angola where oil and war went hand in hand to create one of the longest running wars on the continent.

In 1991, under pressure from the IMF, Kenneth Kaunda allowed a multi-party election to take place. His party, UNIP, failed to get a majority. He went into the political wilderness for a time. And now he has come back, in fighting form, quivering with moral indignation and ready for martyrdom. Only this time the enemy is not the British but fellow Zambians, hot with desire to humiliate the old man.

TWO

Tell Me What It's Really Like

~~~~~

THE GATEKEEPERS

The official funeral oration was delivered by Comrade Lucio Lara, and he could not hold back his emotion. He broke down in tears as he said his farewell: 'Goodbye Friend Neto, goodbye Comrade President. The struggle continues, victory is certain.'

(broadcaster Mesquito Lemos, on the occasion of President Neto's death on Angolan radio, 17 September 1979)

When the father of the Angolan revolution died, the country was engulfed in mourning. Mourning for his death was accompanied by fear of the future: who could possibly take on his mantle? Whose revolutionary spirit could burn brightly enough? Who could command sufficient respect? The man who came forward was handsome, smart, and low profile. Eduardo dos Santos also had a healthy appetite for power, good suits and pretty women. Perhaps a curious choice of successor to Neto, the Intellectual. This charming smiler knew his mind, but was a closed book to the people – no soap-box politician he. It was left to those further down the hierarchy to exercise the rhetoric of revolution. And there was no shortage of fierce gatekeepers to do that, ready to keep the liberal and conservative

41

rabble at bay. And here was I, servant of a western state-funded broadcasting corporation, no radical political credentials to my name, knocking at the gate for entry. My slender contact with Angola on the telephone should have warned me off.

London, 1983. An office in Bush House, home of BBC World Service.

'Don't fucking ring me up to ask me to comment on the claims of UNITA. There has been no attack. They are not a movement, they are just puppets of the South Africans – OK? So ring the South African government up. But UNITA are nothing.'

'But Chloë, just do us a straight piece, saying . . . well, saying what you said just then – expanded a bit and minus some of the language.'

'Don't you bastards understand there are children being killed here, right now?'

'But that's it, Chloë, that's the story we want. Couldn't you just—'

'Oh, of course I forgot the BBC gets its facts from the South African Ministry of Information. Go and peddle some racist crap and leave me alone.'

Angola was caught in the axis of the cold war; Chloë lived in fear of a South African attack. No wonder she had nerves. But we sat at our desks in London in fear of not being able to fill the spaces in our programmes.

This had been our one journalistic link with the government in Luanda for the past four weeks; she was tough, posh and radical, and passing through. The daughter of an earl who had thrown in her lot with the revolution, any revolution. This month it was Angola's turn. Yes, it has to be said that as a PR agent for the MPLA government Chloë Restieux-Baddingley was a disaster. The South Africans couldn't have found a better choice to make the cause of the

Angolan government look mad, drab and unreasonable. Move over, Chloë, I want to see what it's really like.

A gloomy day in London, and I am sitting in the offices of MAGIC (Mozambican Angolan Guinea Bissau Information Centre). This is where you get your visa, if you want to go to any Lusophone country in Africa. It is far from magical, it is ideological and boring. 'I'm sorry your application has not been successful,' says the secretary of MAGIC. She has what is known as a mocking smile on her face. 'I personally lodged it last month, but you have to understand the government has many problems. You are no doubt aware of the recent attack by racist South Africa and the puppet UNITA forces. The added burden of foreign journalists visiting is something it cannot take on at this moment.' Her tone is virtuous and regretful. I know she loathes the BBC, and is perfectly happy for me never to tread Angolan soil.

When it came to Angola everyone took up positions; it was an almost perfect microcosm of the cold war. But nothing's inevitable; there was a time in the 1960s when the MPLA hoped for help from Kennedy against the Portuguese. After all, most of the Protestant missions in Angola were American, detested by the colonial authorities and the Portuguese priests. Kennedy wavered, then cast the MPLA out into the wilderness, and into the arms of the Soviet Union. The moment the Portuguese pulled out, the South Africans were into Angola like a rat down a drain. Protecting South Africa from the red tide was Vorster's view of it, and with diamonds and oil, and the first half of a transcontinental railway, Angola was potentially the richest country on the continent. The Americans fell into line with the South Africans, stoutly ignoring the fact that UNITA's Savimbi was a Maoist by political training. Curiously these cold war alignments were blurred in the minds of some Americans, when it came to the question of oil production.

January 1984, Luanda airport, satellite of the 'Evil Empire' as Mr Reagan would have us believe. I have just arrived.

I look around, step forward and nearly fall through an enormous hole in the wall of the arrivals area; yes, it's a gaping hole from floor level to ceiling. It looks out on to the ragged rooftops of dilapidated airport outbuildings and a boiling grey sky.

Strange voices filter into my head:

'Hi, bud, how y'all doing?'

'Fine and dandy. Good to see you, Ed.'

'You too. Listen, Bud, we'll be taking the helicopter up to Cabinda tomorrow, so I'm going to take you back to the guest house, so y'all can freshen up and rest up a little.'

'Sounds good.'

Ed is wearing a ten-gallon hat.

These are the American oil men, whose engineering skills make it possible to fund the Angolans' war against South Africa, which in turn is being backed by the American government. When they go to Cabinda the American oil men will be protected by Cubans. There's no American Embassy in Angola, there's no American Embassy in Cuba. But petroleum speaks louder than ideology or diplomatic choices.

SLEEPING BEAUTY

Beautiful Luanda by the sea. Built round the sweeping curve of the harbour, the Marginal, which is guarded at its entrance by a sixteenth-century Dutch fort. Luanda stands frozen in time: from a distance it looks like a modern city; look closer and you see that most of the high-rise buildings are only half built, rusting metal struts reaching upwards beyond the confines of slip-formed walls.

In the 1950s and 1960s the Portuguese dictator Salazar and his successor, Caetano, stuffed money into the colonial capitals in Africa, in a last minute bid to appear modern and on the move. And, as is often the case, this last minute yielding to change has served fatally to hasten the demise of the goverment implementing the change. October 1975 and the day the Portuguese pulled out, all construction stopped, cement mixers completed their last revolution, compressors fell silent; for nine years the clinker has lain in piles, overgrown with weeds and moss. Now there are no shops, no cafés; with nobody left to run things the state took them over. Luanda waits to be awoken by the kiss of capitalism.

The view from room 801 of the Hotel Presidente is good. By day there is the sweep of the Marginal and the great Atlantic. At night bright lights take our eyes across to the dockyard, where heavy duty arms are disgorged from Soviet carriers and rumble off to who knows where. Room 801 is heavily air-conditioned. The hotel has just been opened. Things are looking up, they say, with this injection of Brazilian aid. But I'm not so sure. The food we eat is flown from Brazil three times a week, so they say. An Angolan army major perches uncomfortably on the edge of my bed; half of him wants to talk to me, the other not.

'Yes, we saw your application. But the MAGIC office put a "not recommended for visa" note on it.'

'They told me it was you people in Luanda who refused it.' I feel a bit hurt, like you do when you discover someone you know has had a party which they didn't invite you to.

He stares at me steadily.

'Why didn't she want me to come?' I persist.

He shrugs.

We are drinking Coca-Cola with ridiculous amounts of

ice in it. There's an ice-making machine on every floor of the hotel, to me a novelty of which I want to take full advantage. He looks at his watch. I don't want him to go.

'So what's the party really like then? Any good at running things . . . I mean on a practical level – drains, schools, office equipment?' I paint my question with a broad brush, in the desperate hope of getting some insight. I'm amazed he turned up at all. He is a friend of a friend, and good manners are important in Angola.

He shrugs again. 'The party is the party, the army is the army.' He pauses. 'Let us say that when I come to Luanda, I am angry when I see all the holes in the roads. Things falling apart. You know, these are pen-pushers here; they do nothing. In the army, if the road is blown up, or the bridge is destroyed, then we mend it overnight.' He speaks quietly but sounds angry.

'I couldn't record you saying that, could I?' Well, a fast approach sometimes works.

He smiles, amused. 'No, no, no, I must go now.'

He leaves quickly and quietly. I've never been one for soldiers or armies, but the idea of practical competence – to mend, to build – that's very attractive. But here in the corridors of power this competent army major, with much needed skills, feels undervalued.

The major is not alone in not wanting to speak to me. Civilians, too, shy away. This is the land of secrets and conspiracies. Careless talk costs lives. The enemy is outside and within. But camping too long on the moral high ground is corrupting; the viciousness of South Africa has now become an excuse for corruption and deceit. There are rumours of terrible fights at Central Committee meetings over women and land. I don't think this is South African propaganda. Judging by their clothes, the secretaries in the

Ministry of Information have some lucrative liaisons. They wear skin-tight satin jeans and designer blouses. But however big their shopping sprees, they can never feel really safe. The South Africans even plant limpet mines on the ships in Luanda harbour.

If you walk along the Marginal you will find a little seventeenth-century church sandwiched between two high-rise buildings. The walls inside are lined with blue and white tiles. The worshippers are all women. They hold up their arms to the Virgin Mary in dumb appeal, mouthing silent prayers. A man is hanging around the entrance to the church, some kind of party or government agent. He sneers at the women's prayers and watches me with venomous eyes. The Catholic church was notorious before independence for its co-operation with the Portuguese secret service. The MPLA cannot forgive the church.

Anyone here speak English?

'You silly bitch, now you've agreed to record an interview in Portuguese we'll never get any interviews with English speakers.' (Who've been raped, I add silently.) The man from domestic radio has gone scarlet. I want to punch him in the face.

'Haven't you heard of voice-overs?'

'I'm sorry but my editor will not be best pleased by a bunch of voice-overs.'

'In case you hadn't realized, this country is Portuguese speaking, and French is their second language – not everyone in the world speaks English.' I think I am yelling by now.

A third voice joins in, 'Ah so ze BBC fights ze BBC – eez civil war, n'est-ce-pas?' The RFI producer has until now been rather languid, maintaining a smoke-wreathed Gallic aloofness; now he is the jester to his predominantly Anglo-Saxon colleagues. 'Zut alors, it ees lead story. Show me where the nearest telex is, quick, quick, I must file.'

There's some sniggering. It's infectious. But the man from domestic radio can't laugh. He is bitter.

'No – no, it's no good. You've ruined it for everyone. Marvellous, bloody marvellous.'

'Calm down, man.' This time it's Godwin who speaks. 'Listen, this isn't Europe. You've got to have patience, man. These people have got a war on, they can't just rush around finding you someone English to speak to.'

Godwin is the only African journalist among us. He is old and battered-looking, but in reality is only forty. He says he's going to retire soon because he knows too much. He lives off cigarettes and whisky. He is a print journalist. He can compose two-thousand-word stories in his head, word perfect. He boasts that he can get any telex machine, anywhere in the world, to work. His intervention in our argument is kindly. I think he pities Mr Domestic.

Then our minder from the Ministry of Information intervenes: 'OK, so BBC World Service does the interview with the Foreign Minister in Portuguese. We find someone English speaking for you,' she says, addressing Mr Home Service in soothing tones, a nurse dealing with a difficult patient. She is stout, genial, if a little sharp; her name is Katya and she was once a member of the Finnish Communist Party. After a few beers she is prepared (off the record) to be waspish about the mestiço bourgeoisie. But now there are journalists to organize.

'Now please, everyone, listen . . . you must know that we are waiting for the OK from the army. Once we have that, a certain number of you can go down to the south.'

'Today?'

'No, I don't know. Please wait in your hotel rooms.'

I'm getting nervous; two days and nothing on tape. Godwin gives advice. 'You can always try Nujoma. See what he says about the Lusaka agreement. He was left out of the discussions, and he has bases in the south of the country. They are getting tired of him.' The Lusaka agreement has just been announced in Zambia, tying Angola and South Africa into an agreement which will effect the withdrawal of South African and Cuban troops from the country. There should have been a rap written about southern Angola: the MPLA, backed by the Soviet Union, are fighting UNITA, heavily backed by South Africa, which is hunting SWAPO, who are fighting for the independence of South West Africa (Namibia) using Angola (covertly) as a base.

'There are also large contingents of ANC members being trained for the struggle,' says Godwin later that day, 'but that's a secret.'

'Sounds like a good story.'

'Don't.' Godwin is fierce. 'That's a good story for you, yes, but for the Angolans it's a point of security. The South Africans really are bad. This isn't just about Mirage jets dropping bombs. If they catch you and think you are for anyone except UNITA they'll telephone you for information until you beg for mercy.'

'Telephone you?'

'Put electrodes on you, torture you with electricity.'

I feel sick. The South Africans are off the scale. But still they get their point of view across more forcefully than the people they are beating up. Why do the big news editors constantly run South African Police reports and Ministry of Information statements so freely? Answer: because they have telephones, and can write clear English, and know how to deal with newshounds. They are one of us.

REVOLUTIONARY AND RUDE

Today it's going to be an interview in English, no voice-overs. Leader of the South West African People's Organization, Namibian born and bred of a poor farming family, Sam Nujoma is going to be the subject of my interview. Actually he first learned English when he was twenty, so he's not that much more linguistically advantaged than the Angolans. The Namibians are temperamentally different from the Luanda Angolans. They are mainly rural people; in some cases, rural and nomadic. The Europeans they have come into contact with have been Germans or Boers, who value practical skills of hunting, woodwork and farming; they are mistrustful of intellectuals, and disgusted by sex between the races.

The MPLA are overstuffed with ideologues, it's true, but in their favour they are fond of flowers and poetry, history, falling in love – never mind the race – white, black, brown; some of this comes from colonial rule, but honestly it is impossible to say who influenced whom over a period of four hundred years. Among the Angolans of Luanda are grand families who trace their lineage back to the sixteenth century and, despite hundreds of years of Portuguese rule, effortlessly despise the colonizers as socially beneath them. Some are leading MPLA members, and although they talk a lot about the *povo* (the people), for generations their families have not spoken any African language, just Portuguese. The Van Dunems, the Castil Brancos, the Vieirra-Dias. But of course since the revolution this is all a well-kept secret. Besides, many of the daughters of the grand houses have now married guerrilla fighters with more courage than manners. So the snobbery and class values are being eroded. Nobody will talk about this on tape. This is the secret, real world of Angola; we foreign journalists are encouraged to fill our stories with the marionettes and fables of the cold war.

I go to the SWAPO HQ, somewhat miserably, because it's not much of a scoop; Nujoma enjoys giving interviews and is often in London, and when he's not around there are always other SWAPO representatives who will talk. Here we go. The building is modest; a dark brown bungalow set back from the road. Mr Nujoma is waiting inside, smiling a bit like a shark and surrounded by retainers. Within a very short time we both get our needles stuck. I'm trying to get him to admit that he's been snubbed by the comrades in Lusaka. He talks in formulae and replies to every question with a reference to UN Resolution 435, which provides for free and fair elections to be held in Namibia, so ending its status as a South African fiefdom. No fewer than fourteen times in the interview Resolution 435 is mentioned. I am bored; I am bored by the repetition and I am bored because I don't understand power and the exercise of power. I think Mr Nujoma is stupid because he bores me. I am wrong – he is tenacious and wily. This is a man who sticks to his guns, knows he holds the moral high ground, and is clear in his mind that his enemy's sins outweigh any inadequacies he might have as an amusing speaker. I ask a limp question, along the lines of how does he see the future.

'I think the aggression which racist South Africa is waging has been condemned by the People's Republic of Angola, by the entire international community. Therefore South Africa feels very much isolated. And besides that, in this aggression which the Boer has been waging they have lost much power. There are now widows, wives without husbands, children without fathers as a result of this senseless war Namibia is waging. They are losing money and therefore it is right for them to come to their senses and stop this barbaric war.'

Actually, his analysis turns out to be right. Independence for Namibia came in 1990, as much the result of war weariness as of western recognition of SWAPO's rights and the withdrawal of American funding to South Africa.

He smiles at me. His retainers smile. I am not a problem for them. I am a problem for me today. Later I wonder, why didn't I ask him about his family? Why didn't I ask him when he went to school? Why didn't I ask him if he goes into the bush with his men? If he has ever killed a man? Now these would be questions worth asking, but somehow the geopolitics of the situation demand big sweeping questions about policy.

When it is over I stumble out into the humid heat. It is cloudy but bright ... I walk down the path squinting. I light a cigarette, relieved the ordeal is over. A boy jumps out of the back of a four-wheel-drive car. He blocks my path. He is about fifteen, and wears a tiny, trendy pink tank top, all in pink – designer punk, high fashion in a zero economy. The top is cropped short to reveal his lean muscular tummy. The rest of him is clothed in baggy pink punk trousers, with bondage straps hanging between his legs. He says nothing but points at my cigarette; I assume he wants a light. I fumble; he plucks – uninvited – my freshly lit cigarette out of my hand. Then saunters off smoking it. So much for the younger generation of freedom fighters, I think. A year later, over another cigarette I tell the tale to a friend.

'Oh for God's sake,' she said. 'What are you saying – SWAPO members can't wear bondage trousers?'

'No, but when there's a war on, you'd think they'd spend their money on ... well, something more useful.'

'Like what? Solar-powered bicycles? Look, they get an allowance – he probably saved his up and bought bondage trousers.'

'In Luanda?'

'No, in London.'

'So what was he doing there?'

'He's stateless – he's got to go somewhere.'

'But honestly, a pink crop top, and he was so rude ... that's not revolutionary, being rude.'

'Where do you get your ideas from? Who says you can't be rude and revolutionary?'

In search of war

Back at the press office, Katya is being bossy.

'Now we are going to draw straws to see who will go wiz the army to the south.'

'Can't we all go?' asks Mr Home Service querulously.

'No, no, no – the army does not have the room.'

Straws are picked.

'Ah – that is bad,' says the walrus-moustached Portuguese newspaper man, trying to look disappointed. He's done precisely nothing since he arrived; he examines the long straw minutely, as though expecting it to shrink. He will continue to do nothing. I pick a straw, convinced my fate lies in languid Luanda rather than the sizzling south. But alas, I draw the short straw, proverbially and literally.

'Ah,' says the newspaper man, 'you are lucky. You will get a good story now.'

Gulp. Yes, lucky – jolly good. More straws are pulled. My fellow travellers and short-straw-pullers are Mr Domestic, Godwin, a French reporter and a Zimbabwean camera crew. We are all very lucky.

Katya claps her hands and makes an announcement.

'You will fly in an Antonov plane today, maybe tomorrow. We wait for clearance from the Air Force. Then you can see the damage done to Cahama. Please be ready to go at any time.'

'But we want to see the South Africans pulling out,' says Mr Home Service. For once I agree: South African soldiers legging it over the orchard wall, pelted with rotten fruit by FAPLA forces.

'I cannot guarantee this.'

'This is ridiculous, my editor needs to know what the story is before I go.'

'You will have to wait.'

My heart is shrinking as I pack my little bag.

I wish I was in a cosy cottage by the sea, knitting bootees, a warm baby slumbering in its Moses basket, a hot apple pie baking in the oven, giving out a delicious smell. A man (yes, my husband) in a chunky, rough fisherman's jumper comes in, a decent sort of man, kind and brave.

'Mmm, smells delicious, darling. Is it ready yet?'

'You will have to wait,' I say firmly.

'If you say so, darling. Think I'll watch a bit of news, see what's happened to those journalists who were shot down in Angola. They're hoping there might be some survivors. Ghastly business.'

'Don't worry, we'll look after you,' says the white cameraman from Zimbabwe. He is wiry and hard-faced, almost looks like Clint Eastwood. 'Won't we, Jezza? Here, catch.' Jezza is the sound recordist. He catches the Zippo lighter they seem to share.

'Thanks, Mick – yeah, we'll look after you. Just close your eyes and . . . plug into Bruce Springsteen.'

We pile into the Antonov through its rear end, which seems somehow undignified and unsafe. In fact, everything feels unsafe. As well as fifty Cubans (I can tell by their moustaches) there are large quantities of dried fish (I can tell by the smell). This is a cargo plane doubling as a troop carrier; the seats are on the side and there are no safety belts. 'I might as well be travelling four hundred miles by plane with no safety belt,' I reflect absent-mindedly, and then look around. My heart does a triple somersault.

'Pretty sturdy job this,' says Mick, eyes screwed up knowledgeably. 'Mind you, if UNITA get us in their sights . . .'

'Yes, what?'

'Well, if they get us in their sights . . .'

'*What* will happen if UNITA get us in their sights?' He really is an exasperating man.

'Well, you know it's a military aircraft disguised in civilian colours?'

'That's good, isn't it? I mean they'll think we're just a bunch of harmless civilians.'

'No, they've got wise to that game. Four weeks ago they shot down exactly the same kind of Antonov – troop carrier, disguised in Aeroflot colours.' Mick scratches his chest and lights up.

I am not rising to this.

'Oh well, lightning doesn't strike twice.' Breezy on the outside, wheezy within. Quite honestly I think I'll just get out of this plane now and stay the rest of the week in Luanda, maybe find out a bit more about Central Committee policy, take a look at the colonial architecture. I actually get as far as standing up, but the plane begins to move off. Too late now.

'Hey, Jezza, catch.' Mick hurls a packet of cigarettes at him.

'Thanks, Mick.'

'Listen, Pinky' (I am wearing pink socks), 'want to borrow my Walkman?'

'No, thanks.' No, I shall read my Surtees, just to take my mind off things.

Remember well-bred people always take breeding for granted.

Good line that, but after reading it for the sixth time my mind and my eyes wander. The cockpit is partitioned off by a canvas curtain. Through it I can see the Russian pilot playing draughts with his co-pilot. The plane appears to be flying itself. A third man is getting into a white flying suit. He is very tall, with a beautiful complexion, tanned with slightly flushed cheeks, and a nicely shaped mouth. He is staring at me through a fringe of blond hair. I stare back. Anxiety is displaced by lust in an instant. We hold each other's gaze long enough for it to be more than coincidental, and then he very deliberately begins a striptease in reverse, buttoning up his flying suit slowly and gracefully. I am mesmerized. We flirt silently, separated by language, culture, the cold war and the roar of the Antonov's engine. But back in the cottage by the sea . . .

'Apparently, darling, one of the journalists on that plane was having an affair with a KGB agent masquerading as a flight engineer.'

'Well, they *say* she was a journalist – she could have been CIA. You don't know. And anyway they're still looking for the bodies. It's a pretty strange world out there. More apple pie, darling?'

'Yes, please.'

The plane descends sharply. A loud bell rings. The Russian disappears.

The plane ascends, and then begins its descent again. The bell rings. Something of a pattern is emerging.

'What's happening?'

'Oh, the descent's too steep,' says Mick, taping up one of his many boxes. 'That's the warning bell we heard, always goes off if the descent's too steep for a safe landing. Must be an inexperienced pilot.' He finishes taping up. 'Gaffer tape, you can rule the world with gaffer tape, Pinky. Catch, Jezza.' Jezza stows the gaffer tape away. You can rule the world with gaffer tape but you can't land a plane safely with it, I think miserably.

We finally make our landing. Lubango – it is like the promised land, nestling at the foot of a plateau, the Sierra Shela. The air is fresh, the skies are blue, the architecture Mediterranean and everywhere there are small allotments growing maize and vegetables. In 1914 the Jewish Territorial Organization seriously considered this area for a Jewish homeland. After the Boer War Afrikaners trekked here and farmed the land. Lubango once had the finest furniture factory in Angola until it was bombed in 1979 by the South Africans. We are staying at the Pensao Ritz. Katya shows me how to flush the loo by standing on a chair and pouring water (fetched from the river) into the pan from a bucket held high. The Pensao may have a problem with plumbing and it is old and small, but it's one hundredth the cost of the Presidente in Luanda and serves delicious food along with strong locally brewed beer. The capital is pitiful compared to this provincial town.

We eat and wash and then set off to see a co-operative farm. It is a large orchard once owned by a Portuguese family who fled the revolution. The people who live there are rounded up for our inspection. They look bewildered. The apple trees are huge, sticking out in all directions.

'Shouldn't these be pruned?' My question is unanswered. 'You know, pruned; you can't grow fruit trees unless you cut them back every year.'

Katya ignores my question and goes on to explain the principles of co-operative farming. It occurs to me that these trees haven't been pruned since the revolution.

'Tomorrow, if we get clearance, we will go in armed convoy to Cahama,' she says. I know that boys like this kind of expedition because it has a military hardware element.

'So you reckon it's around here that they have the SAM missile installations,' says Mr Home Service, pumping the diminutive and brainy French journalist for information.

'But of course.' He is not willing to divulge more. We are supposed to be competing with one another.

But for now we are forced to do more hanging around, waiting for our armed convoy. Everyone except Godwin is keyed up, restless. I stand on the steps of the Pensao gazing down the narrow hilly streets.

'Oh look, there's a tank,' I shout, trying to get enthusiastic about the military detail.

'It's not a tank, it's an armoured personnel carrier,' snarls Mr Home Service. Years of playing soldiers on his own in his attic bedroom in Cheam have clearly paid off, I think meanly.

I walk outside into brilliant sunshine. Katya clucks for me to come back in. I can't because I am riveted by the sight of poor peasant women wreathed in strings of onions. They wear worn cotton dresses and headscarves. They are white, the first poor whites I have ever seen in Africa. 'Not all the Portuguese had the money to leave Angola at the time of the revolution,' says Katya.

Then suddenly it's time to go. I consider pleading a headache, but since I am the only woman in the group pride gets the better of me. I am not at all happy with the idea of travelling in an armed convoy. It seems somehow attention-seeking. Surely it would be safer to go by bicycle? This way it's 'Hey, guerrillas, hey, soldiers – look at us, we've got rocket-propelled grenades, so come and get us if you dare.'

I find a seat by a window. M. & J. set up shop next to me.

'Chuck us the whisky, Mick,' twinkles Jezza.

'Want some, Pinky?'

'No thanks,' I say primly and settle down to tackling Surtees: *There is nothing certain about a fox hunt, but uncertainty; the worst favoured days sometimes proving the best, and the best favoured ones sometimes proving the worst.*

We have been on the road about five minutes when the driver of our bus begins to get agitated. People are murmuring at the front. I look up. We are trundling down a street on the outskirts of Lubango, and weaving towards us is a large grey metal object.

'Oh my God, it's a personnel carrier.' I am trying to be accurate in a state of alarm; I fail.

'It's a tank actually,' says Jezza.

'But why isn't it stopping?'

There is no sound technical explanation. Could it be the South Africans? UNITA? The beginning of an invasion? At the very last moment the tank swerves out of our way, affording us a close-up view of the driver. He is being throttled by a second man; the tank is dragging a tarpaulin in its wake.

'Katya, what is happening?'

'I do not know.' She purses her lips.

Our convoy rumbles on. There's miles of scrub, and a huge horizon of blue. The journey begins to take on a charmed existence. I abandon Surtees in favour of Bruce Springsteen on the Walkman. (The cottage by the sea seems somewhat poky now, and the man in the chunky fisherman's sweater a bit of a bore, a bit of a fusspot. 'Darling, you're not going out now, are you? It's terribly late and I think it's beginning to rain.')

If I die now, there'll be a smile on my lips. But a few miles later the perfect symmetry of the moment is disturbed by the bus stopping. There is furious conversation on the walkie-talkie.

'What's happening?'

'We are about to be ambushed,' says Mr Domestic with a nasty sadistic twist to his voice. This is the first time he has acknowledged my presence since the great voice-over row.

We are ordered out of the bus by Katya and the soldiers. Out we get. Then I remember I've left my recording apparatus on the bus. I have to crawl back and get it, like those dotty people who go back to a burning house to save their pet hamster. Apparatus retrieved, I join the others. We wait, and wait, and wait.

Twenty minutes later it's all back on the bus. False alarm. I feel nauseous from the amount of unwanted adrenaline coursing through my body. And cheated. To be made that frightened for no reason. This is the second lucky escape. Third time not so lucky, Mr Bond. Yes, the smell of apple pie is calling me back to the little cottage by the sea.

Mick takes another gulp of whisky. 'We'll be going undercover into Matabeleland as soon as we get back. Well, we'll have to turn this lot round first, but that'll only take a day . . . rate we're going half a day. I'm going to give Katya hell if she doesn't get us some decent pictures.'

The bus suddenly stops in the middle of nowhere. A Land-Rover comes into view. An officer jumps out. He looks at us mournfully. His dark eyebrows betray his Portuguese ancestry.

'This is Major Mattheus Coelho Lima of the Cahama brigade. He will now escort you,' says Katya.

'Where?'

'I do not know.'

My adrenaline is stirring again. We all get out of the bus

and start trudging through the scrub. If UNITA doesn't get us, the snakes will.

'Looks like we might see some action, Mick,' says Jezza complacently.

'Think you're right, Jezza. Chuck us your lighter.'

There's supposed to be a ceasefire, but what if they haven't all got the message? You hear about Japanese in far-flung Pacific isles still on patrol thirty years after VJ-Day. Nujoma wasn't even in on the negotiations; he might have told the chaps on the ground to carry on fighting, out of pique. Then an even worse thought occurs: if there is a punch-up, how will I know who is who? This isn't the Battle of Waterloo with soldiers proclaiming their allegiance in a blaze of colour. Out of the whole bunch – Angolan troops and allies, UNITA, SADF and SWAPO – the only ones I could confidently identify would be the Cubans (on account of their moustaches). I can just imagine my report now: 'Some men dressed in military uniform fought some other men in uniform, and then some more men dressed in uniform shot at them. There were ten casualties on the side of the first lot of men dressed in uniform.'

Suddenly the major signals for us to wait. My internal organs rush to swap places. The major beckons us to come forward. We enter a small clearing; he gestures for us to sit down on logs. We sit and wait, and wait. There is a rustle, and from behind a bush appears one, then two young soldiers, dressed in very ragged uniform. They are carrying battered guitars. They begin to sing, voices quivering with yearning and passion. I cannot understand what they are singing about. I consult Katya.

'This song is about a young man,' says Katya. 'He has been invited to a party but he doesn't have a girlfriend. It is a nice party, with plenty to eat and drink, but he is lonely. Then he sees a girl. She is pretty. He dances with her, he falls in love with her, but then she runs away with another man, and he is alone again, with all the fun and music of the party around him.'

'This is all very well, but where are the South Africans?' Mr Domestic is getting restless. We came in search of war and instead found poetry; suits me, but like most journalists in foreign parts, he wants blood.

Later, back in Luanda, as a treat Katya tells me the story behind the rogue tank that nearly ran us over in Lubango. Love and jealousy were at its root. The driver of the tank had stolen it because he had found his girlfriend with another soldier; he had requisitioned the tank in order to mow down the house where she lived. The second man, the throttler, was trying to restrain him. 'The driver will be court-martialled,' remarks Katya in an almost contented way.

THREE

Poor Man's Angola

∿∿∿

No frock, no entry

The security guard at the Ministry of Agriculture is fierce. I know from my Portuguese evening classes he is saying something about me being forbidden to see the minister. But I've got an appointment, hard won with the help of nervous young men at the Ministry of Information, too young for their jobs but trying very hard nonetheless. The guard does not care. He does not like the look of me. I try walking round him, but it's like being marked by the best netball player in the class – he blocks my every move.

''E say, you cannot see the ministero if you wear trousers – you must wear frock.' An interested passer-by puts me in the sartorial picture.

I have come to find out about Marxist-Leninist Mozambique, eight years after the revolution. As in Angola, hundreds of thousands of Portuguese left within the space of a few months, among them doctors, engineers, people who knew the map of the Lourenço Marques sewage system, could take an appendix out, and import glazed cotton for a decent price and sell it for a profit. They all went, so the only option, as in Angola, was to make a virtue out of a disaster. Everything's been nationalized, and capitalism is habitually cursed. Across the Nkomati River are the South

63

Africans, the neighbours from hell: they are there to make sure that small achievements are crushed. It's not a heavy-duty war like in Angola, but rather consists of cruelly unpredictable sniping at clinics, hospitals and, of course, ANC safe homes. But there is a sense of purpose here; socialism is insinuated into people's lives with more care than in Angola. On page ten of *Literacy and Production*, an adult literacy textbook, there's a picture of a soldier smoking a cigarette, with a head dripping with blood on the end of his bayonet; in another picture he's chased away by the people. The sequence is to illustrate the word '*luta*', and the sentence '*A luta do povo e justa*', 'The struggle of the people is just'. On the next page a gentler note is struck: there are pictures of a duck (*pato*), a candle (*vela*) and a pepper (*papaia*).

So socialism sits quite comfortably alongside the everyday. Mozambiquans may, like Angolans, secretly await the kiss of capitalism, but in the meantime they give themselves up, with little protest, to the rough caress of the state. A poor country is more suited to socialism anyway. And FRELIMO started from scratch with no oil as a buffer. This is a country which must be run according to the simple needs of the majority; away with petticoats and antimacassars; fashion is a bourgeois preoccupation. There's none of the secret celebration of designer clothes that I found in Angola; no ministerial mistresses lurking in the corridors of power, dressed in Yves Saint Laurent. Mozambique has neither oil nor diamonds and no frills to its frocks – they are cheap and plain, but they are compulsory. The rules are clear. Women must wear frocks. If they teach, if they go out to work, if they are seeing someone important, then they must wear frocks. But these are my smartest striped trousers and I've got an appointment.

A small crowd gathers. The security guard is anxious.

There is a faint feeling of disorder in the air. I argue more. I wave a business card at him – it serves only to enrage him.

I am just beginning to feel I could burn my striped trousers. The security guard is adamant. I turn away, defeated by revolutionary dress code.

I walk back to the Ministry of Information, trying in vain to hitch a lift. But the very occasional cars are driven by mean aid workers. By now it is four thirty p.m. At the ministry, handsome Raphael, assistant head of the press section, is sitting in his bare office, staring hopefully at a small cutting in a glass vase, willing it to grow big and beautiful. He looks up from his desk nervously. I throw myself into a battered pre-revolutionary armchair.

'The security guard got very cross about me wearing trousers. He wouldn't let me in.'

Raphael frowns. 'That is bad, Fiona. You should wear a frock. You have no respect if you wear trousers.'

'Sorry – could I try again tomorrow wearing a frock?'

'No – tomorrow you can go to Lichinga, in Niassa Province, to see another side of Mozambique.'

'But I don't want to go to Lichinga.'

'You will be safe in Lichinga. The security is good there. You will leave tomorrow at 0930.'

Back at the Pollana Hotel all is quiet. The woodwork in the vestibule is being buffed up with a pungent polish. It's the twilight hour; the gruelling demands of the day have ended but the social rituals of evening have yet to begin. At the back of the restaurant waiters are dozing. In the vestibule the dwarf cashier watches me politely from behind a metal grill, perched on a bar stool. He has an important job. This hotel has its own foreign exchange allowance, which means you can buy food and drink here. It's the only place in Maputo where that is possible. Outside, the market has collapsed, there is nothing to buy.

In the bar is an expatriate. Not the sort who sneers at the
locals and makes a pile of money to retire on in the home
counties – this expatriate is an ardent communist and a
committed whisky drinker (he's from Scotland). He wants
to create a better world for everyone. He's one of a small
band of Europeans supporting the revolution. They are a
mixed bunch: some dull, some priggish, some amusing.
This man asks me what I'm doing; I tell him and he falls
heavily silent. My desire to get to know him better is
defeated by shyness. He silently nurses a whisky and stares
balefully at the Swazi Ambassador, who, perched on a
cocktail stool, is drunkenly pursuing a monologue along the
lines of 'you can never beat the South Africans; they are
ruthless and hold all the economic cards'. I find a table to
myself and order a Mozambiquan beer – come civil war,
come drought, come World Health Organization warning,
it's a comfort to know that whatever adversity is put in their
way, breweries manage to survive and flourish. As I sit on a
bar stool I hear a voice – so quiet and deep, it's like a voice
in my head.

'Have you got any cigarettes?'

I turn. My heart leaps – it's Godwin Matatu. A slow,
appreciative smile spreads across his battered face as I generously give him one of my precious duty-frees. Some say he
was beaten up by Rhodesian security forces, some say by
ZANU toughs, others by ZAPU toughs; no, says another
account, it was East End toughs in a drunken brawl outside
a pub in Shoreditch. However it happened, his face is now a
network of criss-crosses.

I trade more cigarettes for stories: the South Africans are
gearing up for another killer raid, the Soviet Union is secretly
selling Mozambiquan prawns (caught by its vast vacuum
factory ships) to South Africa in exchange for rand. In the
old days white South Africans flocked to Mozambique for a

Riviera-style holiday, courtesy of the Portuguese. My goodness, those Portuguese knew a thing or two about catering.
Portuguese wine in charming tabernas and plates of delicious
prawns. The South Africans no longer travel to Mozambique
for the prawns; they travel here to bomb the clinics and
schools.

A waiter appears at my side. There's a call from London.
I leap to my feet, conscious of duty, and swiftly leave the bar
under the gaze of the Scotsman, the Swazi and the Zimbabwean. Accelerating out of the bar, I fail to see the glass door
and hit it with full force; I reel back, shocked by an
apparently invisible force-field. Then I collect my wits,
galvanized by a deep sense of humiliation, and stride off
nonchalantly with a throbbing forehead. I confer with London on the telephone; it's agreed – tomorrow I'm heading
out of town, going somewhere free from South African
mischief. My destination, Lichinga, is up-country, inland,
and far away.

LAND OF THE DOOR-CLOSER

Sometimes I think I dreamed Lichinga up, but it is there on
the map, eight hundred miles north of Maputo: the bamboo
town (where houses are made of mud straw and bamboo),
and the concrete (or modern) town with its buildings made
of bricks. The streets are long, wide, empty. Silence holds
everything in its hand: tired people in tattered clothes
walking very slowly under a peerless blue sky. Beautiful, but
drained of energy, of hope, of a future. There are shops in
Lichinga, but they all sell the same item. It's the hinged
thing that stops a door closing too quickly – hundreds of
them, made in East Germany, sprayed in grey paint, mocking the casual window-shopper. I discover later they're called
door-closers. There is one hotel in Lichinga owned by two

brothers. Their complexions are very dark, their features Mediterranean; they have wolfish grins and gold medallions. They are the descendants of generations of racial mixings, Africans and Europeans weaving in and out of their family tree. They seem to be the only rich people in Lichinga, but there is no room for me in their hotel. They say I can have breakfast there. I am to sleep in a colonial bungalow down the road. On the outside it is charming red brick and green paintwork framed by trees, with a crazy paving path leading to the door. Inside the air is stale; it smells like nothing has been aired or cleaned since the revolution. Meals cooked eight years ago linger repulsively in one's nostrils. An old earthenware water-purifier stands in the kitchen. It looks like the home of a junior colonial official. I imagine his wife, poorly educated, of peasant stock, distrustful of her mestizo house girl, keeping to herself the painstaking job of soaking the salted fish to make *bacalhau* for her plump and greedy husband. He is, I imagine, a man of small brain and considerable pride, whose tedious bureaucratic existence is punctuated by occasional but urgent bouts of lust for the house girl.

'Please, lock your room at night,' says the sleepy party official who has brought me here.

'Why?'

He shrugs.

There are no sheets on the bed. Just a candlewick coverlet folded at the end. I spread it across the stained mattress. There is a pillow that gives off a strange cloying odour. The colonial official dribbled in his sleep, perhaps. His wife wore strong cheap scent. I fold a blouse round the offending pillow. I put on my nightie even though it is hot. As I pad across the hall to fetch my notebook, I am stopped in my tracks by a spider. It is alarmingly coloured with green and yellow stripes. I'm not usually bothered by spiders, but this one sends warning signals right through my body. My heart races, my hands are shaking at my sides. It's just me and the monster. It's either kill or get killed. I seize the telephone directory for Niassa Province 1972 and throw it at the spider. I am amazed at the accuracy of my aim, but too revolted to examine the effect of the assault. I leave the directory on top of the spider in the middle of the floor and run to my room. I turn on the light by the switch at the side of the door. This is the main light, the only light. I take a mental snapshot of where the bed is, turn off the light and gallop towards the bed, heart still pounding, mouth dry. My shins hit the metal frame with a crack. I lie on the bed heaving with pain. Then remember I am supposed to lock the door on the inside. I scamper back to the door, put the light on. I touch the key in the lock. As I do so I hear a voice and footsteps. I turn the key, switch off the light and run to the bed, fling myself on it, close my eyes and pray for sleep. More footsteps come, more voices, loud, cheerful, then argumentative. Buckets clank, pots and pans are banged. More people pass through. Some pause outside the door to gossip, then move on. And so it goes on all night. The bungalow is some sort of short cut, a thoroughfare linking one *quartier* with another. I feel like the ghost in someone else's house, the invisible troubled spirit trapped in a world of real people leading ordinary busy lives; my night is their day. Morning, please come to break the spell. Morning comes and all is quiet. Perhaps it was a dream, perhaps the house is haunted.

I resolve to put the night of a thousand people behind me and look for fun in Lichinga. At breakfast I am thirsty.

'Could I have another cup of tea, please?'

'No more tea this morning. I'm sorry, we have a problem with the water supply here,' says one of the brothers charmingly.

'Soft drinks?'

'No, I'm so sorry, we have no soft drinks.' I am certain he has a secret cache of liquid somewhere.

'I'm terribly thirsty.'

'Would you like gin? We have gin.' He gestures to the shelf above the bar. There are rows and rows of bottles of Portuguese gin. He is making the best of a bad situation.

'When will the water come back on?'

'Tomorrow morning six a.m.'

I set off to look round town, head dull, mouth dry. I notice I am being followed.

'Why are you following me?'

'I am from security and have to follow you everywhere.'

'Oh, go away.'

He looks hurt, and then becomes sly.

'So why are you here?'

'Because the ministry sent me here. Please go away. I'm going to have a sleep.'

MAN WITH A HANDKERCHIEF UP HIS NOSE

I go back to my colonial residence and wait for an hour, furious and nauseated afresh by the smell. By the time I emerge he has gone. I head off down the main drag. I see a man coming towards me. I move to one side, but he clearly wants to talk to me. He's in a terrible state. Round his head is a greasy, grey bandage, his face is puffy, and flies have formed a moving halo round him. What looks like the corner of a dirty handkerchief is poking out of one nostril.

He is speaking Portuguese slowly, ponderously, with much plaintive repetition.

'Senhora. Please help me. I don't know where I am.'

'You are in Lichinga.'

'Where is this place?'

'It's in northern Mozambique.'

'I don't want to be here. Help me. I want to go home.'

'Where is your home?'

'Please. It is in Maputo. That is my home. Why am I here? My wife does not know where I am. I want to go home.'

'How did you travel here?'

'I went in an aeroplane. They came in the night and they put me on an aeroplane.' He leans forward, putting a gnarled and very dirty hand on my arm. 'Take me home, please.'

'I can't.'

'Tell my wife where I am.'

'Where do you live?'

'In a tall building near the post office.'

'What is the name of the street?'

'Avenida 24 de Julho 1921.'

'Yes but what number?'

'I don't know – you will see it. Please help me. Take me home.'

'I can't take you home but tell me, what is your name?'

'Mateus Goma.'

'Goodbye – I will try and find your wife.'

I leave him standing in the middle of the road, still trying to make sense of his situation, the flies still orbiting his head.

I later find out that he was one of the Unproductive Ones, Os Improdutivos – people with no papers, no work permits, no official designation and living in the city. Meanwhile in the rural areas farmers were unable to meet government production deadlines. Kill two birds with one stone, thought a neat and clever party member, and send the unproductive ones to the rural areas to make them productive. This plan was called Operacão Producão and was drawn up by someone who was very good at equations at school, someone who grew up in a town, someone who didn't know anything about peasant farmers. And so Os Improdutivos were dispatched, but the farmers had no use for crippled carwash boys or out-of-work waiters; they resented the urban invasion.

The most ardent defenders of Operacão Producão are European aid workers. I try to thrash it out with a bright-eyed young woman.

'I heard most of them had jobs of some sort, so why send them off?'

'They didn't have papers.'

'But they were doing something – washing cars, cleaning people's houses – they weren't idle.'

'Look, this kind of work – what is it? Satisfying the decadent whims of the bourgeoisie. They weren't producing anything.'

'Oh come on, they were using their initiative – they had something to offer and people wanted it.'

The young woman looks pained. 'That's market forces at work . . . serving an elite, oppressing the majority.'

'Oh blimey – isn't it better to have a livelihood than nothing at all?'

She's on the attack now: 'That's a short-term view. Fiona, you have to look at it in the long term. This country is underdeveloped. Do you think it should just be a country of carwash boys, housemaids and low agricultural production?'

'But nobody wanted this man in Lichinga – he doesn't know how to dig, how to plant or harvest.'

'There are always casualties when you try and make big changes.'

I think of the man, the dirty bandage, the flies. Yes, revolutionaries can be very heartless.

LAUGHING WITH A STRANGER

Back in Lichinga my encounter with the unproductive one has not gone unnoticed.

'Why were you talking to the man?' The party man has been looking for me. He tries to make the question sound casual and light-hearted. I can't be bothered to be nice.

'I'm supposed to talk to people. That's my job.'

He is reproachful. 'I was waiting for you at the hotel. We had an appointment at Lichinga Radio.'

'I was being followed, spied on actually.'

The party man sighs.

'That is security.'

'Well, I didn't like it, so I hid in my bedroom to make him go away . . . and then I fell asleep.'

'I take you to the radio station now.'

It's a narrow, tall building. The station manager is called Walter. His complexion is very dark but his lips are thin; he has a small triangular face and a goatee beard. He wears a cable-knit cardigan, which makes me think of autumn in England. He is one of those people who is always moving – fiddling with elastic bands, pens, paper clips, moving from one foot to another, pacing up and down. For no reason at all he seems to me completely familiar; like an old friend, a brother. For the first time in two weeks I feel comfortable even if my mouth is dry. He reads my mind.

'Are you thirsty?'

'Yes, I am.'

'I have some small water here for you.'

He pours some water into a small cup from a large metal jug. It is slightly cloudy. He notices my critical look.

'It's been boiled.'

'Thank you – your English is very good.'

'I learned it with the BBC.'

Walter supervises all transmissions from the building. He explains how, under the Portuguese, the radio station was just an offshoot of the metropolis. Northern Mozambique was badly neglected by the colonial rulers, and now the party wants to change that. The policy is for local stations to serve the community, which means broadcasting in more languages and installing speakers in the villages for group listening. Not enough research has been done on the different languages and dialects up here. Some broadcasts are not understood. All this seems a good subject for an interview.

'Walter, can I record you explaining all this?'

Walter smiles, but looks at the floor and pushes a paper clip around with the toe of his battered shoe.

'Ah no, Fiona.'

'Oh, come on.'

'No, I can't. You must ask Comrade Verde.'

'But he doesn't know anything about the area. He's pining to go back to Maputo. Please, please, please, Walter.'

'No, no, no, Fiona.' He becomes stern. 'Now I show you the studio.'

Oh dear, perhaps we're not friends after all.

We move into the corridor. Walter points through the window of the studio door. Inside a young man is mouthing at the microphone, frowning with concentration.

'He is new. He is broadcasting ao viva, living, yes?'

'Broadcasting live, yes. Right.'

'When we go in we must be silent.'

He pushes the door open carefully with his shoulder. The young DJ sees us out of the corner of his eye. Our presence gives added edge and drama to his performance.

'And now, comrades, the latest hit from Fernando Luis . . .'

Walter and I are now both in the studio – the door has sunk back into place with a click. In our effort to be as silent as possible we lower our heads and look at the floor. Gradually I am distracted by Walter's fiddling – he is fiddling furiously with a biro. It cannot be long before he drops it. The DJ is beginning to enjoy himself, spurred on by our interest.

'I hope you liked that music, comrades. I hope it will help you with your daily tasks, contributing to a better, stronger, more productive—'

Ping. The pen does a double somersault, sails through the air and clatters to the ground. The DJ appears not to notice the gymnastic pen. He carries on, but fractionally less certain now in his style. Walter puts a finger to his mouth, as if to prevent the pen from making any more noise; he bends over and I catch his eye. I notice his body is trembling slightly. I look away. I feel a smile spread across my face. Walter's mouth is twitching. I breathe in deeply to calm myself. There's a sharp intake of breath from Walter. I catch his eye again. I can see tears. There's a sort of creaking sound coming from the back of his palate, as he fights the quickening pace of his breathing. I clap my hands to my mouth. The more we think about the importance of the live transmission and the sincere efforts of the young DJ to broadcast nicely, the more we want to give in to the desire to let go. There was no accounting for it; except we knew we shouldn't, and that made us want to all the more. We still manage to be silent, apart from our laboured breathing, but our poor bodies are shaking with the effort of containment, tears pouring down our cheeks. Walter motions towards the door. He pushes it open with his shoulder. I follow. We stand in the corridor shaking and watching with big eyes as the door very slowly falls back into place, again with the minute click. And that's the signal for us to collapse. We sink to the floor, roll around and laugh – like jackasses, like kookaburras, our legs waving around in the air, like ponies enjoying a dust bath. Not for us the tinkling laughter of a drawing-room comedy. No, this is life and death laughter. Noisy, snorting, rough, squealing.

What a truly magnificent place Mozambique is now; and in this moment even Lichinga is redeemed.

Some five minutes later we pick ourselves up off the floor and self-consciously dust ourselves down. We go back, wordless, to the office. I make myself busy looking through my notebook. Walter tidies away some files, then goes to the window and gazes out.

'Comrade Verde is here.'

'Right, I'd better go down. He's taking me to the airport. Goodbye, Walter.'

'Goodbye, Fiona.'

'Good luck with the village projects.'

'Thank you. Boa viagem.'

'Obrigada.'

We shake hands solemnly and I go down the concrete stairs to catch my plane back to Maputo.

I went to Avenida 24 de Julho 1921. I paced round the tallest block of flats near the post office. I asked people if they knew Mrs Goma. Nobody who stopped to reply knew her, others hurried past. The building was at least twenty storeys high, and at least three hundred people must have lived in there. I'm sorry, Mr Goma, I failed to deliver your message.

FOUR

Comrades Complain

~~~

THROUGH THE LOOKING GLASS

*The experiences of revolutionary struggle of the Mozambiquan
people provide an illustration of the struggle for a better future.
Dear comrades, our history validates the thesis that the motive
force of history is class struggle. Class struggle was, and is, a
reality on the African continent.*

(Samora Machel, Berlin, 11 April 1983)

Seven years after my visit to Mozambique, President Samora
Machel is dead and history has turned its back on the
dialectic, surrendering itself to an altogether more chaotic
unfolding of events.

It is to the Soviet Union that I fly in 1990 to find out what
the Russians really felt about their African clients, the truth
behind the rhetoric and the ideology, I hope. Machel, Nkrumah, dos Santos, Nyerere, Kaunda, Mugabe – all of them
were inspired to a greater or lesser extent by what Marxist
Leninism had to offer: for some it meant AK 47s, Antonov
planes and scholarships, for others a coherent strategy (on
paper at least) with which to challenge imperialism and
capitalism. But the rules were strict, the orthodoxies stifling.
Personality, emotions were hidden by the elaborate structures
of the state, and that suited the propagandists in the West. A

listener to the BBC living in Enugu, Nigeria, hits the spot with his letter sent in December 1989:

> *Throughout the colonial period, we were made to understand that the Communists, and in particular, the Soviet Union and her allies, were soulless and were warmongers.*
>
> *It was only a heady few who dared to go there, much more make friends with them. But as we have come to know, the Russians are no more than part of the Human Race. They have feelings. They are capable of hate and love like the rest of humanity. With Glasnost and Perestroika now part of the international vocabulary, the West is fast losing the argument of who should be labelled the villain of the peace.*

It is just two months after the Berlin Wall is breached. Communism is collapsing; there's no return. The biggest bees' nest in the world has been disturbed. The queen bee is in her death throes. A good time to find out about the cold war, while it is still fresh in people's minds and before some new appalling regime gets stuck in.

My first stop in the Soviet Union is External Services, Gostelradio. And there I find a parallel universe; parallel to the one I have known most of my working life. Gostelradio has the same totalitarian architecture as the BBC World Service's HQ, Bush House; the same stone, marble and huge windows, the same splendid 1930s joinery evident in the reception desk (ripped out, alas, by BBC management to make way for the Swedish-Tudor look when the capital budget was found, at the end of the financial year, to be underspent). I feel quite at home in Gostelradio. There are the same unpredictable lifts – rather more in number than in Bush House and smaller in size, but provoking the same grumbles from staff about their slowness. And of course, there is an African Service, just as there is a BBC African

Service. Only this African Service broadcasts in some fourteen African languages, while the BBC has stuck timidly to three. There is a Hausa Service in London, there is a Hausa Service in Moscow.

Mohamed has been a Hausa producer for five years, and he's had enough. We are standing in the cubicle with a Hausa broadcast going out on the other side of the glass in the studio.

'Listen to him.' Mohamed gestures to the Russian colleague doing the broadcast. 'Foolish man. Rubbish. You know this is one of the most popular programmes in northern Nigeria.' Ah, so Mohamed is jealous? Wrong. 'You know why it's so popular? Because it's so bloody bad. Useless. It is so bad it makes people laugh. It's a comedy show. This man cannot speak Hausa. He has never been to Nigeria. Can you imagine I have to put up with this?' This is the first of a great many rhetorical questions *I* have to put up with from Russians as well as Africans. Everyone has discovered they have had enough. Everyone is brimming with harsh criticism, cruel comment and a burning desire for something much, much better – there's not one thing in seventy-three years of postrevolutionary history worth keeping. It's all frightful, and everything in the West is great. Margaret Thatcher is a goddess of wealth, health and wisdom.

But for one person it's business as usual. Revolution or no revolution. Down a corridor in one of the nicely provisioned reading niches, sitting calmly at a small table with a tasselled lamp casting a friendly yellow glow, sits a plump old lady in her seventies. She is reading Charlotte Brontë's *Jane Eyre*. She glances up and smiles vaguely. She is Annabel Litvinov, daughter of Maxim Litvinov who was Soviet Ambassador to Great Britain in the 1930s, later Foreign Minister. Her youth was spent in England and this has given her a passion for English literature. She once worked at Gostelradio, but is long retired; she has her doppelgängers in Bush House: well-educated, frail old ladies in cardigans. Some were announcers, some, despite excellent language degrees, remained faithful secretaries to pipe-smoking, oddly behaved men in charge of language services. Long retired, these ladies come back for cheap lunches and a chance meeting with former colleagues; like homing pigeons they cannot keep away. Yes, Annabel Litvinov is the one serene figure I meet. My guide is no less grumbly than the rest but has a strategic, clever air about him; he's plotting his way out all right. I may provide some help, I may not; for the time being he is keeping his counsel. He is wary of the angry Hausa, who continues to rant.

'Fucking place, I could have a much better standard of living in Nigeria.' Steady on – that's not the sort of language one expects from a Kano man. 'I can buy anything I want in Nigeria,' he boasts. 'But here they are with nothing. And they call us black monkeys.'

Well, he has a point. The previous day I met an Azerbaijani woman, married to another Nigerian, who obviously spoilt her with the sorts of things a lady likes. As we idly consider how hard it is being a woman in a man's world, she confides in me, 'Seventy years of revolution and no sanitary towels.' You can get those in Nigeria, I know that for a fact, even if you pay through the nose for them.

Back at Gostelradio, Mohamed spells out the imminent brain drain. 'Everybody here wants to go. Nobody wants to stay in this place.'

'Will you go back?'

'Sure I will go back, as soon as I can.'

'Why did you come?'

'I came to do Comparative Studies.'

'What were you comparing?'

'Bourgeois journalism and socialist journalism.'

'What is bourgeois journalism?'

Without so much as a hesitation he reels it off: 'Bourgeois journalism aims at mobilizing the sources of production. It is advertising-orientated.'

'What is socialist journalism?'

'Socialist journalism is propaganda.' Then he is off again. 'Now you see what we have to endure all these years. It is different in your BBC Hausa Service – you are professional. Programmes are good.'

I am keen to avoid the subject of job opportunities.

'I'm afraid I have to go now. Good luck.'

We leave the Russian broadcaster still at his microphone, the movements of his mouth just that fraction of a second out of sync with the recording of his voice; it gives him the desperate air of a goldfish trying to catch the fish food as it floats past.

GOODBYE TO ALL THAT

I want to dub some good examples of Soviet propaganda, aimed at an African audience. So we head for the archives. All programmes are listed in what look like large school exercise books. Each programme is entered in neat cyrillic script, along with its duration and transmission date. A straight line runs across each page diagonally from corner to corner.

'What does that mean?'

'Oh, it means the programmes listed on that page have been destroyed.'

'I see.'

We turn page after page, each bearing the mark of destruction. The exercise is proving fruitless.

'What's happened – why have all these programmes been destroyed?'

'You must understand that this was all propaganda . . . propaganda and lies. We are now in a new era. We want truth and democracy.'

'But whether you like it or not, it's part of your history.' An obvious point but one which I feel has to be made.

He is unmoved. 'This is an episode in our history we wish to forget.'

As we talk we turn the pages automatically. Then something flashes past: an unmarked page.

'Stop, stop, stop – turn back.' We shuffle the pages back and there it is, an unmarked page. It has only one entry on it.

'What does it say?'

' "The Life and Death of P. Lumumba. Duration: 15'45. Recorded: 17.01.1963." '

'Can I take a copy of it?'

'Sure,' my guide says, mildly amused as though indulging an eccentric old lady.

Patrice Lumumba, Prime Minister of Congo (assassinated 1961), is an official Soviet hero – there's a whole university named after him. The tape on which the programme is recorded is made in East Germany. The tape speed is the same as in Britain, seven and a half inches per second. The programme is announced with a harsh, unmelodic fanfare of brass that goes from A flat up to the C natural beyond an octave and then down two semitones to B flat, over and over again. Underneath a drum pounds out a monotonous, vaguely warlike beat. The voice of the narrator is smooth, silky, slow and bears the unmistakable accent of a Russian who has learned his English from American language tapes. His name is Yuri Zhukov.

'The National Liberation Movement developed swiftly in the Congo and menacingly. Within a year Lumumba's name had deprived the colonialists of their peace and in the autumn of 1959 they jailed him. He was thrown into a gloomy jail in Jadeauville in Katanga, but it was already too late. The people of the Congo had awakened. Several months later the jailers were forced to release him, and with red handcuff marks on his hands he immediately sat down around the table to negotiate with the Belgian government on the condition of the granting of independence to Congo. And a few months after that he became the Prime Minister of a country which is a little smaller than all Western Europe.'

So concludes part two of Yuri Zhukov's life and death of Patrice Lumumba.

Not nearly as dull as the Soviet broadcasters of my childhood, cutting through the ionosphere on powerful short-wave transmitters with their descriptions of grain production in Georgia increasing by 20 per cent compared to last year's harvest. Given a juicy topic, like an African nationalist hero pitted against the most unpleasant colonial power in Europe, Soviet broadcasting shows quite an aptitude for dramatic effect.

Happy to fail

I am sitting in an apartment by the river Moskva. The ceilings are high and the windows huge. It is the home of Sergei Schlichter, a retired transport engineer. He and his wife are warm and welcoming. We drink tea and eat pickled vegetables. The block which this apartment is part of has a sad history, a monument to the purges. It was here, in the House on the Embankment, as it is called, that leading party members lived in the late 1920s and 1930s, and it was from here that they were taken at night, discreetly, no fight, no pangas, no disembowelling or arson, no garbled government statements, just a tap on the door and a void. Either way fear and death were the end results.

It looks as though the place has not been decorated since those days. Walls and ceilings are grey and beige with the patina of age. The reason I have come here is to get a glimpse of a Soviet view of Africa, a personal view.

I have already spoken to Anatol Gromyko, secretary of the African Institute, the spitting image of his beetle-browed father Andrei Gromyko, one-time Minister of Foreign Affairs and later Chairman of the Praesidium of the Supreme Soviet. Half an hour of special pleading from this armchair African-ist leaves me feeling short-changed: his intellectual reference point on African matters is, interestingly, American: 'W. E. Dubois had talks with Khrushchev; I consider him one of the best.' Yes, but he died at the beginning of the century. How about Malcolm X? He died only twenty-five years ago.

'It is true that Soviet scholarship was cut off from Africa, and studied it mainly theoretically,' he continues, enjoying the sensation of spontaneous discussion, '. . . we have become more serious now . . . we have abandoned stereotypes, we are moving away from ideological position, when everything was studied through the theory of class struggle . . . but now Marxist theory of the dialectic is still helpful . . . the main thrust of our foreign policy in Africa must be co-operation, not confrontation . . . Africa needs help . . . we must get rid of the arms race in the third world . . . it is unfortunate that many countries sell arms and we are one of these countries . . .' He makes a sudden gear change from the geopolitical and the military to the humanitarian. 'But you know, desertification is a terrible menace, leading to famine . . . do you know every two seconds someone dies in the third world, mostly children? . . . we must look at Africa through human eyes, with humanity and compassion instead of confrontation.'

My goodness, Mr Gromyko clearly needs to borrow Mr Kaunda's hankie. But what about his father? Did he ever go to Africa? 'He visited Egypt.' Egypt? Minister of Foreign Affairs for twenty-eight years and he only managed Egypt? Theoretical indeed.

And now here I am in an apartment in the House on the Embankment, Dom na Naberezhnoy, for something altogether more intimate, honest and interesting. And I am not disappointed: Sergi Schlichter captures the thinking of the time more accurately than the apologetic Gromyko. For a start there's the Machiavellian yet ideological strategies ascribed to profit-hungry western businessmen:

'Our approach was that western companies in Africa were neocolonialist – not interested in development, only in underdevelopment.' Milton Obote was in power when Sergei arrived with his family. The government was just turning left, but there were British and French advisers as well as Soviet ones.

'Our image was that the British and French were colonialists and we are sincere, there to help. But when I arrived I understood very quickly that for the Ugandans there is no difference. We were all white people. For me it was frustrating that they did not understand that I really wanted to help.' Soviet aid to Uganda then was not inconsiderable: a cotton plant, a spinning plant, major work on two airfields at Entebbe and Gulu.

But Sergei's chance to show the serious intentions of the Soviet Union came when the government asked the Russians to supply a radio transmitter. 'So OK. Very good project from ideological point of view, so I went to the embassy and wrote an application for a transmitter. Then came the answer: supply to complete in two years' time. "Why so long?" "Because we have a plan and the transmitter is not included in the plan." Finally I got the application through to Moscow and it was approved. After a year the equipment came. Then I felt very uncomfortable when an old British man said, "We used this kind of transmitter twenty years ago in the BBC."' Sergei pulls a snooty face and puts on a disapproving tone, and I can just imagine that sneering Brit.

'So I went to the embassy,' Sergei continues, anxious to unfold the whole story. 'I said, "Look, people, when the President of Uganda came to us, it was an honour – he could have asked Italy, Philips, Sony, but no he asked the Russians, and we failed, and . . ."' Sergei's voice rises to an unhappy crescendo, '". . . and we were happy that we failed."' The experience is clearly fresh in his memory.

What happened when Amin launched his coup? I wondered. 'The people in the embassy locked all the doors and stayed tight. They started packing to go, but they told me to stay otherwise it might be thought a snub.'

Sergei Schlichter eventually did leave the country, hopeful at least that what he had learned about the place could contribute to a larger pool of understanding; it was not to be. 'I was full of ideas about how to reorganize this and that, but nobody was interested. Even when the Ugandan delegation came a few months after I got back, I was not consulted or invited to talk to them. I was surprised when I came back to Moscow how cut off they made me from Africa. You see, they were inventing their own Africa. They didn't want the real thing.'

TAKE ME THERE

'Under the African sky I want to dream of my Russia,' wrote Pushkin. His great-grandfather, Hanibal, came from Ethiopia. He was sold into slavery and ended up in the court of Peter the Great, to become the Emperor's personal adviser, later an admiral. But Pushkin never managed to visit the continent of his ancestor; instead he dreamed of Africa under Russian skies. As did Professor Apollon Davidson, the Soviet Union's leading historian on Africa for at least twenty years. From 1947 to 1967 he studied a continent he was not allowed to visit. For twenty years he studied that massive region in the abstract, his pursuit of history taking on the creative hues of fiction, even poetry. His passion was South Africa. He only visited it for the first time in September 1989, just a few months previous to our meeting.

'It is a little too late now. I am old.'

My heart aches. I want to fling my arms round him and say, 'No, you're not too old.' But I think better of it. It would be an abuse of hospitality. His wife – Professor of Malagasy Studies at Moscow State University – has taken time off from her academic duties to bake such delicious cakes for our tea. In the 1980s Apollon went to Zambia, but saw only the inside of his hotel bedroom and the conference room. His recent trip to South Africa was different. He describes it with fierce tenderness.

'As you know, there was many years academic boycott. But then I get invitation supported by Mass Democratic Movement and ANC. I came to South Africa as first Soviet scholar in six decades. The last delegation of Soviet scholars was in 1929. They organized our programme brilliant. We had the chance to see six cities: Johannesburg, Pretoria, Cape Town, Port Elizabeth, Stellenbosch, Grahamstown, and also people at the university.' But the most important thing of all for him: he had a chance to see life in the townships and in the shanty towns. 'All these decades of my life. And only now I've met Walter Sisulu, Govan Mbeki, and a lot of ordinary people.'

Apollon Davidson allows me to pore over old copies of the *Negro Worker*, published in the 1930s and mainly distributed by Liberian sailors round the world. I look at my watch and realize it is time for me to leave. A final question: 'What do you think about these changes?'

He shrugs.

'You don't seem enthusiastic.'

'You cannot be sure how long this freedom will last. We are the descendants of Ivan the Terrible. You never know.' Professor Davidson falls silent, his brow is furrowed as though anticipating yet another cruel twist to the unfolding historical imperative. Yes, it really is time for me to go.

I collect my things, then that strange sensation surfaces again, the sensation of being in a parallel universe. It occurs to me that Apollon Davidson – by origin a Siberian Jew – has *his* doppelgänger in Britain in the shape of Basil Davidson. Basil Davidson is a little older than Apollon perhaps, but just as passionate about Africa. Both were in the academic wilderness in the 50s and 60s. ('Africa has no history,' the Regius Professor of History, Hugh Trevor-Roper, famously said.) But at least Basil Davidson could travel where he wanted, and by the 70s Africa had become in British academic circles a respectable field of study.

'Do you know Basil Davidson?' I ask as I leave, ready to tell him all about this extraordinary coincidence – another Africanist with the same name. My patronizing impulse is stopped in its tracks.

'Yes, of course I know Basil Davidson,' says Apollon a little wearily.

FIVE

Rare Beauty and Strange Stains

∽∾∾∾

The great hair hunt

'Fiona, you are so lucky to have hair like that.' This is the first compliment Véronique has paid me. We are friends, so frank criticism is part of the deal. As far as clothes and style are concerned I am a sitting target. For a start I don't have proper luggage. Just a holdall and, worse: a backpack. Then again I don't have high-heeled shoes. Or nice cocktail dresses, or nice jewellery. This is a trial for Véronique who comes from West Africa; she is the empress of style.

She is now travelling with me throughout East Africa giving her impressions: West goes East. Her impressions of me come first. 'You're not wearing those shorts, are you?'

'They're practical.'

'You look like some old colonial . . .' Véronique buries the emerging insult in peals of laughter.

Kenyan dress sense gets a rough ride too.

'I'm beginning to wonder if I am in an African country,' she says, giving the passers-by in Nairobi a pitying look. 'They all look so western. Oh my goodness, look at her in yellow and brown – she looks terrible, people would laugh in Cameroun, I'm telling you.' She pauses to take in some more. '. . . well, I suppose a few of them look a bit trendy, but it's not really sophisticated. In fact, they all look very ordinary.'

Nairobi 1992 is a wannabe western modern city with high-rise buildings and marble monuments to power and exclusion. It's a city where the elite fear all the ordinary folk as riff-raff. There's nowhere to sit outside at night and drink a beer; you have to go down, down, downtown, and then you really will meet some riff-raff, so better hide in a huge, gloomy Chinese restaurant along with the rest of the rich cowards. Traditional costume is for the rural people only. Educated people always want to look western.

A woman in traditional Masai dress walks towards us. The man accompanying her wears a battered shiny suit. Véronique steps forward bravely in her best society hostess manner.

'Hello, dear – can you tell us why you are wearing African clothes – you're not wearing western clothes, are you?' The girl titters and stares with large eyes. 'So why are you wearing this? Is it the fashion?'

The man steps forward. 'She doesn't want to talk to BBC.'

I feel a bit scared. Véronique doesn't miss a beat.

'Oh, why not?' The question is delivered in a tone of mild surprise.

The man is surly. 'We are not interested. She does not want to talk to the press.'

I twitter, 'Ask him why he—'

Véronique firmly cuts me off. 'Let's leave it – if they start out like that, they can end up by giving us a punch.' Somehow a short interview on high street fashion does not seem worth a punch.

We set off in search of more promising subjects: boastful opposition politicians, and know-it-all taxi drivers. But every encounter, every commentary is punctuated by Véronique's anxiety about her hair. She left British soil with her hair

relaxed in big curls; the professional-woman look; perhaps a
hint of glamour with that side parting? But now it's drooping
rather, and her scalp is getting itchy and hot, but it doesn't
look that bad to me. 'I'm telling you, it's too hot, it's killing
me.' There are other irritations too. Her bowels. My bowels.
Mine are loose. Hers are constipated. We are doing East
Africa on the cheap and that means sharing a room, sharing
a bathroom, sharing a lavatory. Her sessions are long and
occasional; mine are short and frequent. Sometimes our
bowels veer back to the middle of the bowel behaviour
spectrum. That is, if she eats four slices of pineapple and I
swallow a couple of Imodium pills. But whatever our bowels
are doing, the state of her hair is constantly gnawing at her
peace of mind.

'I have to find a hairdresser – I can't go on any longer –
it's got to be plaited.'

'Well, let's go now.'

'No – you don't understand. We've got to get a weave.
I'm not getting any cheap rubbish extensions here, because
it will be worse.'

'Oh God, can't you wait until we get back? Do you have
to do it now – I mean it looks great.'

'It *does not* look great. And what is waiting? I can't wait
until we get back. You don't understand African hair. You
don't know what a blinking nuisance it is.'

Actually I do know a bit about African hair. Fact number
one: only mad people neglect their hair in Africa. Fact
number two: grooming African hair involves constant effort
and money. Fact number three: the poorest people stick at
it. If your average white English git woke up one morning
with African hair, he or she would be in the loony bin by
day three. Of course there is the short-all-over option, but
that's more African-American LA intellectual; Véronique is a
big hair woman, who sees her hair as her crowning glory.

A hairdresser is finally found. But the price is not right.

'What! For big braids? I could flipping have my hair done in microplaits in Cameroun for that.'

Two days later we head off on the night train for Kisumu.

'You see, I can't wash it. It will look even worse,' she says as she assembles her expensive skin cleansers and moisturizers on the lid of the corner basin. 'You are lucky, you can just wash your hair, dry it and it's fine. But I have to have it styled or braided.'

We've been travelling an hour and the train has just stopped. All Véronique's misgivings about train journeys seem proven.

'You see – and you said train is the only way to travel in the world.'

'Oh stop bloody moaning, get the brandy out and tell me a story.'

'All right. What shall I tell?'

'I don't know. Tell me about when you were little.' We settle down in the unnatural stillness of a train stranded far from human habitation.

'When I was a little girl I lived in the town; I first went to visit my relatives in the village when I was five years old. See, I was just a little girl. Everything in the village was strange. I needed to go to the loo. I thought there would be a toilet. But we were in the countryside and they don't have things like that in the villages. I was told to go in the village pig pen. That's where people went in those days. I climbed over the fence, pulled down my knickers and squatted. The business started to come out. Then I heard this sound; the pig was making that ... what is it? The pig was making a sound through its nose like ...'

'A snuffling sound?'

'Aha – exactly. It snuffled, and then it started to run after me. I could only make funny short steps because my knickers were round my knees, but that stuff was still dangling from my little bum, and the pig wanted it.'

The grotesque image on top of three brandies makes us forget about the misery of broken-down train engines and limp hair.

Véronique tries to steer me out of my laughter and into the terror of the moment.

'I screamed and screamed. My relatives all came out and they watched. They thought it was funny to see the little town girl with a shitty bottom chased by a pig.'

'Well, it must have been.'

'It was terrifying, I'm telling you.'

'So what happened?'

'Oh, someone hauled me out. I did not like village life as a child.'

'But you don't go to the rural areas now, do you?'

'Yes – I go.' Her tone is a little haughty. 'And it's very nice. They are very good people in the villages.'

We finally get to Kisumu, four hours late.

The word is put out – 'Véronique needs a hairdresser.'

We meet a nurse and her daughter on the bus, and invite them back to our hotel room for soft drinks and a chat. The nurse has relaxed hair in a sort of smart bun. The daughter, who is twelve, has her hair done in two big barley-sugar twists and sings a hymn for us in a high clear voice. The nurse's sister does their hair, but she has travelled to Nairobi.

We look for someone to come to the hotel in the evening, but nobody can come at such short notice. And we've got work to do during the day.

'Well, can't you at least wash it?'

'How can I wash it if I haven't found a hairdresser?'

'You don't need a hairdresser to wash it, do you?'

'No but I told you if I wash it it will go crazy. You see, you're European and you don't understand.'

'Maybe we'll find someone in Kampala.'

THE TWINKLING LIGHTS OF KAMPALA

Goodbye Kisumu with your lakeside views and shoeshops, and hello Kampala. Off we go in a taxi flying down the Busia Jinja road to the capital of Uganda, seat of the King of Buganda. We run the gamut of roadblocks manned by boy soldiers who frighten me with their guns and youthfulness, but each time we are waved through. We slide into the twinkling lights of Kampala, welcoming, humming with evening bustle, small bars and stalls lit up and well attended, a city which belongs to the ruled as well as the rulers. But Kampala 1992 is not the height of hair fashion. Most of the women scrape their hair straight back, with no lotion, no curls, no plaits. Mm ... This is a demure Kiganda look, which, along with the long, high-shouldered, high-yoked *basoti*, conceals a tradition of erotic customs stretching back through the centuries. The hair situation is now grave. Many of the streets of Kampala are unsurfaced; red dust is getting everywhere. Half a century ago people suffered from the same problem.

Uganda Herald, 16 December 1936

Letter to the Editor

Dear Sir,
    The dust in Kampala just now is dreadful. At busy times one moves in a continuous cloud of red, irritating and highly germinous dust.

> *What is our municipal water cart doing? Is it true it has*
> *been put on other work? If so, why?*
> *Yours 'choked'.*

And today's dust is particularly attracted to Véronique's hair. So now her scalp is getting in the way of efficient programme making, or so it seems to me.

'Go on, do a commentary to mike,' I, the producer, say imperiously to her, the presenter.

'What?'

'Say something about the market.'

'What do you want me to say?'

'I don't know, but I need some sort of a link to go into the interviews we're doing here.'

'Well, what do you want me to say?'

'Just describe the market. OK, rolling.'

'Um . . . Kampala market is quite big . . .'

'Wait for five seconds. OK, rolling.'

She waits for five seconds. Then: 'Where was I? Oh yes, Kampala is quite big . . .'

'Wait for five, Véro, and start the piece for real, don't start the piece by saying "where was I?"'.

There's a significant and grumpy pause.

'Kampala market is quite big but we have bigger markets at home . . .'

'Yes, but you've got to establish that we are actually here first. Say something like "We're now at Kampala's main market".' I am impossible to satisfy.

Véronique clears her throat, once, twice. It's a sign she's nervous, or fed up, or both.

'Er-erm, erm . . . we're now at Kampala's main market . . .' Silence.

'And?'

'And what?'

'Do a link. Go on to say something about the market – get some detail and colour into it.'

'What do you want me to say?'

The sooner we find a hairdresser and some laxatives the better.

We leave Kampala two days later in sullen silence.

In Dar es Salaam we meet up with our guide. He is a man. And this is just what we need, an excellent antidote to female sulks and feuding. He makes a fuss of us with hugs and kisses. The grumpy spell is broken as we tell him about our adventures. We put the hair problem to him, and before we know it we're meandering down the backstreets and alleyways of Dar, tiptoeing across the rickety planks which span smelly storm drains. A door is opened and suddenly we're in a room full of women plaiting other women's hair. Extensions hang from hooks on the wall like Spanish moss. The air is heavy with lotions and conditioners. It's a harem of hairdressers, and they are the real thing: there are sputniks and twists and microplaits all evolving under deft fingers. But no one is free to do Véronique's hair before tomorrow evening. And tomorrow morning is when we set off for Zanzibar.

We travel to Zanzibar by hovercraft, watching an American shock-horror film with Greek subtitles about a homicidal robot running amok in Vietnam. 'This is the good bit . . . where his head gets chopped off.' Véronique's seen it before, and she doesn't get motion sick. Lucky her.

Ah, Zanzibar. We step off the boat and smell the spices. The effect is exciting and restorative. And there waiting for us (or so it seems), as if by magic, is a 1962 Humber with gleaming chrome trimmings. Its owner, Mohamed, is a taxi driver. And after a bit of haggling he becomes *our* taxi driver. He takes us to the Spice Inn. And the big empty rooms, with carved wooden doors, meet with our mutual approval. We have a delicious meal, the first proper meal in ages for either of us – chicken, coconut, lime, coriander. We really are friends again. Our bowels are also restored to good humour. Our sessions on the lavatory are satisfactory. We bounce up and down on the beds, look out at the streets of the old stone town from our carved wooden balcony, and generally feel at peace with the world. I'm rather hoping we can forget about the hair. But that was a vain and typically European hope.

There's a knock at the door – it's the room maid with a bin for the bathroom.

'Excuse me, I want to have my hair done, you know, plaited. Can you find someone? They must be good and cheap and they must come to the hotel as we are very busy.'

The maid smiles sweetly and leaves the room without saying a word.

'Excuse me,' Véronique bellows and leaps to her feet but she has already vanished. 'I can't understand these people.'

Oh please don't get grumpy, I think.

Five minutes later the room maid appears with a friend. There's a general discussion of prices, and then a deal is struck with surprising speed.

'What is your name?' Véronique asks.

'My name is Naima.'

'Naima, don't be late. We are very busy.'

'Yes, Mama.'

The afternoon is spent looking for extensions. They do not appear to exist in Zanzibar. All inquiries are met with blank or even slightly hostile looks.

Naima comes with not one but three friends. This is obviously a spectator sport.

'We have no extensions,' says Véronique glumly.

'What is it?'

'No artificial hair for the plaits.'

'It is good. Islam say no other hair in your hair.'

Naima begins to plait. This is extra money for her.

In the hotel she earns £8 a month.

'If I keep three months' money I can buy a dress.'

'Hey, that's not true.' Véronique is shocked.

'Yes, is true.'

'How many hours a day?'

'Eight hours a day. The salary is to buy soap. I am with my parents, but they are old, and I buy the soap.'

'Anything else?'

'No.'

'So all your salary goes on soap.'

'Yes.'

'Are you married?'

'I am devoid.'

'Divorced, you mean?'

'Yes.'

'Why?'

'Because my husband's mother is not good. She don't like me. She complain about me.'

'You have children?'

'Three children, but they took them.'

'They are with your husband?'

'Yes.'

'Are you happy?'

'No ... but I happy they are there, because my salary not good. If I take children, what can happen with little money?'

'You visit?'

'Yes.'

'When do you see them?'

'Every Tuesday.'

'Is it difficult to find good husband?'

'Yes – some drink alcohol, some beat you, others look for women, some look for children.'

'What is your ideal husband?'

'I want to stay in peace, I don't want to stay with his parents.'

As she talks, she plaits deftly, but not as fast as the women in the hair harem.

The last plait is done. Véronique takes a critical look in the mirror.

'Oh thank you – I like it. Only it makes my head look bare, because there are no extensions.'

'Hey, you will be a beautiful lady, and if you walk on the street you can get a good man to marry you.' Naima and the girls giggle.

Véronique looks severe. 'I am married already, thank you,' she says primly, handing Naima her fee, equivalent to half of her month's salary. Just as I am thinking how imperious she is, Véronique beckons to the girls. 'Listen, before you go, have a look at those clothes on the bed. You may choose some.'

Véronique has laid out a selection of rather posh ladies' clothes – big jumpers with leather appliqués, wraparound skirts, cardigans with sequins on them.

'Take what you want.'

The girls cluster around excitedly. For the first time they are animated – laughing, whispering. They each choose something and make their goodbyes hurriedly, anxious that their luck might change, perhaps. 'Thank you, thank you.' I come to the conclusion that Véronique is a kinder person than I am.

I too once went in search of an African hairdo. The location was unpromising: a bleak suburb on the outskirts of Moscow. The hairdressers were from Senegal and the Ivory

Coast, and worked largely by appointment to the African embassy wives. The state had a 30 per cent shareholding in the enterprise. The outside was dismal, grey concrete. The interior was palatial – white walls and plush red curtains; everywhere were huge mirrors surrounded by great carved frames.

'You see,' said the beautiful Senegalese co-owner, 'we wanted it to have an African look. So we hired Russian craftsmen and showed them photos and postcards of African carvings. So they did the carving, copying the pictures, and I think it's a good job.' A very good job. Moscow needs a bit of cultural imperialism from down south. When I explain that I want not just an interview but to have my hair done she is amused and interested. 'Thirty cane rows please across the scalp, with shoulder-length extensions.' 'No problem – it will be an hour and a half.' I am given a seat. Opposite me a long-limbed, high-cheekboned beauty is having what looks like one thousand plaits put in, attended by three girls plaiting simultaneously. She stares at me ironically. Is her left eyebrow naturally arched or is it the sight of me? I wonder. A plump young Ghanaian is assigned to me. I can tell she is silently cursing my slippery European tresses.

'Is difficult to get your extension in,' she eventually concedes. Her voice is husky.

'Oh, I'm so sorry.'

She's half irritated and half amused as she tries to anchor the artificial strands at the base of my real hair. Her determination pays off.

An hour and a half later and I am done. I present a strange sight, but rather splendid. I feel extraordinary, magnificent – the cane rows look a bit like a barrister's wig; they feel like a headdress. I imagine myself in the palace of Queen Nefertiti, presiding over fertility ceremonies. I also feel ferociously hungry. The canteen of External Service Radio is still the best place in town to get a cheap meal. Four months after the collapse of communism only the canniest people know where to find a decent meal in Moscow. I queue up in the canteen with a friendly Russian broadcaster. Soon I can feel eyes behind me, boring into my hairdo, into my skull, my soul. Then I hear muttering and a snigger. I turn round. A fat, lardy woman avoids my gaze.

'What did she say?' I ask my fellow broadcaster.

He looks embarrassed. 'She said . . . she said, "Is that a hairdo or a disease?"'

QUEEN OF THE SPICE ISLES

But two years on Véronique is happy with her hairdo. I have a photo of her and me paddling on a sandy shore in Zanzibar, celebrating her hairdressing triumph – a modest twelve-plait job, no extensions. She is wearing a purple dress of tartan design with box pleats. She's smiling generously. I'm smiling with a frown, because the sun's in my eyes. I'm wearing an ill-fitting blouse and a loosely pleated skirt. I look a bit washed out. The scene suggests some sort of encounter between North and South: a visitor from the British Foreign and Commonwealth Office (me) being shown round by the Minister for Women's Affairs perhaps?

After our paddle we go on a grand tour with Mohamed, the taxi driver, past old Arab palaces and through avenues of clove trees. He likes history and takes us to the Zanzibar museum. It's a heady mixture of day-old chicks pickled in formaldehyde by the Revd Caldicott in the 1930s and photos of slaves shackled in preparation for sale by Arab traders, a reminder that Zanzibar's beauty was founded on cruelty and greed. And in the corner, a symbol of salvation: a familiar figure, obscured by a rash of advancing mould. Yes, it's the queen, Her Britannic Majesty. Oil on canvas, heavy gold frame. She's in full ceremonial dress – diamond crown, slightly ill-fitting oyster-coloured satin dress, white gloves and blue sash – but she is on the floor. It's surprising that she wasn't burned back in the 1964 revolution. Perhaps she was banished then, only the faintest ghost of colonial loyalty preserving her from total destruction. And now she's been brought out of the cupboard, propped up against the wall; not quite rehabilitated, but almost. The green mould has certainly got a grip. It has advanced diagonally across her sash and is threatening to engulf her throat.

Empires come and go, as do revolutions. Outside a two-hundred-year-old tortoise takes it easy with some cabbage leaves.

THE CURSE OF THE INFIDEL

We arrive back at the Spice Inn hot, tired, but happy. We pay Mohamed our daily fee and trip up the steps.

'Fiona,' Véronique whispers theatrically, as we approach the reception.

'What?'

'Look behind you.'

'What?'

'Your dress – it's covered in blood.'

Oh hell.

'Now you've done it.'

'What do you mean?'

'See – it was all over the car seat.'

'What???'

'I'm telling you – a great big patch on his white covers.'

'Oh no.'

'Didn't you notice?'

'No – I thought it was just sweat; I didn't realize it was blood. I've got to get to the bathroom.'

'He'll never drive us again.'

'What do you mean?'

'Mohamed – he's Muslim, and now you've defiled his car with menstrual blood.'

'Don't be ridiculous.'

But the fact is, her words have a horrible ring of truth about them. I know of pious Muslims who won't sit next to a woman on the bus, in case she's quietly menstruating – and now I've succeeded in daubing my menstrual flow all over our driver's dazzling white seat covers.

Our mood turns to gloom. Véronique's convinced we'll never get another driver as good as Mohamed. I secretly believe her, but argue in favour of redemption. We bicker and then lapse into silence. I am feeling listless and dizzy. No wonder there were so few female explorers in the past.

We sit at breakfast in glum silence the next day. It's eight thirty-two a.m. – Mohamed was supposed to come at eight thirty.

'See – he won't come now. We'll have to find another driver.'

A man appears from reception. 'Please, Mama, your driver is here.'

The words sound magic to me, unbelievably wonderful.

'Probably come to give you a punch,' mutters Véronique.

'We're not in West Africa now,' I say primly.

'What do you mean?'

We're heading for a row. I get up from the table. Mohamed is here and nothing can proceed further until I've apologized to him. I grit my teeth and head for reception.

He is smiling benignly.

'Oh Mohamed,' I'm gibbering, blushing, 'I'm so sorry about the um . . . mess on the back seat. I didn't realize until afterwards. I'm terribly sorry.'

Mohamed smiles without any embarassment. 'Please, no

problem. I am a taxi driver, I am used to such things. Where would you like to go today?'

If only Mohamed weren't married, I would marry him. What a man!

We gather our things. We're back on form. Hurrah. Véronique is pleased too, I can see. Inside the Humber there's another set of gleaming white covers on the seats. I am kitted out in the best sanitary protection the West can offer. And today Zanzibar is our oyster.

SIX

Merchants of Style

〜〜〜

REINVENTION OF TRADITION

Six years on from the great hair hunt I am sitting in a small workroom at the back of a shop in Nairobi. I want to find out what's fashionable these days in Kenya; is it still the Freeman's clothes catalogue look? The answer is no. A young woman called Linda is stitching a beautiful hat. She is freshly graduated from fashion school. The hat is part of a wedding outfit and goes with a sort of detachable yoke, decorated with cowrie shells, and then of course there's the dress. Linda is very petite and has a tiny voice.

'The style of the hat is Xhosa. We brought hats back from South Africa to copy this kind of shape. The material comes from West Africa, from Mali – it's called mud cloth, and the design of the dress and collar is done by my boss – she's Kenyan, she's called Mollie.'

Mollie is young, clever and ambitious. She has a business designing clothes and importing Dutch wax prints from the Netherlands. These are the materials which reign supreme in West Africa; the Dutch textiles companies have been making them exclusively for West Africa for one hundred and fifty years. They are catching on in South Africa and now in East Africa. Mollie is sole agent in Kenya.

'People of a certain class want the African look now. They

don't always want the big white wedding dress with the white
veil. You saw the mud cloth outfit, didn't you? It is not cheap
but it is high quality. I feel it's my duty to spread the word
about these beautiful fabrics. When people buy material from
me I ask them to get their tailors to tell their other customers
where it comes from. The men are more difficult to persuade.
Kenyan men are not as . . . not as flamboyant as West African
men. But some of them will wear Mandela shirts, you know
the colourful shirts that Mandela wears?'

Yes, it's goodbye polka dots and hello damask. Rich
Kenyans are discovering their Africanness, which under
colonial rule was so reviled.

TAILORS FOR TWO THOUSAND YEARS

For the men of East and southern Africa the European suit
is still an important purchase. But most are bought off the
peg. Times are hard for the bespoke tailor. In Bulawayo,
Zimbabwe I find one such marytr to mass manufacturing. I
find him by crossing the wide Bulawayo streets with their
porch-fronted buildings, and turning into Robert Mugabe
Street, once Gray Street, to contemplate number 89, Naran's
Gents Tailors, established 1912. In the windows are faded
pictures of European gents in a range of outfits appropriate
for different social occasions in the 1930s – tennis whites,
plus fours, formal top hat and tails.

The proprietor is old and bent, and infinitely sad. His
name is A.N. Naran. He is cautious, but having agreed to
talk he states his position with one magnificent historical
sweep. His opening announcement catches me unawares.

'We have been tailors for two thousand years.'

'Two thousand years?'

'We are tailors by caste, you see. My father was born in
India. I was born in India, and came here aged twelve. This

shop was started in 1939 but before that we had a shop next door, established by my father in 1912. I make suits, jackets, trousers, waistcoats, and I do altering.'

'Isn't it too hot to wear suits and things in Africa?'

Mr Naran fixes me with a beady eye. 'Thirty years ago they were tailor-minded people in this country. When they came to me it was all for made-to-measure suits. It was mostly Europeans then, but some Africans also.' Mr Naran sighs. 'Now our business is slack – too much ready-made clothes from the factory, mass-produced goods. But the quality is not so good. Ours is the best quality. You see, when the old man died he passed his suit on to his son. We used to get material from the UK, but I'm not making many suits now, just alterations and repairs. I suppose my customers are mainly old Europeans and old Africans. I'm well known for a long time and they come by recommendation. My eldest son is in tailoring. My younger son has a factory making dresses.'

Mr Naran bows his head and falls silent. Perhaps the admission that one of his sons has thrown in his lot with the world of mass manufacturing leaves him feeling mournful. At any rate it is now clear that my audience with the proprietor of the oldest tailoring business in the world is over.

A FINE THING TO HAVE IN YOUR PARLOUR

Let us leave dry, clear, modern Zimbabwe, with its white landowners and race anxiety, and return to the humid coastline of West Africa, where the climate and the mosquitoes conspired so successfully against European land ownership. The year: 1989. To Freetown, then, capital of Sierra Leone, and a certain hotel, the Brookfields Hotel. There you will find a monkey, and I swear that monkey bought his suit from Mr Naran. He looks a very 1930s colonial figure, sitting there smoking a pipe, wearing a cloth cap, a jacket, a waistcoat and a bow tie, with a yellow flower in his button-hole. He was painted by one of three triplets. Alusine Bangura paints for his own pleasure. He uses household gloss paints. The style could, I suppose, be described as photo-realistic, African pop art. Painting is not just a pastime for him, it is also his job. He teaches prisoners in Freetown main prison. His passion for art had little standing in a professionally minded culture like Freetown's.

'At first I worked privately at home and my mother said it is not a good work. I used her cloth to wipe my paintbrush, and she said I must pay for it. My twin partners stopped school from standard four. I stopped from five before my father died. My mother said my twin brothers had started work and why did I not.'

His pupils in the prison have committed a fine spectrum of crimes. Their murky pasts do not seem to worry Alusine at all.

'Some of my pupils committed larceny, I have one who committed a murder, the other two just committed minor crimes of stealing. They did not have any idea about art. I have to show them the human figure. If you want to draw the head of a woman, you use an egg. If you want to do a young child you use a square, and for a young male you do it in three stages. I taught myself.'

He clearly believes art can effect a moral transformation.

'I think my pupils will be better people because they do art. When they finish their prison term, they will live with me until they know a bit what to do. I feel that art gives the love of the job. I would like it if the outside world would ask me to do my work and send it to an exhibition. I am a sergeant in the prison service. I have trained about eight prisoners.'

I ask about the monkey at the Brookfields Hotel. I imagine it is a satirical figure – perhaps political, or perhaps a general comment on human folly. But Alusine's explanation ambushes me with its literalness.

'I painted the monkey in the Brookfields Hotel because I wanted to imagine how a monkey can be like a human being if he is trained. They say that the monkey comes from our early people, so I think that it's a very good thing to train a monkey – you can see how he can ride a bicycle and go to market. A picture of a monkey is a fine thing to have in your parlour.'

I wander around his studio. The walls are painted with a dense brown gloss. The whole surface is stippled with white paint. It's hung with icons spanning time and place: Lionel Ritchie, President Momoh, Indian film stars and the Mona Lisa.

'In your version of the Mona Lisa the colours are much brighter.'

Alusine is happy I have noticed her. 'They say that Mona Lisa was the finest queen in world. I got the picture from a book. I copied this from a picture one inch square, like a stamp. And they say whatever place you stand, she will see you. And I tried to do this. I also paint these Indian pictures, because I love Indian films. I remember one film called *Dream Girl*. This is an Indian film star from that film. I love American films and Indian films.'

We leave Alusine's studio and walk across an area of scrubland to a low building. It's the prison officers' canteen. The walls are full of paintings. I meet a colleague of Alusine Bangura, a stout, genial figure in uniform.

'Yes, Alusine's my colleague. His art is very fantastic. How do you observe his pictures?'

'Great – I like the roses all along the wall, then there's the fruit . . .'

'They attract you too?' He wants to pin me down.

'Yes. And they're very funny – this one. Bush Cow Game – the two monkeys playing.' I am quickly corrected.

'No, they're baboons.'

'Ah well, they're kissing. And this one's smoking a pipe and drinking a beer. There's a monkey at Brookfields Hotel like that one.' But these are not the prison officer's favourites. He impatiently moves me on.

'How about the beautiful ladies? Oh, that one attract me too much. She's more better than my wife.' He chuckles. 'Alusine's a very great man. Hey, what about the President over there? What is your position now? You should invite Alusine to go to England. We want him to go to England, so that people can know that Africans can draw marvellous pictures.'

Yes, I really should. But I am a fraud, that is my position. I come, an emissary from a mighty organization, with my microphone and curiosity, raising hopes wherever I go. But it's impossible to explain that when I return to British soil I shall shrink in power; I shall climb on to a treadmill of relentless programme making and mothering. Snip goes the razor on the magnetic tape, squelch goes the changed nappy; the talent scout of African photo-realistic pop art will fall into bed exhausted after singing 'My Bonnie Lies over the Ocean' ten times.

REVENGE OF THE DEMON LAUNDERERS

I bid farewell to my prison officer friends. I am sweaty from tramping the streets of Freetown, so it's back to the hotel to change my trousers – the Brookfields Hotel with its besuited monkey. This is a hotel that knew better times once. It's shabby and cheap now, but very popular with the Rotary Club, and a place where men in power meet to drink and gossip. I find my laundry on my bed – starched and ironed to perfection by the look of it. It's a reminder that credit is never given where it's due. In all the reports I've read by the World Bank, IMF or aid agencies, no one ever mentions that the continent of Africa has the best launderers on earth; not so much as a footnote is devoted to the ace ironers, who tackle every frill, every pleat and every pin-tuck fearlessly, and can smooth out the rouched topography of a child's party dress in minutes. How neglected they must feel. They are a central pillar of civilization, but go unapplauded. Ironed clothes, along with well-groomed hair, are the benchmarks of sanity, civilization and competence. My departure was once delayed from a house in Kampala, at the very threshold, because the hostess considered my blouse inadequately ironed. 'Take it off,' she commanded. 'I shall have it ironed for you.'

That day at the Brookfields Hotel the laundry looked brilliant as usual, but beneath the starched exterior lurked a dreadful thing. My trousers looked perfectly washed, starched and ironed, but closer inspection revealed a monstrous blue blotch on the back of one leg. Annoyance takes a toehold. I make for the reception.

'I can't pay for this. In fact, you better pay me if you can't get this stain out. Those trousers cost forty pounds.' I am ready to luxuriate in a tide of apologies, but the receptionist remains inert. My verbal assault loses itself in a vacuum. She eventually stirs herself.

'I call the housekeeper,' she says sluggishly. The housekeeper appears. She is very tall and very fat. She studies the trousers unimpressed.

'I call the chief laundress.'

The chief laundress appears. She is belligerent. 'This was here before.'

'No, it wasn't.'

'We did not do this.' The assistant laundress joins in.

'You must have done.'

'We did not. In fact, that boy saw that stain on your trousers yesterday.' Hang on a moment. What boy? And what does the housekeeper know about all this? She's had absolutely no opinion on the subject up until now.

'What boy?'

'That boy. Lansanna – come here!'

A boy of about fourteen dawdles over from behind the bar where he's been polishing glasses.

'You see this mark on this lady's trouser yesterday?' bellows the housekeeper.

'Yes, Madame.'

'Whaat? I've never seen him before. I wasn't even wearing them yesterday.'

'Ehen, he saw the mark,' says the chief laundress with satisfaction.

This is getting a bit distasteful. It's as though I'm in the dock, caught out doing something disgusting.

'I want you to pay for my trousers.' My last attempt to gain the moral high ground.

'We no pay am,' says the housekeeper harshly. Silence. The housekeeper, the chief laundress, the assistant laundress, the receptionist and the pot boy all stare at me. Five to one. This is a conspiracy – the great stain conspiracy.

'Well, I certainly won't pay my laundry bill.' I stalk off with as much dignity as I can muster. Alusine's monkey surveys me calmly as I go back to my musty room. He is my only friend in the Brookfields Hotel today.

SEVEN

Car Culture

〰〰

CRUISING FOR STYLE

Most of urban Africa is gridlocked – cars, buses, minibuses, coaches converge every day in ritual frustration. In Lagos beggar mothers breastfeed by the side of the road in great clouds of exhaust puffed out by huge and tattered juggernauts. In Kampala bus boys scream, wail and sing for customers who, once tempted inside, pay half a dollar for the ride from hell. And everywhere potholes and dust.

In South Africa the roads are beautiful, so beautiful that every year thousands die in high speed crashes. Are cars worth the bother? For years I have been keeping track.

> *I want to take a taxi from Freetown to Kilimanjaro,*
> *I need a new Pajero to cruise across Sahara.*
> *Car wash are you ready? I want to pick my lady.*
> *Oh I need a car, I am a driver in a car.*
> *Whatever the cost I am a doctor on the move.*
>
> *Make I little wonder what the driver told me,*
> *Trouble with the motor car, trouble with the engine,*
> *Trouble with his master at the filling station.*
> *When I hear insurers, do you think I need a car?*
> *With the cost to keep the action, do you think I need a car?*

Mr Bigstuff and the Goddess of Charm

With gasoline a nuisance, do you think I need a car?
In the Third World of Africa, do you think I need a car?
                    (lyrics by Charlie Haffner, Freetong Players)

The answer is yes. The car reigns supreme everywhere, a
sign of status, sexual attraction and power. More people die
in car accidents than of anything else in Africa. In 1998 the
Red Cross launched a campaign for road safety, but generally
motor madness doesn't tug at the heart strings in the same
way as famine, cholera, war. And it's hard to imagine the aid
agency publicity:

'Eight-year-old Amina was orphaned by a car.'

'Twelve-year-old Yeboa has asthma – help reduce the car
population in her area: donate a bicycle.'

Not likely.

The first cars came to Nigeria in the early years of the
twentieth century. William Akinola Dawodu was king of
cars back then, the first person to make a business of
importing cars. He was born in 1879 and educated at the
CMS Grammar School in Lagos. What a fine man he must
have been to master the complexities of automotive tech-
nology, newly sprung from northern climes, and make a
trade out of it. He set up a small workshop in Lagos in 1905
and by 1907 his business was booming.

In those palmy days, says his obituary in the *Daily Times*,
Nigeria, 7 January 1930, *he had another store at Egerton
Square, and a shop under his two-storey building at Bishop
Street. A pioneer in vehicular trade, he introduced the famous
Ford cars in Lagos, and by 1919 he was sole agent for American
Firestone Tyres, Dodge, Charlotte and Reo Motors, and for the
English Star, Humber Premier and Hobart Cycles.*

But the car king was eventually dethroned: *Like many
pioneers he suffered terribly from the loss of his important motor
agencies, which European firms eventually captured . . . he will*

114

long be remembered as one of our great captains of industry, and as a good and useful citizen.

Everyone in the world loves cars. You can be selfish in a car, cut off from the rest of miserable humanity. A car is a suit of armour, a weapon and a house. Of course, in Mr Dawodu's life cars were still reserved exclusively for the toffs, be they in West Africa or in the east of the continent.

Uganda Herald 9 December 1936
A collision occurred on the Kijura Road, near Kahangi, between cars belonging to Mr M. Stead and the Kahuma of Burahya. One side of the Kahuma's car was badly bent. Mr Stead's car had one wheel almost torn off. The collision occurred on a fairly open bit of road, and it is understood that legal action is pending.

Who won? I wonder. Colonial servant or local ruler?

Sixty years on, car ownership has in some measure been democratized. But a car is still special enough to make a difference to how people see you if you own one.

'The ambition of everybody when you leave school,' says one friend, 'when you leave university, is to have a car. As a matter of fact the man who has a car now has a higher status than he had ten years ago.'

Your position improves but it's still a horrible expense. A businessman whom I quiz at Freetown airport sums it up as follows: 'To own a car is a necessity, that's one side of it. But the other is: to own a car is seriously a luxury – to maintain a car in Sierra Leone you can feed a family of four or five.'

A car becomes as essential as a pair of shoes – people don't have to have shoes, especially if it's hot, but people will think the less of you if you don't have shoes, and the same goes for cars. So people buy cars who can't afford them.

Mrs Coker does not own a car. She lives in Tooting Bec. She left Lagos over thirty years ago but goes back to visit, and is disappointed with consumer values.

'You go into some houses in Lagos now and you want to be sick. They are so dirty and untidy, dark and poky. But outside there will be a car all right, probably a very smart one.'

Sam Tumoi does not own a car. He is on his third beer, sitting in a small drinking hole in a narrow street in Freetown. He has already annoyed me by asking me to buy eleven pairs of the best quality football boots I can find for his local team, the Wellington Wanderers. His request follows a lecture on the plight of the masses and elitist tendencies in Sierra Leone. I primly point out that money can be better spent on books than expensive boots. He reviles me for my patronizing, neo-colonialist ways. I bring up the issue of cars as a way of steering the conversation out of a gloomy North–South cul-de-sac. And what he has to say about cars makes sense.

'If you had buses, if you had trains, if you had sufficient taxi cabs, then there would be no rush for everybody to own a car. There is a class – Ngugi would call it the Wabenzi class, or the nouveaux riches, or the political elite, the up-and-coming men who've made it – who imagine that a car goes with status. For them the car is not wanted or needed for its utilitarian value, instead,' he takes a sip of beer here, 'it is a question of class, of fashion, of fancy.'

He spits out 'fashion' and 'fancy' with fine contempt. Rather my point about the boots, but then again boots don't need petrol, boots don't kill people at high speed.

In Uganda I talk to a retired lawyer about cars. He is a man who has no time for fashion or fancy. But he has a Mercedes

Benz. And Kampala is the sort of place you could walk or bicycle round quite easily. He's a decent sort of man who knows all the ethical, political, environmental arguments of the West, but has gone to considerable expense to buy a car. 'You see, people won't take me seriously if I don't have a car. Oh, I would like to walk but it's not on. You see, I was away fifteen years. When I came back I went about my business in town on foot. My friends had to take me aside and say, "Look, you can't go around town on foot." Status is important. If I drive a small car my clan will feel I am letting them down. Listen, in England it's just a few fellows who will mock you in the pub if you have a small car. I have to deal with the whole clan – now that's a different kettle of fish.'

The lawyer mops his brow, exhausted from justifying to me the decisions he has made.

There was, I think, only one head of state who didn't succumb to the big posh car syndrome: Thomas Sankara, leader of Bourkina Faso, once known as Upper Volta. Capital: Ouagadougou. Sankara died young and handsome with revolutionary credentials intact, assassinated on 15 October 1987. When he came to power he wanted to break with the past; not for him the black shiny limo escorted by outriders, sirens wailing. He didn't even have a driver. He drove himself; and the choice of vehicle? 'Le Car' – a little black Renault 5, *without* air-conditioning. His ministers were obliged to follow suit.

The Mercedes still reigns supreme among heads of state and those aspiring to take power. The two stages of a run-of-the-mill *coup d'état* involve: 1. grabbing the radio station, 2. driving round in a Mercedes showing everyone who's boss.

But for a faux-functional look (Sankara style without the discomfort) the Pajero is a winner. This and other four-wheel-drive cars are just as expensive as Mercedes, but look more workaday. Like trainers, they pretend to be functional but really they are just expensive style accessories, flaunted from Cape Town to Muswell Hill. The powers that be in the third world – African and European – can always justify the expense by pulling a serious face and pointing out that it's the only vehicle that can manage the potholes. The new four-wheel-drive cars are the descendants of the hardy Land-Rover with its sharp metal corners and unupholstered interiors, the original pothole buster. The new generation retain the outward boxy appearance of the old Land-Rover, and the high clearance, but inside all is luxury – there's everything bar the cocktail cabinet.

CRUISING FOR SPEED

The Toyota Landcruiser, circa 1987, was midway between modern Pajero and old Land-Rover. In Somalia it was nearly the death of me.

Mogadishu. March 1987. I lie on my bed in the Croce del Sud Hotel with a ferocious cold. But I can't complain; the Croce del Sud is the nicest place in the world. Managed by an Italian lady, Madame Briata, it was built on the off chance that Mussolini might drop by. He never did. But it ended up as a beautiful hotel, designed in the Islamic manner with high-ceilinged rooms round a courtyard. On the walls hang what look like early medieval religious scenes painted on wood. I assume they are reproductions; an American (ex-Vietnam veteran), who is staying at the hotel while he teaches Somali Air Force pilots, says they are real. He also says that flying jet planes is PFM (Pure Fucking Magic), and for that reason I'm not entirely sure I can trust his artistic judgement. (I was always too shy to ask Madame Briata if her paintings

118

were real. It would have been a bit like asking if she wore a wig or had false teeth.)

So there I was sneezing, snorting and pondering the authenticity of the paintings, the confident manner of Americans, the architecture of the hotel, Mussolini's invasion of the Horn, and the vileness of the vultures (these were the only unpleasant aspect of life at the Croce del Sud – they perched in the trees in the courtyard and dropped their bones from on high on to the tables below). Then the phone rang.

'Fiona. Henry. We leave one hour for Kismayu.'

'Can't. I've got a cold.'

'But it is arranged.'

'I'm ill.'

'But you must come.'

Henry is now pleading. We are in a country which is very close to civil war. The border with Ethiopia is disputed. There is still order, but only because the ruler is ruthless and unpredictable. Siad Barre was the only head of state to cross the iron curtain, from pro-Soviet to pro-Western, while still in power. Henry works in the Ministry of Information. He speaks the language of the enemy, Amharic, which makes him useful but a potential traitor. His real name is Ahmed but Somalis, like Angolans, are fond of nicknames, which they acquire in adult life and use rather endearingly in official circles.

'You will see nice projects. Good development. It is green in the south. You have to come.'

Henry is a nice man, a funny man, and a frightened man. I will get him in trouble if I don't go.

An hour later we are heading south to Kismayu in a white Toyota Landcruiser. There are four of us. Henry and I, a young man who is supposed to be the driver's mate but behaves like the dormouse in *Alice in Wonderland*, curled up in the back, sleeping. Then there's the driver. He's not 'The Driver', he's a nephew of the deputy minister of information, and he likes driving cars. That's the problem.

Abdul – for that is his name – is a speed freak. The other problem is his clothes. How can you trust a man who embarks on a 300-mile car journey in an all-white suit? Finally, Abdul is stupid. He has no conversation, just laughs like a hyena and drives. Somalis are supposed to be knights of the road. Employed by hauliers all over southern and East Africa for their stamina and dependability, driving non-stop for days at a time, chewing the narcotic leaves of the khat bush to keep awake, brilliant at mending their vehicles single-handed in the middle of nowhere, and generally being unstoppable. My dream had been to make a road movie traversing the Cape to Cairo. But Abdul would not be taking the lead. The moment we are out of Mogadishu he's like Mr Toad – mad and excited at the wheel. Again and again I ask him to slow down. He turns to me, laughs, eases off the accelerator, but within minutes the dial is creeping across the speedometer. We are travelling down the Mogadishu–Jilib road. Built by the EEC in 1982 at a cost of $90 million, it's another example of jobs for the boys masquerading as aid. No proper foundations, no kerb, just macadam poured on to the sandy soil. The local joke is, it wasn't built, it was painted on.

I must be fair: Henry and Abdul are trying very hard. There are plans to make southern Somalia a tourist attraction. It's more fertile and wetter than the north. Today I am a sort of proto-tourist for them to try a few things out on. The car draws to a jerky halt.

'Now you are at the middle of the earth,' says Ahmed, making big eyes.

He jumps out of the car and scuffs his shoes on the faded white stripe painted on the road to represent the equatorial line. Very nice, I suppose, if you like jumping backwards and forwards over a dusty line in the road saying, 'Now I'm in the northern hemisphere, now I'm in the southern hemisphere.' I know I am disappointing them with my sullen behaviour.

Back in the car, and we rattle along for another hour. Then we stop at a lonely wayside inn; outside, one table and three chairs. We are offered watermelon juice and bananas. 'Freshly picked from the trees,' says Henry significantly. Yes, these boys really know what's good for a jaded European tourist. Another hour later we sit in a coconut grove drinking fresh coconut juice. 'This will make your cold very good,' says Abdul. Then we get a flat tyre and have to change wheels.

We arrive on the outskirts of Kismayu as the sun sets. We stay in a hotel built by the Chinese. Huge, octagonal, almost splendid if it weren't so faded and dusty, it has no context; it's built in the middle of scrub, with no connection to the town. We are the only guests. The food is little in amount, and has obviously been husbanded for us alone. This is a hotel which never had a heyday. The only regular visitors are large greedy baboons which frighten me at breakfast. The next day we visit a Dutch fish-freezing plant. There's a plan to introduce fish into the diet of inland Somalis further north. But they are nauseated by seafood. So, what with feasibility studies and fish acculturation programmes, this one could run and run, I think to myself grumpily. We try to visit a rice project but can't get the authorization. I knew this trip would be pointless. Time to go. I'm still fretting about the car. I look at the tyres.

'That one's bald. We can't travel with that.'

It must have been the spare.

'We cannot change it because we have no free tyre.' Abdul laughs.

'Well, I don't want to go with that.'

Henry looks embarrassed.

'There is no choice. There is no car going north.'

'No train?'

'No.'

'No plane?'

'No.'

So we set off. Abdul and I perform our double act of reproach and defiance. Only this time he goes faster. He's become immune to my nagging. He dodges the cracks and gaps in the road surface at forty, fifty, sixty miles an hour. Then he misjudges: CLUNK – the soaring momentum is interrupted. Something has given way. The car whisks itself off the road and thunders through the bush – thorn trees scratch the paintwork, rocks batter the suspension. We sit wordless, amazed at the loss of control. Then the car swings back across the road, to explore the bush on the other side. And in one sick-making rush, it curves round and throws itself over on to its side. I'm going to die in a bloody car crash. BANG.

Silence.

Golden dust motes float through a shaft of sunlight. I'm alive – that's good, but do my bits work? Toes? Yes. Fingers? Yes. Now what? Oh Christ – this is when the petrol tank explodes. Got to get out. Up and up I go through the strange architecture of a turned-over car. Out through the window I go, and plop I fall on the ground. Can't stand up. I can only crouch like a frog. I try to stand up again. No. My left side is in a rictus, my arm won't move above my elbow.

A lorryload of workers stop and people gather round to observe the scene, especially me, white frog-woman.

Abdul for once is silent. He is in shock. The driver's mate

appears to be still asleep. Henry looks at me anxiously. I try to tell him how I feel.

'I think my arm is dislocated. It hurts in a vague way if I keep very still, and a lot when I try and stand up.'

Henry nods. The lesson of this tale is never self-diagnose, at least not aloud. Henry talks to the crowd. A woman steps forward.

'She knows about bones,' says Henry.

She grasps my arm firmly and yanks it up in the air with all her might. My poor arm, I later discover, is fractured in about ten different places. For the second time that day I think I am going to die. The scream that comes out of me has a life all of its own. I am an inert object, silent and numb, but the scream bolts out of my body like a mad creature and circles round the crowd wildly, thrilling and terrifying them. Even Dr Bones is alarmed. She drops my arm like a hot brick; it falls to my side useless. Another scream-creature leaps out of me. Then the scream and I both fall to the ground whimpering rhythmically. Someone throws a bucket of water over me. Silence. We wait in the sun. The crowd goes back into the lorry. There's no room for me. As I lie on the ground in the dust, I realize that my cold has vanished, completely.

Half an hour later a juggernaut appears on the horizon, big, handsome, articulated; to my surprise it draws up alongside and the driver gets out. Now here comes a real knight of the road – gaunt, wiry, with a magnificent set of khat-stained teeth. He agrees to take us to Jilib where there may be a doctor. They heave me up into his cab and he gives me one very small aspirin, but my mouth is too dry to swallow it. He then tries to drive very slowly and carefully, but I am like the princess with a pea under her mattress. Every pebble we drive over is a chisel hammered into my shoulder.

We drive around for three hours. Pain ebbs and flows. I am alternately perky and speechless. I am decanted into the local commissar's four-wheel-drive car. We head for the Jilib river and down the bank. The commissar prods the driver.

'He wants him to test the depth of the river to see if we can cross it by car,' says Henry.

The driver looks very unhappy.

'There are crocodiles in the river,' Henry explains.

The driver is pushed riverwards by the party official. He rolls up his trousers and wades in. The water is shallow enough for the car, and there are no crocodiles. I am delivered up to another fascist legacy: a leper colony which Mussolini commissioned in the 1930s. It's situated in the middle of the river, and originally housed all the lepers in the country. It's still a home for lepers, but just the local sufferers. Evangelical missionaries run it now. I have always disapproved of the kind of missionaries who see their main aim as conversion; and when they choose to evangelize in a Muslim country I doubt their sanity. But when you're in agony you stop sneering and start being grateful. He who holds the painkillers is most definitely in the right. The missionaries are young, calm and American. They give me a delicious morphine cocktail, well over its sell-by date and thus fit for donation to a third world country. But who cares? It works. For one and a half hours I am restored; then it's another one and a half hours of agony before I'm allowed to pop another pill.

The next day more kind people organize a plane to take me out of Somalia and to a nice hospital in Kenya, which I have the money to pay for. It's pointless trying to be heroic abroad if you are white or rich, or both, you will always get rescued and returned home well treated and fussed over. But it's easy enough to tell the folks back home that you had a very big adventure. As I get into the Cessna, Abdul gives me a friendly pat on my broken shoulder, and I am transfixed by a shaft of pain; my eyes fill with tears.

'Don't be sad about us, Fiona. We find another car to drive back.'

Henry waves mournfully, and up we go; no potholes, no swerving, no other traffic, just beautiful blue sky.

Later I was sent a photo of the Toyota: collapsed bonnet, skewed wheel. The BBC's stringer Abdulkadir Noor stands by it, as though it were some big game trophy. Did it ever see active service again? Probably not. If you're flooded with aid you just wait for the next car to come along. Somalia even then was the poorest country in the world, according to the chaps in Washington. And that meant it got an awful lot of aid. I couldn't understand this, because the market-place was awash with state-of-the-art ghetto blasters, Walk-mans and FM radios, but of course it was black market stuff and so officially didn't exist. Yes, another four-wheel-drive car would surely replace that Landcruiser.

That was in 1987. The Croce del Sud still exists – not a hotel, but home to displaced people. Mogadishu is now in ruins. The pressure cooker finally blew, the clans went to war, and Siad Barre fled. I hope Henry is all right. I'm sure Abdul is fine – there's such strength in stupidity.

CRUISING FOR SPARE PARTS

These days more aid money goes to petty tyrants in eastern Europe than petty tyrants in Africa. And generally times are hard, so no one can afford to write a car off, least of all in Nigeria. There was a time when people bought cars here and didn't know they needed oil; cars with wrecked engines were abandoned on the roadside. These days car owners are wary of their own ignorance and put their automative fate in the hands of skilled mechanics. And some of the finest in the world are to be found in Nigeria. The Nigerian car mechanic: high priest of the road, the heart surgeon of transport. Cars that would die in northern Europe, cars that would defy the deftest mechanics Kwikfit can offer, have life breathed into them in Nigeria by mechanical geniuses.

Sola Odunfa stares at me solemnly. He is huddled in a trench coat, protection against the cold weather in London, and perhaps protection against me. He does not like being interviewed. He asks the questions. He is a crack reporter who roams the streets of Lagos, looking for stories to make into dispatches. These he pours down the telephone line like so much liquid gold to grateful BBC producers. Now he is in London, trapped by me in a studio. His car is essential to his job, so he has agreed to talk to me about his mechanic. Sola owns a Peugeot 405. When he talks his tone is reverential. I am mesmerized.

'He's a young man. I'm not sure if he's ever seen the inside of a classroom. He went into the trade through apprenticeship. Now several times I've watched him, not only repairing my car, but working on other people's cars. He has something about him which . . .' Sola pauses and gazes dreamily into the middle distance. '. . . something which I cannot place my hand on. If I drive in, before I tell him what is wrong, just listening to the engine, he already knows what is wrong. I think he has a gift with cars. There's virtually *nothing* he cannot do with a Peugeot. The only problem is . . .' Sola smiles affectionately here, '. . . he believes he knows much more than the manufacturers. Once in a while something goes wrong and I say, "Oh could you please change this part?"' Sola adopts the soothing but controlling voice of a temptress, a Circe of the mechanical world, as he imitates his mechanic. "Oh yes," he says, "you *must* change it. Ah, but you see the part from the old model is much better than this. If I put this one in you will enjoy the car." Then I say to him, "Look, the people who designed this car put this particular part in for a purpose." He says, "No, don't mind them. They just want to deceive you – they want to take your money. I will change that shock absorber and put in the one from the old model and you will enjoy it." '

Sola's mechanic always has his way.

CRUISING FOR LOVE

'Let's face it,' says my actor friend from Iboland, 'you won't get anybody if you don't have a car. Especially in Lagos where the traffic is very bad. Every girl wants to move about. If you have a car, you are in, if you don't' . . . he pauses here melodramatically, 'if you don't – too bad.'

So what's the girls' point of view? I turned to Funke to find out if girls really love cars as much as the boys think. She's a dress designer, and has been living in London these last two years. She is married. She is quietly spoken, and addresses the problem very carefully: 'A girl from a good background would not attach importance to a car.' Aha – you see? I didn't think they were so materialistic. Funke continues steadily, 'But your average Nigerian girl would not like to go out with a man without a car. It's part of the relationship.' Oh dear, it *is* like the boys say, not that a Nigerian girl would want to admit to cars being such a priority. 'Some will tell you it's not important, but deep down they know that it is.'

I thank Funke for her clear summing up of gender and cars. I go back to the office. There's a cassette waiting to be listened to on my desk. It's come from Freetown. It was sent by a reporter called Fode Fofanah. 'Find me a man', I had said to him, 'who thinks having a car helps him attract women.' He had found such a man. I put the cassette into the machine to listen. I let myself imagine the man he was interviewing: immensely fat, perfectly pleased with himself. And a big liar. I had better call him O. or, perhaps more generously, Mr Bigstuff; if I don't disguise his name, he's sure to sue me – Sierra Leoneans are famously litigious. Whatever his morals, his outrageousness has me gripped, as do Fode's short laconic questions.

Good afternoon, what is your name?
    'I am O.'
    '*What's your job?*
    'I'm a civil servant by profession.'
    '*What is the make of this your car?*
    'It's a Japanese car – 626 Mazda coupé.'
    '*Very flashy, indeed.*'
    'Of course.'
    '*All the girls in Freetown must be yours?*
    'Exactly so.'
    '*How do these girls get in touch with you?*
'Some of them just fancy getting a ride. For instance one day I was cruising slowly along Siaka Stevens Street. I saw two beautiful girls. I stopped and beckoned to them. In a flash of a second they are inside my car. I took them to the Gem Restaurant. I treated them. This was the very first time we met. I took them home. We had a good time, then I gave them appointment that I would meet them in the evening, but I never went. The next day the same thing happened. This time it was by Barclays Bank. I met again two beautiful girls, I called them, I took them to the restaurant. You keep on doing this – it's not a problem as long as you have a flashy car.'

128

'*It must be very expensive though if every day you have to pick up new girls, take them to restaurants, take them to night clubs. Where do you get all this money from?*'

'Ah, don't get me wrong (*little chuckle*). Now that's what most people think. But when you own a car you don't need to have money, because most of the girls will go all out to provide for you. They even get you money to get petrol.'

'*What about repairs?*'

'Same goes for repairs. About two weeks ago I had a breakdown. All the girls were not happy and went all out to get money for me to buy the spare parts.'

'*And that way the car was back on the road?*'

'Yes. In fact we made a small party. All the girls were very happy the car was back on the road.'

Oh yes, O., we know the kind of man you are. Behind four walls your wife probably beats you up every night and you have to make up for that somehow. But we enjoy your strutting peacock display. Of course, for every braggard peacock there's a sparrow with a tale of woe. Mr Bigstuff, take heed . . .

Women loved me too much
Women loved me so much because I was extravagant, a rascal and entirely too much without responsibility. My real name was Mr Belgian but women did not like this name and stopped me from answering to the name. They gave me two names. One was M. W. which meant Master of Women, while the other one was B. L. which meant Boy of Love. I accepted these strange names and did business with women. I forgot myself and my people. I could only think of women every minute of the day. I also took to drinking. I used to finish 24 bottles of beer daily, and dancing was also my hobby. Within a few weeks of my dealings with women my pocket dried up. My girls boycotted me

because I could no longer spend money. I am now living a miserable life.

(ex No Condition is Permanent *revised and enlarged by the Master of Life, J. C. Brothers Bookshop, Onitsha*)

EIGHT

Beautiful People

∼✍∼

THE HUMAN SUNDIAL

'We don't need him.'

'Listen, he's a good bloke.'

'We haven't got a budget to pay for a fixer.'

'Listen, he knows everyone. 'Sgot contacts.'

'Christ, what do we need contacts for? We just want to record the kiddies and get a bit of publicity.'

'That's it – he knows how to get us publicity.'

'Well, so do I – just ring up the paper.'

'Naah – got to do it face to face and we haven't got time. The beauty of Sam is he works odd hours.'

The beauty of Sam . . . well, yes, that was it; for me Sam's beauty was the problem.

We had come to Ghana to promote the golden art of radio among the younger generation. We had five days in which to build a studio at the National Theatre and record a thousand Accra schoolchildren. Sam has been recruited to help. He is a fitness instructor, and thus has a perfect body. But he doesn't just lie around showing his body to best advantage; Dan is right, he is a mover, and within hours he turns himself into a studio manager, adjusting the microphone for shy nine-year-olds, toughing it out with stroppy fourteen-year-olds addicted to Snoop Doggy Dog, and generally keeping order. For four days I am cooped up in a makeshift studio with Sam. Dan is outside encased in his headphones, master of his control panel and his destiny. I am a victim of my pheromones, cooped up with male beauty, taut, shining, smiling. This is how they get pandas to mate in the zoo, I muse: put them together in a confined space and wait. It's only a matter of time. Every day Sam asks me out. On day five I crack.

We meet for beer in the evening. I am almost too tired to move. He looks sad. There's a small streak of what looks like the sediment of dried tears in the corner of one eye. I resist the temptation to wipe his face with my napkin. He is subdued, but rallies when the waiter produces a beer.

'I like you.'

He gazes at me with tawny eyes, unblinking. I take a sip of beer, and witter on about the enslavement of Ghanaian youth to rap music. He presses his suit.

'Seriously, I want to make love to you.'

Ho hum. It's the sun. If it was hotter in England, English men would be like this. Sam stares at me harder, then turns away and sighs. He seems to be wavering between passion and gloom.

'My life is not easy – you think I just meet rich women and sleep with them?'

'Well, yes, I do rather.'

'You do not understand.' He looks down at his beer with a despairing look. 'I had a French girlfriend. She was old like you, but I loved her. Then she played around. I want a good woman.'

The tawny eyes gaze at me again. To my annoyance and despite his unintended insult, my loins are stirring faintly.

'Look, I don't think I'm quite the ticket for you. You need some young, perky thing.'

'The young girls are all greedy and unkind. They want me to spend all my money. These young pretty girls are very bad.'

'Well, don't get sad because of me.'

'I am not sad because of you.'

A spike of disappointment.

'Well, you look sad.'

'That is something else.'

'What?' I am beginning to feel muddled by this conversation.

'See this mark?' He points to the streak under his eye.

'What is it?'

'A gecko walked over me in my sleep. I have to visit the medicine man or I will die.'

'Die?' I am not ready for this.

'The mark will grow, it will make a circle round my face. If it completes the circle I will die.'

Sam's head is bowed. Any stirring of the loins is draining away, and yet I don't believe a word of it.

'Can the medicine man prevent it growing?' After all it's rude not to take someone seriously.

'Yes – it is easy. He just catches a gecko and kills it, then says some words.' He gazes at me again. 'What are you doing tomorrow evening?'

'Um . . . well, I've got to listen to a few interviews . . . and then, um . . . nothing much.'

'I will come to see you then. I need to be near you.'

'Well, let's meet up and then we can do that interview about how to become a fitness instructor.'

He has finished his beer. He glances at his very heavy, expensive-looking watch and with a soulful look excuses himself.

'I see you tomorrow six o'clock.'

I watch him head off into the slipstream of traffic until he disappears. Sunday passes quietly. We dismantle the last of the studio.

'Good bloke, Sam. He's got a great piece for us into the *Graphic*, with a photo.'

'He's got the hots for me, and the problem is I—'

Dan cuts in quickly. 'Yeah, well. Watch yourself. Fancy a cup of tea?'

Standing on the balcony of the Penta Hotel, I can see Sam bounding up the road. The sky is dark and purple, the street busy with people on the loose.

He strides on to the balcony.

'I am so happy to see you.'

He smiles and gazes at me. My heart is pounding. The smoky grey trail has grown another inch.

'You haven't been to see the medicine man yet?'

'No, not yet – it is OK. I told you, as long as it doesn't make a circle I am all right. Where shall we go?'

'Well, we could do the interview . . . in my room would be best.'

Sam's father was a boxing manager. Sam toyed with the idea of following in his footsteps, but then hit on the notion of combining acting (no pay) with fitness instruction (low pay but big tips). He has a nice voice and speaks fluently. He gives a precise and engaging account of his life.

'To me as an actor, you need to look fit. You need to train a lot. Myself I train three hours every day except Sunday. Every day I have a part of my body that I do. I don't do all the body every day. Maybe for Monday I take up the chest, I work on the chest with the bench press. Some muscles need to relax. You see when you work all the body in the day, you overwork it.'

I feel tender, but hurry on to extract a picture of his clientele.

'I have people from the Dutch Embassy and British High Commission. More women than men,' (lucky women, I think) 'because they are really worried about their body' (then again, unlucky women, I think) 'they want to slim their waist and butt. When people first arrive they are very frightened. In the first place they are shy. You need to approach the person so that they know there is hope. You don't give him a heavy programme, you need to take him cool, then he won't be shy.'

Sam watches lots of American films, and that is where he gets his inspiration for acting.

'What I want is to set up my own business, but acting is what I like best. And if you take into account people like Arnold Schwarzenegger and Jean-Claude van Damme and co., they are very good, because they are huge and good-looking. I want to be like them.'

Huge and good-looking – well, he's on the way.

'Sam, thanks very much for this interview.'

'Thank you too.'

I wind back and check the last few seconds of the recording. When I look up from my machine, the grey trail has moved. I believe in the gecko's curse now. Sam's face is a sundial, exchanging light for life, shadow for death; the trail is beginning to curve round to his chin.

I am frightened. He stares at me hungrily. He takes my hand.

The phone rings.

'Your other friend Mr Dan is waiting for you in reception.' The voice of the receptionist has a nasty edge to it.

'I've got to go. Dan's waiting.'

'Ah, my friend Dan.' Sam smiles and closes his eyes briefly with pleasure. 'I come with you to see him.'

'Promise me you'll go to the medicine man.'

'I will go tomorrow and I will see you tomorrow night,' and then tenderly, 'your last night.'

I have forfeited the good will of the entire hotel staff by having a man in my room. Slow service and frosty looks are my lot. Joseph the waiter, once a friend, will not look me in the eye. There's no omelette at breakfast – they have run out of eggs. Well, that's their story. I didn't notice there being any egg shortage the morning after the gold prospectors brought their floozies in to stay. Double eggs all round, sunny side up, more like. Oh well, one law for ladies and one for gents. Frankly I don't give a damn, as long as Sam lives, as long as beauty beats the beast. That afternoon I pray.

I am waiting in the reception of the Penta Hotel to say goodbye to Sam the fitness instructor. Two American rastafarians are arguing with the receptionist. They have come to find their roots, and take in the sights of a Pan African arts festival endorsed by Stevie Wonder.

'Come on, man, you telling me you don't take American Express. What is this? You call yourself a hotel?'

Sam arrives. I am relieved the receptionist is too preoccupied to notice our reunion at first, but I'm wrong. Despite the credit-card fury, he sees Sam out of the corner of his eye, and hisses something at him. Sam spits out a contemptuous riposte. If it came to a fight between the puny but vindictive receptionist and the magnificently fit Sam I know who would win. We go on to the balcony and watch the ebb and flow of the street. I order beer from a sullen waiter. Sam is solemn. He produces a ring. It is large.

'It was my grandmother's.'

'She must have had huge hands.'

'It is made of white gold.'

I feel mean.

He stares at me steadily. I return his gaze, and then I notice – the mark has gone.

'You went to the medicine man?'

'Yes.'

'And did he sacrifice a gecko?'

'Of course.'

'How long did it take? Did the mark go immediately?'

'I want to visit you in London.' He says this seriously and slowly. But I want to know more about the gecko-banishing ritual. I hold back, fearful of sounding prurient.

'Oh well, you're welcome any time to come and stay – any time. You've got my address.'

I feel happy. After all, Sam is alive, he isn't going to die. But I don't really want him to visit me, and I don't want the ring . . .

'Listen, I can't take the ring.'

'You must take it – with this ring you cannot forget me.'

'Oh all right then.' I put it on my middle finger but it's still too loose. 'Good luck with the fitness instruction, and I hope you find a beautiful lady.'

'I will find her, and we will have many children. We will come and visit you in London.' He wasn't meant to say that, but no, I don't want to marry Sam. My sights are set on going back home; back to the land of dull diseases and powdery, bloodless cures, back to the land of cautious, cold-blooded men, and privet hedges that always need trimming. The thing is, I could do with a bit of a rest, a rest from all this passion, beauty and magic.

GODDESS OF CHARM AND GOOD MANNERS

If you aren't born beautiful, you can at least learn to be charming. Amina Patel will teach you, if you're still under twelve. She runs a charm school. She's targeting the privileged urban child: spoilt and brutish, cut loose from the heavy discipline which is rooted in tradition and the rural community. Privileged urban African child has all the pleasures the electronic age can offer: satellite TV, video, gameboys, CDs, computer. Driven from A to B in a four-wheel-drive car, the child's feet hardly touch soil. Life is a perpetual round of visiting one high-fenced, security-patrolled house with a swimming pool after another. Gone is the time when the children of eccentric, posh Europeans went out all day, ran wild in the bush, climbed trees. Rich children – African and European – are little prisoners. Amina Patel will make them polite little prisoners.

Amina Patel is the goddess of good manners and etiquette. She is so beautiful I could watch her all day. She is somewhere around five foot ten inches tall, with heavy straight black hair; high-breasted, wasp-waisted, long-legged. Her hands are immaculately manicured. She wears big, bold bangles on slim wrists. Her posture is that of a dancer. Both parents were a mixture of African and Asian, earning them the official category 'Coloured'.

Many people have told me that Zimbabwe is the most racist country in Africa, more so than South Africa. Historically Rhodesia had very few whites fighting minority rule; Rhodesia had no substantial intellectual or artistic community subverting the laws of petty racists, neither did it have crack black journalists holding the system to ridicule . . . no Can Themba, Arthur Maimane, no *Drum* magazine with saucy pix and investigative stories. No, white Rhodesia combined racist cruelty with spectacular dullness. Amazing that such a brilliant bloom as Doris Lessing could grow on that soil. (Although, of course, she was driven out; no question of her thriving underground.) In Harare I meet black Zimbabweans, I meet white Zimbabweans, but I rarely meet them together. The children of the rich hang out in racially separate gangs. People are rarely horrible to one another, in public at any rate; they just avoid one another. White–black couples are very rare. I meet the black wife of a white Italian, and she explains why they moved to Uganda: 'I know for a fact that one of the white mothers with a child in my son's class asked the headmaster if her son could be moved from sitting next to my son. The headmaster said it wasn't that kind of school. The mother took her son out.' There are rumours of new schools opening which advertise their facilities only to whites, private clubs established just for whites. Nobody will talk much about race, except one old Serbo-Croat in Bulawayo who complains loudly to me that they breed like bunnies. When I tell him my partner is African he appears not to hear.

But go to Amina's charm school and you will see: children of mixed race, white children, black children, Asian children. Amina has triumphed against the tramlines of racial hatred, and now her services are courted by mothers across the ethnic spectrum. A plump white Zimbabwean with an Alice band and pink lipstick has sent her daughter on Amina's course as a Christmas present. 'She loves prancing around. Now when Amina tells her how to present herself, how to walk into a room nicely and all that, she takes it very seriously.'

A heavy black Zimbabwean mother is eager to confess her loss of parental authority. 'I have no control; my daughter always drinks sodas and eats sweet things, but Miss Patel can stop them from going to that fridge. She tells them Coke is bad for them and they listen.'

Amina Patel covers all aspects of moral and physical behaviour.

'I can offer a ten-year-old the children's modelling and grooming course. This includes opening and closing doors properly, sitting, using correct cutlery, and correct treatment of skin; black skins tolerate sun better of course. And black children should use vaseline. But parents are becoming more westernized. Sometimes they drop the vaseline out. Same thing happens with breastfeeding. We only do this course during the school holidays and this gives parents some time off.'

Amina talks like a white Zimbabwean – with a slightly jerky, high voice, the end of sentences marked with an upward inflection. In other respects she defies any category. She's Muslim by upbringing, while being hugely glamorous. And for me, there's something touchingly Victorian about the way she puts health and moral decency together. I keep expecting her to mention regular bowel movements. She does, after all, come from a medical background. She originally trained as a midwife and nurse. She puts her good posture down to her father's strictness and is scathing about modern manners, or rather the lack of them.

'I think manners are atrocious now. I don't know who makes the rules. If you have basic good manners you can't go wrong. And I think it's the same in all the ethnic groups. It's always easier for somebody else to tell children what to do, so children who defy their own mother will listen to me. But it's not just about manners.'

As she talks she emphasizes her points with her slim hands, accompanied by the delicious shunting sound of all her bangles. Her thick glossy hair falls from side to side as her head moves.

'This afternoon we're doing personality – getting the children to think about nice and nasty. And then we're

140

going to think about diet – they have to write down exactly what they had last night. Some are grossly overweight; they eat too many cakes and sweets and Coca-Cola, but the nice thing about kids is they are so honest, so they will tell me just how much they eat.'

She is driven to teach children the minutest social manoeuvres, whether they be plain or beautiful, clumsy or grateful.

'Modelling is a misnomer because that makes you think you have to be gorgeous. What I am concerned with is presentation; presenting yourself well. I have boys as well as girls – I'm very old fashioned and like to have car doors opened and chairs pulled out for me. The children love it to bits. My parents were Muslim – a very respectful culture. The table manners I teach are western, but good manners fit in any culture.'

The next day I come to watch Amina as she winds up the class for the day.

'What I want you to do for your homework ... ah, Joshua, never put your hands in your mouth ... what I want you to do is bring magazines with pictures of people in fashionable clothes, posing. And then we'll try out some of the poses for your photographs. Then I want you to think about what makes people nice or horrible. Can somebody give me one thing that makes you nice?'

'Manners?'

'Yes, manners make you well liked. Something else?'

'Kindness?'

'Good one, kindness.'

'Respect?'

'Yes, respect. If you show respect, people will show it to you.'

A tiny voice volunteers an idea. Amina strains to hear.

'I can't hear you. What are you saying? You know what is also good manners is speaking out. It's good manners to be heard. OK? Now let's talk about things that are not so nice. Any bad behaviour you can think of?'

'Fighting?'

'Yes.'

'Stealing?'

'Yes.'

'Untidiness?'

'Yes, untidiness means you don't care about yourself. Oh and standing up like that is rude.'

Muffled voice pleads necessity.

'What, again? This is the third time this morning. Someone take her to the loo.'

A small mite is led away.

'Any more bad things?'

'Killing?'

'Yes, killing, that's very bad – and even watching those killing movies is bad . . . Isabel, do not dig your nose – that's a bad thing, that's a bad grooming point.'

'Sucking your thumb?'

'Yes, don't suck your thumb; don't suck any part of your body.'

The children are getting restless. The mothers are grouped outside, fondly looking through the window for their darlings.

'All right, you can go now. Don't forget the magazine pictures I told you about. See you tomorrow. You can all stand up now.'

A ragged lilting chorus responds:

'Goodbye, Miss Patel.'

If only Miss Patel could be Prime Minister; if only Miss Patel would make me good and charming. But I think it's too late as far as I'm concerned. Disconsolate and hungry, I wonder off into the street and find a baker. There's the usual colonial legacy of greasy Cornish pasties, buns iced in lurid pink and white. Amina would be dismayed. I close my eyes and it's 1963, a hot day in Reigate. We are at the baker's, my mother and I. She is buying bread and making harsh remarks about the English cakes. Lazy wasps crawl over the powdery, synthetic meringues.

'Of course when I was a child in Zürich we went to the Sprüngli every week – proper patisserie. It was so delicious. Not this ghastly . . .'

I hear an impatient click behind me. I turn. A thin, lined, white face scowls at me. I turn back, and a plump, dark brown face scowls at me from behind the counter. I put on my most charming, anxious-to-please voice:

'Two iced buns please, and a Coca-Cola.'

NINE

White Ghosts and Kaka Devils

∽◦∾

VIVE LA FRANCE

'Mille soixante-six.' If only I'd paid more attention to numbers when I was learning French at school. This is what I was thinking one very hot afternoon in Djibouti. But numbers hold very little interest for me in any language. And now the Attorney General of Djibouti is looming over me. His jowly face hiked into a smile, his eyes as wide as dinner plates.

'Mille soixante-six,' he repeats, adding, 'Ne vous inquiétez pas, mademoiselle – je suis de Normandie, vous êtes anglaise.'

'Mille soixante-six.' I try hard to make it out. One thousand . . . one thousand, sixty-six. Oh no, he's making an indecent suggestion. Is he? No, that can't be right . . . one thousand and sixty-six. Got it. Of course – 1066. And Normandy . . . Normandy. Norman invasion. Of course. Why, me and the Attorney General of Djibouti are practically first cousins, so that's all right then. This meeting should not be regarded as an interrogation, more of a coming together of two great cultures. But the problem is he is on home territory. I am not. This much I had discovered about Djibouti in the five days I had been there: the President was very short-sighted, and the French ran the show. This means

144

that in this tiny East African country bordering on Somalia and Ethiopia, there are French soldiers, French marines, the Foreign Legion; French wives, French children and a French Attorney General, Le Procureur Général. My Norman acquaintance. The French like to be in control, independence or no independence. My stay in Djibouti coincided with a temporary loss of control. But first to set the scene.

THE LEGION IS MY FAMILY

My first evening in Djibouti in the small, shabby but clean Hotel Siesta, and I am given a rose by the cook. 'How romantic,' I gush. He shrugs, 'Non, c'est l'habitude de la maison.' The roses are flown in several times a week 'coupé'. None could grow here because Djibouti is a desert moonscape; like a geological textbook – all layers and configurations of rock, occasionally softened by sand, but plants and trees are not a feature. It imports its vegetables from one particular part of Ethiopia on a great steam train. In another part of Ethiopia people are starving. Here in Djibouti it is very dry and hot. And despite this stifling heat I must get to work. I ask the manager if he can fix up an interview with a legionnaire. There's been a death in the Legion, here in Djibouti, maybe a murder, according to the *Daily Mail*; the victim is a British legionnaire called Honeywell. I am rapidly establishing myself as a favoured guest at the Hotel Siesta; experience has taught me that in the long term this favoured guest status tends to backfire, but for the moment I'm in, so the manager gives me a contact . . . a legionnaire who will talk.

Actually, my main task is not to chase men in uniform but to observe Djibouti playing host to warring neighbours: Somalia and Ethiopia, and other countries in the region – Kenya, Uganda. It's a big occasion for little Djibouti. Somalia and Ethiopa are still technically at war over the Ogaden region. They are ostensibly here to come to an agreement on regional development, but the hidden agenda is diplomatic and the main thing is they are breathing the same air. The second day of my stay is devoted to listening to ritually affirmative speeches: one extravagant development project after another is wafted before the assembled delegates, every one guaranteed to pay off the mortgages and school fees of western consultants and aid workers. Each project is described in paralysing detail, and comes with a massive price tag. For example, a project to examine the reproductive cycle of the camel comes with an estimated cost of $1,200 million. Why, you could set up a computerized dating agency for camels *and* aid workers for that kind of money. But at least the Ethiopian and Somali delegates, while not exactly swapping cigarette cards, have not walked out on one another. The Ethiopians have a particularly haunted look. Mengistu runs a marginally tighter ship than Siad Barre, being ideologically lined up behind the Russians. They are more anxious about representing their government abroad than the Somalis. The Somalis feel more at home here since a large proportion of Djiboutians are actually Somali. Before independence Djibouti was French Somaliland.

In the evening I return to my jolie maison by the sea. The legionnaire is waiting for me. He is sitting on a stool, his kepi or hat on the counter. He is very brown and handsome. He doesn't look English. He grew up in Cornwall – his father is English but his mother is Mauritian. I am surprised and a little disappointed by his politeness. I was expecting a terrifically rough diamond, spitting on the floor and calling the cat a bastard; this would give me the chance to be rather ladylike and shocked, perhaps even tremble a little. No, he is very polite, and quite comfortable chatting to me about the Legion. 'The days of taking on hardened criminals are gone – you've got to have a clean nose to be a legionnaire,' he explains calmly. He then goes on to talk about his life in a series of Foreign Legion formulae: 'The Legion is my family. You leave your past behind you, even your name is changed.' He is egged on by my wide-eyed fascination and a second bottle of beer; then the contradictions flow thick and fast. 'We are completely independent of France, we hate the French. Yes, we do go on manoeuvres with the French army; it is true the top posts in the Legion are held by Frenchmen, but most of us are not French.' He uses terms which he knows I won't understand, then enjoys explaining them: 'seville' means on leave, 'tenu' on leave not in uniform, 'permission' on leave in uniform.

Enough of the formalities – what about women? He takes this in his stride. 'I haven't slept with a single local woman since I arrived five months ago. I wait for the American ships to come in ... you know, American servicewomen. The local woman are all circumcised, from Ethiopia, so they don't enjoy it.' I am trying hard to imagine healthy, young, American servicewomen with good teeth and marvellously frilly genitals beckoning the young legionnaries as soon as their ships cast anchor. Courtship and congress must be swift and energetic. Then I wonder why he joined the Legion in the first place, before it became his family etc. 'I wanted to join the army, but they told me I was too old.' This is obviously a lie, since he is only twenty-six. A hint of melodrama has crept in. 'So what can you do if your country doesn't want you?' Well, quite a lot really I'd have thought, besides joining the Foreign Legion.

'Of course I've done other stuff – modelling.'

Now I'm impressed.

'Modelling? What, clothes?'

'Yes, clothes. Nothing naughty. I'm the only legionnaire I know with an Equity card.' He smiles a smile for the imaginary camera. Dreamy. We're each on our third beer.

He bows his head and delves into his kepi, lifts up the headband on the inside and fishes out a photo of a young middle-aged woman. 'My mum – I miss her.' A poor quality colour snapshot of a smiling plump woman, tousled black hair, summer dress, bare arms, lipstick.

'She looks nice.'

'They were furious when I joined, my mum and dad.'

'Thought the Legion was your family.'

'It is now,' he says abruptly. There's a pause in the conversation, the first for a good half hour.

'Um . . . so what happened to Honeywell?'

The legionnaire draws himself up straight. The photo is reinserted in the headband. He's not as tiddly as I thought.

'No comment.'

The hackneyed phrase makes me want to giggle.

'Oh come on – what happened?'

'Can't tell you.'

'You knew him?'

'Yeah, I knew him. Knew his family.'

'Was he murdered?'

'Not saying.'

'Sounds like the Foreign Legion living up to its murky reputation.'

'If you say so.'

Huh! Bet he doesn't know. Just making himself sound interesting.

'I was told he was beheaded.'

He smiles. 'Do you want to see some night life?'

I hesitate. 'All right.' I fall in with the change of subject, resolving quietly to follow up the Honeywell mystery later on. First stop is Le Scope. A single long room lit by a red light. There are two posters with page three girls on them to get you in the mood. The only other customers are two

French soldiers. But the place is full of women. We walk in and they all shout 'Johnny'. They get up to kiss him four times on the cheeks backwards and forwards. Then they kiss me. They are enchanting and beautiful with fluffy hair, kohl-rimmed eyes and damp cheeks. Then Gina arrives – his favourite, he explains. She is especially beautiful, her cheeks are extra damp and her hair forms a halo of curls. She's twenty-four and left Ethiopia three years ago. He later tells me that she had offered to sleep with him for his pleasure; he declined on account of it being a one-way business. So the attraction is confined to poignant encounters in the red glow of the disco.

I want to know from Gina what it was like living under the regime of Mengistu Haile Mariam.

'Why did you leave your home?'

'Because of the government.'

'Why because of the government?'

'It's communist.'

'Yes, but what don't you like about it?'

'The politics.'

'How did that affect your life?'

Gina drifts off, bored and irritated by my questions. For the first time Johnny looks agitated. He hadn't anticipated this line of questioning. 'Leave it,' he warns me. A legionnaire joins our table. He is French. He has a shaved head that looks like it's been attacked with a jackhammer and then left to scarify on a hot day in the Sahara. His arms are covered in tattoos. He's quite a rough enough diamond to make me tremble. Bet he doesn't have an Equity card. Keeping to form he pulls out an untipped Gauloise. He pauses before lighting it and looks at me with hard blue eyes. 'Est-ce-que je vous dérange, si je fume?'

The rough diamond turns out to be a gallant chevalier. I am disarmed. 'Pas de tout,' I twitter.

Gina comes back with a drink; she has forgiven me my cold war interrogation. We talk about men.

'What about him?' I gesture towards my guide.

'Il est très bon, très bon.'

'Better than the others?'

She bursts into peals of laughter. The chevalier laughs and listens. She says she's not interested in marriage; she's doing everything for herself. She goes to church every Sunday, three miles out of town, passing a military checkpoint. Why are there checkpoints, I wonder. 'Because that's what it's like here,' says Johnny. I look at him critically. Here he is in his kepi, shorts and socks, having sworn his oath of fealty. How much does he really know about the politics of the place? Not a lot, but he knows where the guns are pointing, I suppose. We move to another bar. There are big white men here – French, I think, and behaving the way European men do when they are far away from their own womenfolk, and are letting their hair down with women they normally can only fantasize about. One gives me a glance of contempt mingled with embarrassment. They paw the delicate Ethiopian girls, who smile but give angry little wriggles with their shoulders; this only serves to inflame the beasts. Suddenly a figure comes whirling towards us, like a spinning top. This is Mama Fanti. She is a seventy-year-old prostitute. These days she does more drinking and dancing than screwing. She wears traditional Somali dress – she is not Ethiopian – and is a celebrity. She comes up to me and kisses my hands with leathery lips and then spirals off again. Two legionnaires come in. They are British. They greet Johnny unenthusiastically and ignore me. Johnny does not introduce me. They are white and flabby. They use the words 'cunt' and 'fucking' while they wait to order their beers. These I understand, the word 'Bobo' I don't.

'Oh that. Well, it's a sort of word for the locals.'

'Like nigger?'

'Well, sort of – everyone uses it.'

'Everyone white uses it, you mean.'

Johnny looks blank. The English legionnaires burp loudly. I wonder if they have any idea how repulsive they are.

Time to go. It's Monday night, not a great time for living it up – the girls outnumber the men. We walk along the sea road in silence, both, I think, well pleased with each other's company.

'Thought you were going to be a bloke when the manager said a British journalist wanted to speak to me – prettiest bloke I've ever met.'

I feel a dangerous little glow – the moon, the sea, the heat, a man in uniform, with an Equity card . . . No! No, absolutely not! It'll only get me in the most frightful trouble. We reach the vestibule of the Siesta and kiss each other chastely on the lips.

AGENT OF DESTRUCTION

The development conference dawns another day, with more self-important wittering about soil erosion, rinderpest vaccination programmes, Juba river irrigation schemes, reforestation – on and on. I return to the Siesta tired and irritable. I take my key at reception and Johnny comes running into the bar.

'Got a good story for you.'

'Oh yeah.' I'm not up for anything much in this heat.

'Bomb's gone off in town, six dead. I can't hang around. I shouldn't be here – I'm on alert now. See you.'

Not just Johnny on alert. The mobilized military might of the French is evident on every road, at every corner.

The business of the bomb takes over the rest of my day and night. It was planted in a popular café in the centre of

town. At least five people have been killed. Elections are
coming up so it could be the opposition, but it could be
anti-French, pro-Iranian. For Djibouti is strategic for France.
It's not an official naval base but an important stopover, and
there are plenty of ships docked. I inspect the café and the
crater. There are tiny scraps of flesh and blood about the
shattered structure. The bodies were removed within twenty
minutes of the bomb going off – by French security, I'm
told. I want to cry. It could have been me, I think . . . and
what an evil thing to do, how cowardly. All attempts to
approach people in the crowd with my microphone are
rebuffed. Then a big blond man appears, like a character
from an Astérix cartoon. I ask him timidly, 'Did you see
what happened?'

'No.'

'How many people died?'

'I'm going to the morgue to find out. You can come with
me if you want,' says the large blond man.

It always amazes me that anyone wants to help a journalist. He is, I discover, the British honorary consul and his
name is Godwin Cattle. I've often wondered what they do,
honorary consuls. Mr Cattle works hard most of the time
at some importing job. He is not even British, although he
speaks good plain English. He is Belgian and he looks
harassed. He now has to make time for chasing round
morgues identifying dead bodies. We go first to the military
hospital to see how the wounded are doing. It's a filthy
place, but better than the general hospital, Mr Cattle tells
me. A French surgeon appears covered in blood, still wearing
his swimming trunks. He is enraged at the sight of me and
my microphone. He begins to scream. It's a grotesque
combination: a man screaming in French, wearing only his
swimming trunks, dripping with blood in the suffocating
heat. I still have the cassette recording: the surgeon screaming

so loudly his voice is distorted, Mr Cattle further away and quieter, trying to appease him, and then there's me breathing heavily very close to the microphone, occasionally saying rather stupidly, 'Oh dear.' Poor Mr Cattle. Bet he's regretting bumping into me. His attempts to calm the surgeon down fail. He goes back to his surgery.

We head for the morgue. Outside the big blue doors of the building women sit and chat quietly as though waiting for a show. There's no weeping. They can't be bereaved relatives. Perhaps they are professional morgue attendants. A stillness seems to emanate from inside, the irreversible stillness of death. A boy sits on the roof of the generator hut, the generator which keeps the refrigeration going inside. He wears a scarf round his mouth and nose, and picks his toes. Mr Cattle has to go in and see if he can identify any British nationals. He's joined by the American and British ambassadors doing the same thing. Bet they are scared, but they've got to do a job. I pray I don't catch so much as a whiff of dead rotting bodies. I'll be sick if I do, I know I will. I wait and wait, and don't smell a thing. Perhaps I should have gone in with the men to see the damage. Be the detached observer. Oh no, I can't. I don't want to see mutilated children, and adults torn apart and bloody.

At last Mr Cattle emerges. His head is bowed. He manages to tell me in a slightly wobbly voice that there are five dead; two are unrecognizable in terms of sex or race.

I set to, filing a report down the phone. Quite why, I don't know; I am not really a reporter. I make features, but working for the BBC I somehow feel I should turn my hand to whatever the situation demands. Nobody's even heard of me in the BBC newsroom.

'Now, dear, are you sure it's not a gas canister? It's no good sounding off about bombs if it's a domestic explosion.'

'No, it's not a gas canister – the police and the army say it's a bomb.'

'All right then . . . where did you say you worked?'

'The African Service.'

'Right.' Did I hear a sceptical note? 'Listen, love, we'll take your piece in half an hour; nothing longer than one minute twenty seconds.'

The numbers keep changing as others die in hospital. Another less sceptical and more kindly sub-editor in the newsroom points out that the figures can be kept in the presenter's introduction; I don't need to keep updating the story on account of another death. The final death toll is one legionnaire, three German scientists, two French sailors, one French professor, two Djiboutian waiters, one Djiboutian policeman and one French civilian. A shabby deed.

TUNISIAN NIGHTCAP

I get back to the hotel at one a.m. There are French soldiers at the door, part of a massive security operation which is going on throughout Djibouti. They examine my bag and equipment. The night receptionist is awake and looks at me mistrustfully as he gives me my key. I mount the stairs and a voice calls over my shoulder.

'Bonsoir.' A tousled man, Arab in appearance, comes alongside. 'Ça va?'

Well, since you ask, not brilliant, I think to myself.

'Vous aimez Djibouti?'

Not at this precise moment.

'Vous aimez Djibouti?'

He's exasperating.

'No,' and I add rather between clenched teeth, 'Everyone's a bit anxious at the moment.'

'Ah, you are English. I am businessman from Tunisie. You visit Tunisie?'

'Yes, once.' Why am I talking to this man and where has he been the last ten hours? He's certainly out of step with the mood of the moment.

'You drink whisky with me?'

What?

'No.'

'You will like it, drink whisky with me in my room.'

'No.' I hurry up the stairs pursued by him. He's drunk.

'Come on, baby – whisky with me . . .'

Aghhh. I make a rush for my room and with shaky hands turn the key, slamming the door shut and locking it from the inside. Then do that thing heroines do in films, leaning with my back to the door, my arms splayed out, glancing up to one corner of the door frame, panting gently. Finally convinced that I am safe, I lie down and sleep very heavily.

I'm up at five. Having starting the ball rolling with the reporting, I find I have to keep going; it's a bit like feeding a baby.

'So if we can take a minute for the 1100 Reel and if you get anything for the 1300 give us a call at 1230.'

The question now is, Who did it?

The mood in the hotel has plummeted. My status has been transformed from honoured guest to liability; an English journalist who has witnessed a blow struck against French power and prestige. In the run-up to a press conference a French journalist working for RFI attacks me and the BBC for being 'implicitly pro-Soviet'. He records his interviews on an enormous machine, and asks the Foreign Minister big floppy open-ended questions. By comparison, I reflect, my machine is small and virile – my questions short and sharp. Neither of us gets any nearer to knowing what happened. The military and police are still on full alert in case more bombs have been planted. The hotel has been visited several times during the day by important Frenchmen in uniform. Each time Cocoa the manager looks more depressed. Dinner is no longer served outside under the canopy. The front windows are locked up. People huddle in groups inside. I try striking up a conversation with a French couple at the bar in my bad French: 'Vous êtes en vacances?'

'Non.' Their faces remain impassive, and they move to their seats in the dining area as fast as they can. I later discover that the hotel caters more or less entirely for the families and partners of the French military and navy. I'm tired and pining for someone to talk to. I sit alone and bored, pushing around my delicious carranx ungratefully. A shadow falls across my plate.

'Can I join you?'

My heart leaps. 'Rather.'

A man with a brown face, one gold earring and very fair hair politely waits for an invitation he can understand.

'I mean, please, yes, take a seat.'

He sits down. It seems as though we've always known each other.

'They're not very friendly here,' I venture.

'They are French. You are English. The French run everything.' He is Romanian. He was born to a circus family. He had an equestrian act. The horses were bought from Hungary. When he was twenty-five and touring in Spain, the circus tent caught fire and most of his relatives died. 'No more circus. Now I travel round the world delivering boats. I'm always moving. I have no home, but I have a bank account in Thailand.'

'You speak very good English.'

'I speak English, Greek, French of course, Romanian, Italian, some Spanish but not so good.'

He is a difficult mixture of melancholy and boastfulness.

'Don't you miss the circus?' I regret the question as I ask it, remembering the fire and his family.

'No, but some traditions I keep. Like this earring. It's put in when you are two or three years old. But every five years you change it.'

'Why?'

'The gold in the earring absorbs all the evil in you, all the bad things. And when it fills up I go to a lake in the south of France and throw it in. I'm not superstitious, but I still do this. I won't stay here long, I'm just dropping off a boat for a French army man. This place ... well, there's too much difference between the rich and the poor.'

We spend the rest of the evening turning over that theme, occasionally making a detour to remark upon the ruthless way the French go about pursuing their interests abroad. I decline an invitation to share his bed; he accepts the refusal with good grace. I go to my room and have my first proper long sleep in two days.

The next morning I ring up the newsroom. Would they like something about an opposition statement made in connection with the explosion? 'Sorry, dear. I don't think it's quite hard enough to run. We're very full at the moment with the Czech Prime Minister. If they nail anyone for the explosion give us a ring.' Having been run off my feet with news bulletins and radio newsreels I feel rejected; it's like unrequited love. I'm a reporter now. Not hard enough? Well, really!

There's a big uniformed guy in reception, speaking French fast and furious. He carries a big cardboard box. I hear the word 'Tunisian'.

'So what's he want?' I ask Cocoa.

'He has photos. He wants us to look.'

'Oh, can I?'

'No, no. It is for staff only.'

'Was he asking about that Tunisian? I met him, you know . . .'

'No, no. It is nothing.'

Hmm. I ring Godwin.

'Any new developments?'

'No, not really.'

'Who knows exactly what's happening now? I mean, who could give me a proper update on where the investigation stands?'

'The French military attaché.'

'At the embassy?'

'Yes.'

Of course they'll give me the brush-off like everyone else, I think self-pityingly. And to begin with the French military attaché *is* a little frosty.

'I'm sorry, Madame, we have no comments for the BBC.'

'Listen, I know you're after a Tunisian . . .'

'Sorry, Madame – we are not talking to the press.'

'. . . and I know he was staying at the hotel . . .'

'Madame, please . . .'

'. . . and the night of the bombing he tried to get me to drink whisky with him. So you see—'

'You met him?'

'Yes.'

'What time?'

'One in the morning after the explosion, and all I want is—'

'Please remain where you are.'

'What?'

'We shall send someone round to the Hotel Siesta to talk to you.'

'Why? Is it him? I'm busy, I can't hang around all day at the hotel.'

'But we need to interrogate you, Madame, today.' He puts the phone down.

Hang on a moment. This is all the wrong way round. I'm supposed to be asking the questions. I'm supposed to be chasing the story. Now me and the story are beginning to merge in a most disconcerting way.

1066

The very portly, very tall Attorney General looms over me. He smokes a pipe. Of course, mille soixante-six is 1066. And he is from Normandy and I am English so really we can both be friends.

'Now I want you to show me what happened.'

'Well, I was just going up to bed when . . .'

'No, I want you to show me exactly where you were standing.'

'Well, I was in the reception at the bottom of the stairs.'

'Let us go.'

'Now I was here.'

'On the third step of the stair?'

'Maybe the third, or the second . . . no, hang on a minute – I turned to face him here on the fourth step. But I first heard his voice with my left foot on the second step and my right foot on the third step.'

The Attorney General is lapping it up.

'So then what happened?'

'Then he asked me if I was tired. I said yes. He said he was a Tunisian here on business and then he offered me whisky in his room.'

'And did you accept?' The Attorney General's eyes are glittering dangerously; he takes a tremendous puff on his pipe.

'Of course not.' Talk about misreading a girl's character.

'Are you sure?'

'Of course I'm sure . . . he was drunk. I don't go into men's rooms. I said no and went to my room and locked the door.'

'Did he try to get in?'

'No.'

'Now let's go through this again. Let us start again at the bottom of the stairs.'

I'm feeling miserable. At best it's a bit like rehearsing on stage for a particularly complicated farce, blocking the movements to perfection for a tyrannical director. At worst it feels like the Procureur Général thinks I'm a silly English tart trying to cover up her tracks.

We go through the whole procedure again. And this time he pursues another line.

'Did you enter his room?'

'No.'

'Had you entered his room previously this week?'

'No, I'd never met him before.'

'But he had been staying here all week.'

'Well, I never noticed him.'

'But you are a journalist . . .'

In time even the Attorney General can see I have had enough.

'Thank you – you have been most helpful. This afternoon, Commander Bouchoux will come and speak to you. Oh and by the way, please do not make this a story for your people in London. It would not be nice for you to be interrogated by Djibouti security – their methods are not as nice as ours.'

IT WAS HIM!

Of course, a really brave person, or even a professional journalist, would have been on the phone straight away, filing live. But I am not a professional journalist, and not a really brave person. I am a coward, so instead of filing about the Norman encounter, I cower in my room. Then I ring London.

'What shall I do?'

'Keep a low profile,' says my boss.

'But do you think I should file something?'

'Just keep a low profile. Answer their questions and don't do anything.'

After a wretched lunch of warm Coca-Cola, the phone rings in my room.

'Commander Bouchoux is downstairs.'

The one thing I shall remember about him is that his uniform stands out for the thickness of his knee-length socks; he looks a bit like the illustrations of Philippe's father in my French textbook at school. His hair is black and parted to the side and combed with a bit of Brylcreem, or whatever the French equivalent is. He has a nicer manner than the man from Normandy. He is carrying a large cardboard box. We are assigned an empty bedroom by a glum-looking Cocoa.

'So what happened on the night of the explosion?'

'Well, I was just about to climb the stairs. My left foot was on the second step and my right foot was on the third step when—'

'You were approached and he offered you whisky.'

'Exactly.'

'So did you go to his room?'

Sacré bleu, they are one-track-minded, these French.

'No, I did not.'

161

'You did not spend the night with him.' His voice is calm, disinterested – none of the lasciviousness of the Attorney General.

'I certainly did not. I didn't know him. He was drunk. I locked myself up in my room.'

'I am sorry to ask all these questions, but we have to be precise about what he did after he . . .' He stops, smiles and takes the lid off the cardboard box. 'Now I have some photos I want you to look at.'

'Righto.' This is awful. Suppose I pick out the wrong bloke? I try to remember what he looked like. He had a moustache, black hair, quite a narrow face. Practically every single photo that Commander Bouchoux is spreading out on the table depicts a man with a moustache, black hair and a narrow face; OK, perhaps a smattering of fat blokes thrown in for interest's sake.

Row after row of slightly shifty-looking men are laid out. Then suddenly, bang. There he is. Black hair, moustache, narrow face, but it's him. I surprise myself with the swiftness of recognition.

'Him.'

'This is the man?'

'Yes.'

'You are sure.'

'Yes, completely.' And I am completely sure, but that certainty comes with a terrible pang that only the tender-hearted female could feel. (It's the same thing that stops a woman from gouging out the eyes of the man who's about to rape her.) He looks dazed and vulnerable in the photo. Is his mum still alive? How did he get mixed up in this pickle? What will happen to him?

'Was he the one who did it?'

'Yes, Madame.'

I am taken aback by the honesty of his answer.

162

'But how do you know? Did he confess?' Stupid question – they must have knocked the shit out of him.

'Yes, he confessed. But there is forensic evidence against him too. He left some of the equipment in his room. You know he was lodged directly above your room.'

Crikey.

'So what happens now?'

Commander Bouchoux smiles politely. 'Thank you very much for your help. You are leaving soon?'

How does he know that? I wonder.

'Yes.'

'Have a pleasant trip to Somalia.'

Commander Bouchoux gathers up his photos and leaves.

MEDALLION MAN AND FOREIGN OFFICE MAN

I am trying to write up my notes. My last day in Djibouti.

'Can I buy you a drink?'

On the one hand I am feeling rather thirsty, on the other I don't accept drinks from strange men.

'Let me buy you a drink.'

The voice is insistent but friendly, Oh, what the hell. I'm feeling demob happy.

'All right then – tonic water.'

He looks like a beach bum – shorts, shades, medallion.

He returns with a tonic and introduces himself as the assistant to the chief of security. My tonic water freezes in my throat. He stares at me through reflective lenses.

'You spoke to the Attorney General?'

'Yes – so what?'

'We are exploring a Djiboutian connection.'

'But you've got your man, he was in the—'

'We've been watching you.'

What?

'What do you mean you've been watching me?'

'You have been dialling the same number, all the time. We know that you are in contact with the opposition.'

It's the last straw that broke the camel's back. I rise to my feet. I'm so cross that my eyes are pricking with tears.

'I'm going to ring the British honorary consul,' I announce theatrically and sweep out of the porch and into the hotel.

'Who have you been in contact with, Mademoiselle Ledger?' calls out the medallion man demonically after me. 'Who is your contact?'

Back in my room, and straight on to the telephone: 'Mr Cattle – sorry to trouble you again, but this French bloke in shorts started accusing me of . . .'

An hour later Godwin Cattle appears, with a cheery Englishman in tow. French medallion man has gone by now.

The cheery Englishman introduces himself as being from the Foreign Office.

'Just come from Aden – extraordinary place. Been giving you a hard time here, have they?'

I narrate my story of the three interrogations.

'But you see, my dear, everyone's looking for promotion. Your latest chap in the boxers has heard about you. He knows you're English and a journalist, so he's beastly to you – makes him feel big.'

I can detect in myself a horrible weakness for this Englishman's posh, rather pansy way of speaking, everything made into a joke. A raft of jingoistic, patriotic, elitist feelings are rising up inside me. Yes, the man from the Foreign Office is here; I am safe from all these nasty French people. At last someone with a sense of humour, a good command of English and, it turns out, a fondness for history. We order beers all round. The bartender gives us a filthy look. The man from the FO likes talking.

'You see, the French believe in total control – of all the European powers to rule in Africa, they're the most cynical – you could say honest. But the English are . . .'

'Frightful hypocrites,' I throw in.

'But endearingly amateur,' he responds.

'Yes, endearingly amateur – that's all . . .' How nice to agree, how nice to enjoy your own capacity for self-effacement.

'Now the English view is life's a bit of a dress rehearsal – give it a whirl, see what happens. But you see the French take it all frightfully seriously.' The two of us have a good laugh, the FO man and me. God knows what Godwin Cattle thinks. I don't think he's bothered – being Belgian he stands somewhere in the middle.

'Of course the Germans were brilliant in Togo and quite appalling in South West Africa . . .'

More beers all round. By eleven o'clock we have moved on to Portuguese colonial style (deeply inefficient, ambiguous attitude to race). Godwin has gone.

'Deux bières encore, s'il vous plaît,' I call gaily. I really am enjoying myself.

'Il n'y a pas de bières,' says the bartender sourly. Hovering in the background I can see the now grim-faced Cocoa.

'They're just trying it on. Ask them for a bottle of wine – they'll have that.'

'Une bouteille de vin, s'il vous plaît.'

'Pas de vin.' This is a great big fat lie. You could not run a hotel for French people with vases of cut roses and no wine.

But when people lie there's not a lot to be done.

'I should be going.' The FO man stands up and sways. 'Jolly good, jolly good,' he says over and over again. And then he goes to wake up a slumbering taxi driver.

The next day a Fokker takes me to Somalia, where being European counts for a great deal less than it does in Djibouti.

TEN

Neat Streets and Mean Minds

~~~

'Go on then.'

'What? What?'

'Let's see you do it.'

'Do what?'

Francis is big and chuckly. He sells liquor in Dar es Salaam. He's been drinking steadily all evening, and he is teasing us with a tale from his childhood. This is my best night yet in a city where the most interesting dramas happen behind closed doors, and I'm always on the wrong side. Nobody shouts at each other in the street. No Mr Bigstuff struts his stuff. The rich keep a low profile. Love is discreet.

'I made good money.'

'People actually paid?'

'Yes.'

'Go on then.'

'You want me to . . .?'

'Yes, yes. Go on. Please,' we chorus with squeaky voices.

'You have to give me a pen.'

'Here you are.'

Francis has finally agreed to draw a white lady for us. This used to be his main source of income in secondary school forty years ago. His drawings of white ladies were – according

166

to Francis – legendary. With all the careful deliberation of the drunk, he resumes his old money-spinner.

'What are those things?' Véronique is already scoffing.

'Her legs,' says Francis. His tone is mellow and content. He has been transformed suddenly by the business of drawing.

Véronique bursts into laughter. 'They are stick legs.' She puts her face close to his. 'Is that how you think white women's legs are?'

Francis pauses, his concentration broken. Through his drunken haze he is aware that he is in the company of one white woman (me).

'This how some white women are constructed,' he replies diplomatically. 'Very nice long legs.'

Then he carries on, once more entranced by his own work.

'Oh my goodness – her eyes are like saucers,' says Véronique.

'That is because she is surprised,' says Francis calmly.

'Why?'

'Because I am drawing her.' It's a good answer that puts a temporary halt to Véronique's criticisms, but not for long.

'Why does her hair go down and then up like that?'

'She has nice European hair and a nice sharp pointed nose.'

'And she has stick arms.'

Francis preserves a dignified silence.

'What is this thick thing on her skinny arm?'

Now this demands a response.

'That is a Rolex watch.'

'A watch?'

'It shows she is a rich white woman.'

Another peal of laughter.

'You sold this for money?' The tone is incredulous.

'My fellow pupils were queueing – very difficult to satisfy demand.'

'Why?'

'Because nobody else could draw white ladies.'

Francis completes the portrait. And there she is, vixen-faced, with her Doris Day flick-up hair, very thin flat chest. She's wearing a sort of shift dress. She has Olive Oyl shoes – long and curving at the toes, with heels added on as an afterthought. And there's the massive Rolex watch.

'Can I have her?' I ask eagerly. Véronique gives me a pitying look.

'Of course.'

'How much?'

'You can have her for free.'

'Thanks.'

It isn't a brilliant drawing, I'm not sure why I wanted it and still have it in my address book, but looking at it now a memory is stirred: Ndola 1983. The International Hotel. Francis's white lady looks remarkably like the proprietor.

Flora Thirkettle owned a hotel on the Copper Belt. It had the most popular bar in Ndola. And that's because it never ran out of beer. The price you paid (apart from a few kwacha) was first, a gloomy ambience – the walls painted dark brown, the drinking area poorly lit by naked bulbs. Not such a high price for hardened drinkers; it's a fact they like a place to be a bit run down. They feel good, drinking in the gloom; they don't want prettiness, frills, ornaments. They want to be hard men, with beer providing the pleasure. Second, there's Flora's ferocious temper, the biggest price of all. But the customers keep coming because she delivers the beer. I am staying just a couple of nights. My bedroom is dull but spotless. The sheets are stretched tight across the bed. They have been efficiently darned. It takes me some time to realize that I am Flora's honoured guest. She is not keen for me to lurk in the drinking area downstairs. But I am sticking it out, for a few beers at least; young enough still to imagine that girls can be 'one of the lads'. I am wedged between Mr Saki and Mr Phiri. Mr Saki runs a private school, with rather more status than facilities. Mr Saki is trying to convince Mr Phiri to join the party. They are both trying to take no notice of me – partly, I think, because Zambians are a little shy, and partly because I am a white girl who has no business being here, making men all self-conscious when they should be relaxing after a hard day's work. Actually, most of them are relaxing after the effort of last night's relaxing. There is little work here; copper is still dug up, but the mines are hardly breaking even. Flora knows. She came here from Norfolk with her husband in the 1950s to make money. He on the mines, she running a night club for white miners. And then it all went sour. Or rather the currency went non-convertible. And their investments vanished. She's widowed now. Thin and wiry, like an old vine. Stuck on the Belt.

There's a ripple in the room. Flora has entered. Coquettish in her black skirt and frilled blouse, she marches across the room purposefully. Mr Saki and Mr Phiri look up, momentarily worried. Then take her on.

'Here's Flora looking radiant as ever.'

Flora's expression doesn't change.

'A toast to Flora – who makes more money out of us than all the other shebeens in this town.'

Flora tilts her face back and smiles a tight little smile. Then she beckons to me, with just the faintest gesture, but it is perfectly clear she wants me to come with her.

We weave through the round tables and puddles of beer.

She leads me upstairs to her suite of rooms. The style is early 1960s. Plenty of cream and black. Ladylike. There's a cocktail bar – black plastic, studded. She puts on a diaphanous pink dressing gown – or is it an elegant housecoat? – and pours herself and me big martinis. She rifles through her record collection and selects some Mantovani; with precision she sets the needle on the record. She sits down, fluffs up her home-rollered hair with well-manicured hands and lights a long cigarette with a small, gold lighter. She's a frightful battleaxe, but she's so ladylike. Her accent still carries a slight Norfolk burr but she's a lady, like Diana Dors was a lady, or Kathy Kirby, or Barbara Windsor – with an eye to neatness, big hair, manicured hands and a small waist. I look down critically at my Indian cotton dress and slightly dirty nails – really it's about time I packed in the ethnic milkmaid look, and tried acting my age. I don't think Flora's the least bit bothered. For her purposes I'm white company, however unladylike. I'm tempted to feel sorry for her, but shan't. Independence or colonialism, low or high copper prices, she has more status and power here than she would have in the suburbs of Norwich. She's a European, beached in foreign parts it is true, but she hasn't gone to seed. Her bedlinen may have holes in it but it is properly darned.

I feel I must give her value for money, and strike up a conversation.

'They were talking about the Party downstairs . . .'

'The Party.' Flora spits on the P. 'It's the parasites that join the Party. Fools like me work me fingers to the bone. And what have I got to show for it?'

'The hotel's very popular.'

'But I can't sell it. And if I could sell it, I could only get kwacha for it – toy money. This country was a good country once, it was rich. And then Mr Kaunda decides the currency should be non-convertible.' I feel the conversation could get stuck in a non-convertible groove.

'So what was it like in the fifties?'

'Oh well,' Flora smirks, 'we had a bloody good time. This country had something going then. You think this hotel is popular? You should have seen my club. People came from miles around.'

'Zambians? Europeans?'

'You joking? Europeans of course. Men that worked on the mine, with money to spend.'

There's a roar from downstairs – it could be approval, it could be dissent. At any rate it involves a number of voices and has penetrated Flora's boudoir. Flora slams her martini down. She looks mean. She's probably had a few already, I think anxiously. It is one o'clock in the morning. And there's a little scratch on the Mantovani record – just where the words 'distant shore' would go, if it were a vocal.

She shouts, 'Oh no – they're not getting away with that . . . destroying my peace and quiet in my room, destroying my evening.'

She's a good deal more like a next door neighbour than the owner of the joint. She gets up. I follow at a discreet distance, fear yielding to the prospect of a spectacle. Down the dark, dreary stairs. The door to the bar is flung open. Flora stands and gazes. Some drinkers have caught sight of her and look uneasy. There are phrases from Flora's Norfolk past, phrases like 'last orders', 'time, gentlemen, please', which might be appropriate at this moment, but she forgot to take them with her to Northern Rhodesia, she forgot to pack them when she headed south, past Caister St Edmunds, past Cairo and on to the Cape, before doubling back up to the Belt. The drinkers are now being treated to Flora's shorthand equivalent of these time-honoured phrases.

'Get out, you bloody bastards,' she screams.

Bodies shift.

'Out, all of you, out.'

She picks out a drinker to make an example of him. She advances on him.

'Out! Gettit?'

He's actually a bit too drunk to get it. A thin, wiry arm shoots out of the fold of her housecoat and stops short an inch from his face. She growls. He moves, alarmed. Slowly, but agitated enough.

'For the last time: out, the lot of you – you've got your flaming independence but you're not enjoying it at my expense tonight.'

Fifty or so cheap pairs of shoes shuffle gradually across the black lino floor, smearing puddles of beer as they go. A thin smile sets on Flora's face.

'I think I'll be going to bed, Flora.'

It seems it would be just too easy to cross her now. She takes no notice of me, just stares the men out of the room.

The next morning I am summoned to her bedroom. She is sitting up in bed against piles of pillows. It's one of those all-in-one beds with an elaborate, padded headrest and fitted side tables with gilt mouldings in a vaguely Georgian imitation. Her pale blue negligee is cut low, with ribbons threaded round the neckline. The room smells of hairspray. She has put lipstick on.

'Slept all right?' she asks warily, perhaps anticipating complaint.

'Oh brilliant,' say I, anxious to reassure her. But actually it's true. I did sleep well, perfectly confident that her tyranny meant the sheets had been changed, the room was clean, and there were no cockroaches.

'Can't get decent hairspray these days. This comes from South Africa but it's not up to much.'

She picks up a make-up mirror and scrutinizes the lined face.

'Bone structure – stays with you for ever.'

Still gazing at herself, she reaches for a cigarette. She puts it in the corner of her mouth and lights it, swivelling her eyes so she can keep taking stock of herself. The moment of contemplation runs its course and the little mirror is flung down on the pink counterpane. She takes another drag on her cigarette, sits bolt upright and roars a command.

'Paper!'

Cigarette smoke drifts out of her mouth like resonance. There's an anxious patter of feet. The door opens. A house-girl gently places the paper at the end of the bed. Flora picks it up.

'Getting thinner all the time. Always the same crap. Central Committee this, Central Committee that. Need a bomb put under their arses.'

How intolerable Flora finds it all. She came to make money – energetically and efficiently. And then twenty years down the line there was nothing left to take except small change, beer money. She should have loosened up in my opinion. Gone to a few Nsaka evenings, sat on a log under a decent moon watching comic sketches, drinking, having a laugh. Tuned in to Alick Nkhata and the Lusaka Radio Band, stepping out in style with their hit number 'Taxi Driver', Englishman Dick Sapper on keyboards. But I fear Flora would have sneered at all that; sneered at BBC producers on secondment for a year, fervent in their belief that radio was a tool for achieving democracy and independence. Flora was busy re-creating 1950s Britain in Northern Rhodesia: cocktails, expatriate flirtations and perhaps, occasionally, in a quiet moment, she made room for an Empire Service broadcast, but I am only guessing. All her life in Africa, Flora, like many Europeans, has dealt almost exclusively in deficiencies, arguing with dull-witted, greedy government officials and with drunken men, and each day they hem her in more and more.

Broken heart

If you want to know more about another country, another culture, then conducting a love affair with someone from that place has much to recommend it. But be prepared for the inevitable transition from ecstatic insights to agonizing heartache. Long ago I fell in love with a writer. He was very clever with words and I confused this with kindness. Not that he was a bad man but, like many men, he needed a lot more kindness than he could ever give. More to the point, he'd grown up inhaling the poisonous vapour of apartheid. This extraordinary system, concocted from cruel imagination and self-preservation, crushed many a spirit, but not him. He was clever *and* defiant, sharp-wittedly boxing and coxing the white men in charge, who, for all their meanness, were often foolish and unworldly. They tried to ignore their neighbours on the continent throbbing for independence. And that's what the majority in South Africa wanted. Such optimism. I wish I'd been there.

The Very Clever Writer has given me a book to look at about *Drum* magazine, with lots of hard and beautiful black and white photos. There's Arthur Maimane looking me straight in the eye, over the shoulder of the girl he's dancing with in a Sophiatown club, cigarette hanging obliquely out the corner of his mouth. He's wearing what looks like a sailor's hat, with the inscription 'In the Groove' on it. There's Todd Matshikiza, half silhouetted against the stage lights, looking happy. And there's Juby Mayet, *Drum* cover girl, in a dress to die for. And Jim Baily, editor of *Drum*;

he's white but he knows where he's going – he's got a mission. He doesn't need to stop and wonder where he fits in – he's going for bust like the rest of them, even if he knows the price they pay is higher than anything he is likely to experience. Oh yes, I wish I'd been there – on the cusp, in the 1950s, before the government machine became steely efficient, when it still looked possible to win, to spear the growing octopus of apartheid. But I am white, and to be white meant always to hold the power, whether you thought it wrong or right. The dinner party ends and you send your African guests off with affection, but first you sign a letter saying you had to keep them working late; this they can produce if they are stopped at the roadblock on the way back to the township after hours. The photos mislead me with their glamour. I don't understand quite how cruelly the logic of apartheid slices through everything. I close the book of photos and try to think of something pleasing.

'I've bought a Christmas tree – shall we put it up?'

He's amused. It has been a difficult week since I've arrived. There have been some very tender moments, and some drunken quarrels. My problem is, I think I understand about this race thing, but I don't. I think that love conquers all; it doesn't. I am young, bumptious and want to cross borders for which I have no passport and no map. Every morning it rains outside. The bougainvillaea bow their blossoms to the water and we are tender and happy; by teatime the beer has started to flow and we are quarrelling or there is silence. I thought I knew how deep the scars ran, and what caused them, but I didn't. And he was trapped between a desire to love and a perverse desire to wound. That morning he reads a letter from an American student, a former lover; it's erotic, intimate, clever. 'Last night I dreamt of you, your back covered with cicatrices...' I listen dumbly, trying to be stoic, brave; frightened that if I say anything, I'll cry and sound jealous. Now the Very Clever Man looks at me carefully with a disarming sweetness.

'The flower's bought a Christmas tree. Go on, get it out.'

I go to the bedroom and unpack a twelve-inch-high Woolworth foldaway tree with green tinsel and plastic snow. I bring it into the room in triumph.

'And not only that, I've brought crackers.'

'Crackers?' There's a note of admiration in his voice which I haven't heard since he first saw me naked. 'You have brought crackers.'

I am pleased. A bottle of beer is opened and the first cracker is cracked. And a cracker cracked in southern Africa is worth ten crackers in England. They are quite good quality too. He gets a tiny notebook and pencil, which makes us laugh, and I get a pair of earrings. We put on our hats, and pull another cracker. We are having fun. If only we could always have fun. Pull another cracker. There's a rumble of thunder. The rain starts to beat down. To hell with that – let's have another beer. And another cracker. Crack. Bang. Bang. Now there is knocking at the door. He gets up to open it, leaving me holding my half of the cracker. A young woman walks in and holds him with her stare at the door. The thunder rumbles, which is just as well because it's awfully silent now. Her voice is heavy with hurt.

'You said you were in Zimbabwe for Christmas.'

The accusation hangs in the air. I take off my paper hat. She looks at me.

'Who is she?'

I could ask the same question.

'She's just a friend, honey.'

Oh yes, just a friend who popped in from England with a box of crackers and a small foldaway Christmas tree.

'She's sleeping in the spare room.'

176

My cheeks burn with anger. The woman begins to cry.

'Why have you come here? Why are you here?' he says to her, going on the offensive.

'Vicky said she saw you, and Joseph is sick, he is very sick. The doctor thinks it is cerebral malaria.' She begins to sob, her head bowed.

'This is serious,' says the writer grimly, turning on me now, challenging me to strike up an argument about the two-timing that's been going on.

'He is so young.' The woman collapses on the sofa in sobs.

The writer starts to comfort her. No contest. I'm off for a swim. I'm no good at scenes. I can't bear the sight of women weeping over men and children. And I'm no good at fighting for my man.

The hotel pool is empty because it is raining. I long to see the impassive, walrus-moustached face of Lord Lucan again, calmly parting the water with his large white arms; that would take my mind off this rotten affair. Up and down I swim until I'm quite exhausted. By the time I return to the flat, the writer is very tired and emotional. Gladys – for that is her name – is plain emotional. The sight of me makes everything worse.

'Where have you been?' he explodes.

'I have been swimming, trying to stay out of your way,' I say with as much dignity as I can muster. Gladys looks like she could give my dignity a big kick up the jacksie.

'And now I am going to bed to read.' To be honest, I'm marking my territory: the mistress taking up position in her lover's bed. I sweep out of the sitting room and into the bedroom. I can hear rumbling, shouty noises from the writer and more sobbing from Gladys. I put on a nightie. Now what's it to be: *The Golden Bough* or J. G. Farrell's *The Troubles*? I think I shall go for the J. G. Farrell. I settle down, fingers in my ears to block out the noise: *The Irish, as far as he knew, had always had a habit of making trouble. That was in the nature of things. As for the aim of their unruly behaviour, self government for Ireland, that seemed quite absurd. What would be the advantage to the Irish themselves? . . . So thought the Major anyway.* The tale is interrupted by the door bursting open. The writer is now a vengeful bluebeard. He roars. I ignore him. He picks something up from the end of the bed and hurls it at me. I deflect it with my arm. And before I have time to take further pre-emptive action he leaves the room with a great banging of the door. I pick the missile up from the floor: Frazer's *Golden Bough.* Luckily it's a paperback edition.

But now sang-froid is giving way to a pounding head and heart. I don't like physical violence. Just as I am considering what to do next the door bursts open again and the writer seizes my case and throws it into the next room. I get out of his bed clutching my *Troubles* so to speak, and follow my luggage. On the way I take in Gladys, now pleading. She wants the writer to take her home.

'Bloody, bloody women. You can fucking go on your own. Or sleep on that sofa. I don't want either of you women near me. Fucking women.' He finally retires to his room, striding past me without a glance. The door closes with another great bang.

'Um . . . Gladys.' She turns her head away from me, disgusted. 'Look . . . I don't expect you to like me, but we're both in the same boat . . . um, situation . . . so why don't we bury the hatchet . . . um, sorry, that's an English expression. I mean there's no point in you and me quarrelling . . . well, not now. Look, why don't you . . . why don't you let me take you home?' Why I am offering to do this is not entirely clear to me at first. But then I see it. I want a

178

little control. Besides, a bit of sisterly solidarity might teach the clever writer a lesson. Ha!

Gladys is quiet. She doesn't say yes, she doesn't say no. I go to the spare room and put on jodhpur boots and breeches to make myself feel brave. I consider popping my head round the door to tell him what we are doing, but think better of it.

It is New Year's Eve, and just coming up to the midnight hour as we set off across Lusaka. Everywhere you can hear people carousing, enjoying themselves. In Nigeria, I later discover, they are having a coup. We walk across the university campus, through the night silence. Then curiosity gets the better of me.

'Where are we going?'

'To my brother's.'

'Does he know about . . . ?'

'No.'

'Where's your little boy?'

'In hospital.' Not being a mother, I can't think of anything else to say about this.

'My name's Fiona.

'My name is Gladys.' We stop to shake hands. Gladys is tall and trim, not exactly slender but broad-shouldered and small-breasted. She wears a floral dress, a cardigan. Her hair is in big gerry curls with a fringe. She teaches small children, she tells me.

'How long have you known him?'

'Two years.'

'Oh, I've only know him about two months. But you see, he never mentioned you.'

'He said he wanted to marry me.' Her voice wobbles, and now I am truly sorry. She begins to cry and has to stop walking. I give her little pats on the back.

179

'Oh dear. He never said he wanted to marry *me* . . . but for you, that's awful . . . he raised your hopes. Well, at least we know what he's really like now . . . I mean, he's not really marriage material . . . you've got a kid . . . you need a really reliable chap.'

'It is true.'

We reach Gladys's brother's home. We hug by the gate. Totally reconciled, the jealous toxins drained away.

'Good luck.'

'Thank you for taking me home. What will you do now?'

'My plane goes at the end of the day. So I'll go back and pack and find somewhere to hang out until it's time to go to the airport.'

I trudge back to the flat. The moment I enter there's a roar from the bedroom – it's five o'clock in the morning. His energy seems limitless.

'You fucking women destroy my life.'

I pack as quickly as I can, my hands are shaking, I'm suddenly tired. There's no point in saying goodbye. He has become a monster, and I do not love him enough to wait for him to change back to the quiet, clever, witty person I first met. I manoeuvre the suitcase out of the door. Bumpety-bump down the stairs and on to the street. I hail a stray taxi and go to the BBC stringer's house, not that I know him very well, but it's either that or the British High Commission, or the chairman of the Gymkhana Club. I sit on the BBC stringer's doorstep and begin reading William Boyd's *Ice Cream War* for comfort. The sun is quite hot already. I read two lines and begin to cry. I am still crying when the BBC stringer discovers me. He is embarrassed. He has a guest staying; I get the feeling that anything would be better than my tears: the front line under enemy fire, for example. But I cannot stop the tears. I cry until my lids are swollen, my head is pounding and my tummy feels sick from all the tears I've swallowed.

ENGLISH ROSES

My liaison with the Very Clever Writer had been a disaster. But it was part of an honourable tradition, I reflected, a tradition that goes largely unrecognized. I've read quite a few books on what brought about the end of colonialism. Among the reasons: the Second World War, the Soviet Union, socialism, communism, better nutrition, the example of Israel, better education, the press. No one ever mentions sex, or the English roses. But it was a small army of English roses who donated typing skills, soap powder, food, adoration and loyalty to a small army of African nationalists. These English roses were clever, well educated and understood the issues: racism, imperialism, discrimination. They toiled over Remingtons during the day and, I like to think, had totally brilliant sex at night. Not that English roses were primarily concerned with sex; their first concern was *justice*, next to buying more typewriter ribbon and getting the laundry done. This allowed their partners the freedom to talk and to dream: to melt down the colonial shackles into pangas for harvesting the maize with; to imagine a new world order – factories belching smoke, full of happy workers surrounded by fields of wheat; courts dispensing justice where being pale-skinned was no advantage; and of course not a European man in sight. Many dreamers were cruelly disappointed; some drank their lives away. Some took temporary leave of absence from their roses, going home to test the water, conduct feasibility studies, so to speak, see what professional advantages independence might bring. And meanwhile the years slid by.

'This is the year when you will come to Africa,' the man

says every year to the family he has left in England. And the wives and children wait; time robs them of their passion, but they wait. And they have other things to worry about: the children are, on account of their looks, made to understand they are guests in their own country; they are at the mercy of the whims, taste, prejudices and education of the English locals; they are variously seen as 'exotic', 'amusing', 'frightfully clever for someone who looks so different', 'not bad for a nigger', or just plain 'foreign', 'dirty', 'brown'. Their dad really does mean to rescue them from the peasant attitudes of northern Europeans, but now he has another family and if the government changes, there might be chances, openings, who knows . . .

Not all of those clever nationalists drank the dregs of disappointment of course. Seretse Khama of Botswana brought the fair-haired Ruth back as his bride, against a wall of disapproval and obstruction supplied by the British and South African governments. She lives there even now. His power was rooted in history. Other leaders sprang from obscurity to taste success and power; they became fathers of the nation – Nkrumah, Kaunda, Nyerere. And when they did, they appointed competent, well-educated English women as their secretaries. And as far as we know these women were utterly devoted and chaste in all their duties. But the English roses have their memories.

A TIDY TOWN AND ITS RUBBISH

Twelve years later, I am in southern Africa again – completely dry-eyed, and shopping for underwear in Windhoek. Nothing frivolous, nothing silky and skimpy; Windhoek isn't that sort of town and this is a strictly practical mission; my luggage has been lost in transit. As I go from the pharmacy to another ladies' dress shop I notice everything's written in German. *German*, not Afrikaans. The German community have survived reparations after the First World War, ostracism by the British in the second, colonization by white South Africans. Despite all this, it is German culture that dominates the capital. Windhoek looks like a Hanseatic town: buildings carefully painted, road surfaces flawless, road markings clear. There's no patina of age, everything is new and standardized, as though from a kit, a German city kit. In fact, smarter than anything you'll find in Germany. Of course, climate is on the side of the municipal maintenance department. It is very hot and very dry. By contrast, on the coast of West Africa the killing combination of heat and damp corrodes and damages everything: machines, clothes and buildings. But here the heat preserves.

'So this is Africa,' says the sound recordist as we wake up for our first working day.

'Well, not really. You see, in West Africa it would be . . .' I'm really searching for words now. '. . . it would be more rumbustious, um, more African. There wouldn't be all these white people walking around doing business and operating cash tills, there would be more shouting, more people. It would be more organic, more messy. You'd like it much more than this sort of German stuff.'

The sound recordist listens politely, but I know I am sounding muddled and churlish. And I nervously imagine a West African getting very cross with me: 'We've got the skyscrapers and computers too.' While a Namibian might say: 'How African do you like your Africans? More drums? Tribal costume?' Oh dear, generalizations do tend to offend.

Anyway it's very hot, this sound recordist likes the sun, there's a swimming pool, and there's a very large Herero seamstress/laundress downstairs, wearing her Victorian hooped skirts and a big head-tie – clear evidence that we are not in Germany. I inspect the tiling and grouting in our bathroom: very high standard, no mashed-up tiles shoved into awkward corners, no standing next to the lav to wash because the shower head's been fixed at the wrong angle.

The marble floor in the breakfast room is perfect. A waitress appears with fresh coffee; she is straining to do everything perfectly. Her employers, the owners of the bed and breakfast, are German; she is African. My host appears, an unremarkable, sunburnt, balding German; he has come to make sure all is 'in Ordnung'.

'Our room is very nice. You have a very high standard of craftsmanship here – lovely bathroom too.'

He is pleased. 'Thank you, thank you. But you know it is very difficult, very hard. You see, the African . . .' he pulls a face like he's bitten on a lemon peel, 'the African: keine Ahnung, no idea. We use a German firm, the boss is German. The workers are Bastards.' He looks at me solemnly. I realize this cannot be an insult.

'Bastards?'

'Ya, Bastards – they are good Coloureds from the north. You see, the Coloured here in Windhoek,' another citric wince, 'they do nothing but drink – drink, drink, drink. Useless. But the Bastards are different.'

'Of course, the Bastards. I remember now.' The hierarchy in Namibia goes something like this, I later learn. No. 1 Germans, no. 2 Afrikaners, no. 3 Africans, No. 4 Coloureds. And in a class of their own for grouting and tiling: the Bastards of the north. There are a good many African expatriates, particularly from Uganda. They remain outside the hierarchy, but tend to make friends with either Germans or Afrikaners rather than Africans or Coloureds.

I finish my hot chocolate and salami on black bread, and get ready to meet Frederick Philander. I have come to the cleanest, tidiest place in the world to do the dirtiest, smelliest of jobs: to record Frederick Philander's radio drama. It is set on the Windhoek municipal rubbish dump. It's about two scavengers who live off the rubbish. There's the pleasure of authenticity, and an element of vanity has settled itself at the heart of my plans. Yes, I can hear the fascinated voices already: 'What? You recorded a play on a rubbish dump? Really?' 'Yes, we actually recorded the play on a rubbish dump.' Well, as we all know, pride comes before the fall; fragrant smells before fetid ones.

Freddie is a giant – well, not quite, but he is very tall with a beer belly and he has a loud voice as though he is always talking for the benefit of the man in the back row. He swears, burps and smokes continually. He is a playwright and actor, who has to earn his money teaching geography. He was born in South Africa over forty years ago, classified Coloured. His face stands in total contrast to his manner, it's so mild and fine in its features. His lips are thin and form a melancholy shape; his eyes have bags under them, but turn up gracefully at the corners, giving him a feline look. Much of the time he seems to be staring at an invisible horizon. This shut-offness, combined with the very loud voice and the size of him, is discomfiting. The louder he is the quieter I become. And my quietness makes him louder.

'What I want to get clear, here, is the publicity. Now I've told the local papers about the recording. They've already run some stories this month. They will do follow-up publicity when the play is transmitted.' He produces a beautifully bound file of press cuttings in German, English and Afrikaans. 'See? The second thing I want to discuss with you is this: when we have done the play can you help with contacts in the UK?' Freddie is bellowing now.

My mouth has turned into a cat's bottom. 'Um, would you like a drink?' I ask.

'I'll have a beer – because we need exposure, and you coming here from the BBC is going to be good for us.'

With misgiving I hand over a beer. He's going to drive me nuts. He burps loudly and with satisfaction.

'Now here,' he says, producing another clear plastic wallet, 'is the official permission from the company who have been contacted by Windhoek's municipal council to deal with the rubbish. This permission allows us to record between the days of January 6th and January 14th. I know you won't be staying that long, but just in case,' he's shouting again, 'just in case there's a problem, we have a bit of leeway, right?' He stares at me hopefully.

'Right,' I say primly, 'well, that's terrific. You've been very efficient.' Which he has. 'Can we go to the dump now?'

'Sure – we can go now. It's not a problem.'

We leave the toy town and head for the township to pick up beers. The township – a poor child's building kit. This is where poor people live, along with people who are professional like Freddie: professional, but historically the wrong colour. The houses are small rectangles stretching for miles. Dry, neat, proper roads, superior to any slum in East or West Africa. Every road seems to be punctuated with a little corner store selling food and booze. It's all very orderly, but the despair of the disinherited hangs in the air. All about is broken glass. People in the corner store watch us quietly and glumly as we stock up with soft drinks and beer. I have to make a little speech about beer being off limits while recording takes place.

'But you know, here, beer is a soft drink,' says Freddie.

Fifteen minutes later we are curving round the path to the dump. The road is lined with rows of neatly stacked tyres.

'So many tyres.'

'Have to put them somewhere. You can't bury them. See?'

'Why not?'

'Because it doesn't matter how deep you bury them, they work their way up to the surface.'

'Like worms?'

Fred's not taken with the simile, or maybe he misheard. He's shouting again.

'If you put the tyres underground they move to the surface. You can't fucking bury them.'

We reach the site office of the dump. There are five of us: Fred, me and the sound recordist. Then there's Felicity (Fred's partner and cast member, someone you'd like to be your best friend. She looks mildly Mediterranean – I later discover that she too was classified Coloured) and David (scrawny, twenty-one-old, shy African). A white man in a short-sleeved shirt comes out to greet us; behind him is a landscape of towering rubbish and behind that the blue, blue sky. The white man shakes all our hands – and a flurry of jollity erupts. 'Very kind . . . bit of an unusual request . . . marvellous . . . if there's anything you need . . . watch out for trucks coming in.'

'Thanks for setting all this up for us,' I conclude unctuously. I am secretly rejoicing at this unusual marriage of art and civic propriety. I should be thanking Freddie. Clever and organized Freddie. His manner may be strange but he delivers.

We leave the man in short shirt sleeves and head for a flat clearing among mounds. We need a bit of solid ground for recording on.

'None of this is solid ground,' says Freddie. He knows because he's spent days taking notes about the place in preparation for writing the play. 'Look,' he gestures beyond the bushes. I look and see we are high up, standing on one very large old rubbish mountain. The accumulated detritus of all those tidy people in town, of the township, is below us, above us, on either side. There's a special place for old cars – they have their own little graveyard.

Where the ground is flat, between the mounds and mountains, old wires and cables poke through the surface; tyre-surfacing syndrome again. And on the slopes of the largest mountains, dressed in uniform blue, are the real scavengers on whom Freddie has based his play. They work slowly, picking up, discarding, picking up, discarding. The harvest is lean.

Very occasionally they make a find: a piece of cloth, a metal widget, a wheel; later I see a whole chair, not a three-legged chair or one with no seat but a perfectly proper kitchen chair, perched uncertainly on a hill of rubbish. Yes, the play, the location, all in all a very satisfying convergence of art and life. But there's a price to be paid, as I am beginning to find out. The others are waiting, waiting for me to make a move. But I'm held back by a strong, foreign smell which is snaking its way through my nose; it baffles the olfactory section of my brain with its strangeness. It's certainly a quiet sort of smell. It doesn't have the immediate impact of a ripe nappy or an open drain – that's a smack-in-the-face sort of smell. This is more of having-your-stomach-squeezed-slowly smell. It isn't a constant presence. Sometimes it hangs back, making one think it's not that horrible. Then it surges forward – organic, cloying, sweet – decay shot through with a mechanical tang – a terrible mixture of old pants, rotting meat and perishing rubber – all baked at 120 degrees Fahrenheit.

'So, Fiona, what would you like to do now?' asks Laura, the sound recordist, neat in cotton shorts, and too well brought up to start moaning about the smell.

'What?' It seems as though the smell has made me deaf. She tries to make it easy for me.

'What would you like to start with? Our furry friend is all ready for action,' she says, patting her big stereo mike with its fluffy windshield. 'Bit of wildtrack? Sound check? Rehearsal to mike?'

Everyone looks at me expectantly.

'Um – let's just rehearse to mike the, um . . . first bit where . . . um . . . all three of you come together.'

'We don't,' says Freddie.

'What?'

'We don't ever come together, not at the same time.'

'Oh well, you and Felicity's first bit together . . .'

The smell has now settled on my tongue and is dissolving in my saliva, so I am tasting it as well as smelling it. I fight the desire to retch.

I put on my headphones.

'OK, from . . . um . . . page . . . page five.'

Freddie produces his finest backrow bellow, Felicity tries to keep up. Neither has been placed properly round the microphone; I have failed to explain about the importance of making intensity do the work of volume. I have no one to blame but myself when my headphones fill up with a cacophony of exploding P's and a torrent of metallic distortion. I leap in the air like a cartoon character. For one moment, sound drives away smell and I come to my senses.

'Right. Fine. Let's leave that for now. I think we should spend the rest of the day looking for a quieter, less smelly location for the dialogue. We'll come back here tomorrow to do wildtrack and truck manoeuvres as spot effects.' I make a mental note to bring a large silk scarf soaked in scent.

DEMON DRINK

Day three. Half the play is done. The wildtrack, ambient sound, truck manoeuvres and half the dialogue have been recorded. No more smells. We are back at the best location so far: a water reservoir. It's eight thirty a.m. – we are running late. We wanted to start at eight to beat the wind in the trees and the traffic, which gradually escalate as the day proceeds. David is walking slowly and wobbling.

He's drunk.

Freddie is mad. 'We told him, "Friday night and you must stay at home. Don't go out and drink." He's done it before. And what did he do? He goes out fucking drinking all night. Got back this morning at six thirty a.m.' He releases a torrent of abuse at David in Afrikaans. David recoils, smiling slowly and stupidly, barely able to twitch a muscle in his face. And now one bad thing leads to another. A whisky bottle has somehow found its way on to the picnic table among the props and spare scripts, and adds to the drama. It seems to me the whole production is drowning in alcohol.

'I'm confiscating this.' Even I am surprised at the harsh tone of my voice, as I whisk the bottle off the table and put it in the boot of the car. Freddie and David are momentarily united in disbelief. (Was it Freddie's whisky? I then wonder.) My heart is pounding with anger. I am a colonial madam; they are foolish natives. I am angry at the sight of the whisky bottle mingling so intimately with the spare scripts and all the props seeded for sound effects – the policeman's whistle, the nylon nightie and the bottle with a cork in it. A bottle of whisky has no place there. I try not to show my annoyance.

'OK, let's go for a take. One rehearsal then we'll record. From the top of scene five then.'

David sways.

'"Come in and jump on my lorry . . ." ach, sorry, man.'
This is not promising.
'"Come up my lorry and jump in . . ." Ach shit . . .
"Come, my little sweetheart, and jump my lorry to town."'

'Can we go for a take? If you stumble, then pause and go
back on the line.' My voice is excessively calm.

'"Sweetheart, jump here and take my lorry to . . ." ach
voetsek. "Sweetheart, jump into my town and . . ."'

Take two.
Take three.
Take four.
Take five.
Take six.
Take seven . . . oh, fuck this.

'Don't you have any pride? This is going to be broadcast
to 120 million people and we've only got two days to get it
recorded – and you go out drinking all night. Just go away,
stick your head in some water and come back in an hour. If
you're not sober then you're out.'

My face is red. David's face is stony. He's heard it all
before. He's twenty-one, he's got rotten teeth, two kids by
two different women, and he can't stop the booze. But
David comes from a good home, his father is a preacher and
a salesman. So there's no point in crying tears for him.

An hour later he returns from dunking his head in the
reservoir. He is perfectly sober. His performance is on the
button. Four hours later the play is recorded.

We sit in Fred's small township house. The front room is
almost entirely taken up with a table. This is a place for
sleeping at night, not hanging around in. The lino is badly
torn, the walls scuffed but lined with posters of past plays.
All is mellow now. The colonial madam has caught an
Elder Dempster steamship back to the old country. The

natives have set off down invisible paths and are now scouring the horizon for game. We have cracked open a few beers and are rejoicing in having done the job, and done it well.

'So, David, what do you want to be in your dreams?'

'In my dreams, I want to be a movie star . . .' David is smoking, squinting at me pleasantly through the smoke. '. . . and an international soccer star.'

Freddie snorts. David smiles, perfectly aware of the incongruity between fantasy and reality.

'What do your parents think of your acting?'

'They think it's excellent. They think it keeps me off the street.'

But not off the booze, I think. It's Freddie I really want to talk to. I assume he'll give me the run-around. Bluster, evade or bludgeon me with words. He does none of this. He concentrates hard on trying to answer my questions as best and honestly as he can, his voice straining, hesitant.

Why did he write the play?

'I have such a weak heart, me. Maybe I'm a very aggressive person on the surface, but when it comes to these hardships and sorrow, it moves me. One day I went to this dump and sat for five hours. The first thing I said to myself was, "Thank God it's not me." They were fighting with vultures and baboons. And I thought this story has to be told.'

That tender side is there when he talks about his dad, a policeman who was in the Second World War.

'He used to sing these songs. When he had a drink . . . it used to bring back memories. There was one he used to sing when my mother wasn't around . . . about how they queued in some Egyptian town waiting to get their turn in the brothel. Then he used to sing these beautiful love ballads. "Red Sails in the Sunset", "Way down by the Sea" and all that.'

His tone hardens as we leave the childhood idyll behind.

'I would tell you I consider myself to be in exile in Namibia. In 1979 I worked as a teacher and on the newspapers. But this apartheid thing was beginning to get to me. I consider myself a victim of that apartheid system. I was never political, but always involved in activating the community. I started a group of actors whom I first taught to read and write. I've done quite a lot of social work. That's my little community.

'In Cape Town I got involved with activists. Then the situation became too hot. So I said to myself I'd rather leave South Africa.'

When Freddie arrived in Windhoek, there was no home-grown drama. Neither African nor European. A splendid theatre was built to play host to companies from South Africa – that was the great point of cultural reference.

'How did we persuade them to put on a play? To this day I don't know. Look, I went there, I said, "Listen here, I want to rent this theatre to do a production." And they looked at me, and this one white guy said he had to contact his superior and I had to see him again about this. He said to me, "What are you people trying to do? This is not your line of culture." I told him, "Then we make it our culture now." I rented the theatre for two days. We got big audiences, so big, people were sitting on the steps. I said to the theatre, "Listen, our people will be coming." The first evening it was 90 per cent white and the next it was 90 per cent black, because everyone realized their own people were on the stage.'

I wonder how Freddie's work is received today.

'The critics give their views: very biased; they're mostly white people. I normally have a good laugh, and when we do a play, I tell my actors don't expect any glowing reviews. Then we take the play to South Africa and it's usually acclaimed. Then we come back and it's a success.'

Felicity gives Fred a tender look, which absolves him of all sin. A dart of envy passes through me.

WHOSE IS SHE?

My first time in South Africa. It was 1993. No majority rule yet, but the white South Africans have voted in a referendum for an end to apartheid. We are on a South African Airways flight – myself and my daughter. I have bought her a very well turned out Barbie doll. We are both excited, for this is her first big trip to Africa. Now we are travel companions; no aching goodbye this time as I set off in search of adventure. We are travelling together, to the continent where Daddy was born and lives. Except we're not seeing Daddy, that bit of the plan hasn't worked out. So we arrange the next best thing: to visit his lovely cousin and her husband in Lesotho who have invited us to stay. My daughter's plaits are tight and shining, her knees nicely oiled. The plane is cramped and old. The air hostesses are all white, heavily made up, like whorish Russian dolls. One of these strange creatures comes towards us beaming.

'I like your pletts. Who did them for you?'

My daughter smiles angelically but forgets to reply in the way five-year-olds do. The air hostess picks up a plait and lets it drop, mesmerized by its texture and weight, it seems. I step in.

'I did them.'

'Oh . . . so you're looking after her?' Her voice is typically high and on one note.

'Yes, I'm looking after her.'

'So who is she with?'

'She's with me.'

'Yes, but whose is she?'

'She's mine.' By this time my voice is just a little louder than necessary.

'Ya, but where are her parents?'

'She's mine. She's my daughter.'

The air hostess gawps.

'Oh . . . well, nice pletts.'

I realize then that she has a problem imagining a white woman with anything but a white child.

We arrive in Johannesburg. The airport is bare and empty. It reminds me of Moscow in 1983. I never thought I would miss advertisements, shops, rampant consumerism, but I do. We are in transit, going to Lesotho. We go through customs here; although Lesotho is nominally independent, it is part of a customs union with South Africa. It's also a question of security. Lesotho is surrounded by South Africa, and the government want to be sure that there are no bombs or guns lurking in their midst. I put our hand luggage through the X-ray machine.

'Not all at once,' snarls the supervisor.

'You'd like our items of luggage one at a time?' I say in my best lah-di-dah voice.

She doesn't reply.

'Mummy, are we in Lesotho?'

'Not yet, my mousekin, but soon I hope.'

In a voice constricted with anger and irritation, the supervisor tells me to put the other bag on the belt. 'Not that one,' she says through gritted teeth. She's going to explode with hatred. So what's her problem: spot of PMT, or a spot of racial prejudice? Somehow I don't think it's hormone levels.

'What do you want – all, one, some? You're not being very clear.'

She makes a guttural noise of annoyance.

We finally get through.

'She's a bit of a crosspatch, isn't she, Mum?'

That's right, a bit of a crosspatch.

Grumpy, provincial, unsophisticated, curious in a cack-handed kind of way. These are South Africa's ordinary whites – cursed with a Pavlovian hostility towards dark skin. Black is 'out there', 'other', 'difficult', 'stupid', 'dangerous'; white is 'trying hard', 'sensible', 'reliable', 'home'. They are not very educated, these whites, not like the whites who write great academic treatises and draft endlessly complex legislation on why separation of the races is all to the common good; different again from whites in power who torture behind closed doors; different from clever white liberals agonized by the desire to succeed and prosper with a clear conscience. The whites that interest me most work at cash tills, in restaurants. They are the majority.

I am on my own buying a biro in a shop in beautiful East London – a South African Eastbourne but much tidier, cleaner and better maintained. I want to pay; the cashier grabs my wrist and selects a finger on my hand.

'That's pretty. Is it an engagement ring?'

'No,' I reply unencouragingly. Where is her sense of boundaries, I think priggishly.

Late that afternoon we walk along the beach, a multi-racial group – me (European), my daughter and her cousin (European-African), her other two cousins (African). I lag behind, lazy. A pretty young white girl – about seventeen – follows me. She's looking at me, finally she plucks up courage to speak.

'Yooeythim?'

'Sorry?' I can't make out what she's saying.

'I said, yooeythim?'

'What? Oh yes – I'm with them.'

'Y'all right? I said y'all right?'

'Yes, thank you. They are my family.' My cold tone blocks her interfering intimacy.

'Oh.' She looks crestfallen. Crestfallen, I think, because I don't need rescuing, and crestfallen because she has annoyed me.

The next week we drive to the Orange Free State to visit a game farm. We go to a supermarket in Zastrom. We comprise two Europeans, one Sotho (that's three grown-ups) and one Ugandan and two Ugandan-Europeans (the children). We push our trolley round. People stare. The women really are thin-lipped, with dry, lined skin. The hostility is palpable. I've never felt that before, eyes really boring into you because you are in the minority, despised, disliked. And what do they know about us? Nothing. But however much they knew, nothing would ever register in their minds more than the colour of our skin. The anger I feel now is visceral – the anger of a mother whose child is in danger. We go back to the farmstead, have a few beers.

Spoilt silly

My next visit to South Africa is four years on. I'm alone, so I don't have my daughter to worry about. I'd heard about the high standard of living among the professional classes, both white and black, in South Africa. I'd been dead jealous of visiting journalists, victims of apartheid, who cursed the government but moaned about the upkeep of their swimming pool. But nothing prepared me for the high life in Cape Town. I'd been sent to direct a play. The flights and accommmodation have all been arranged for me. The hotel is swanky, decorated in the English country house style: heavy curtains tied with great swags at the side, big sofas and armchairs, flowers in vases. The hotel looks out to the Atlantic. Around the corner is the Indian Ocean.

And from my window I can see Robben Island, hazy like a mythical place. At the hotel there are a lot of old people staying; then there are tall spiky women in their thirties with posh luggage. White Cape Town is permanently going to the races or some such function. Women wear over-smart clothes, and gold bracelets which jangle, silk blouses, and a tad too much make-up. It's tempting to make fun of them. There are no African guests at the hotel. In the restaurant the staff are a mixture of white Afrikaners, white English South African, African and mixed race. The reception has mainly whites with a few mixed race staff. Already by day two the sound recordist and I have managed to annoy several of the receptionists with awkward non-touristy requests. There's one with glassy green eyes and red hair. My companion calls her the ginger Rottweiler; she hides her contempt with politeness.

'Can we borrow a plug?'

'With pleasure.'

'Can you route all calls to our mobile? This is the number.'

'With pleasure.'

'Can we have lunch brought up to our rooms?'

'With pleasure.'

'Can we hire a conference room for ten people with light refreshments for a play reading?'

'With pleasure.'

She enunciates the phrase using the same three high notes, with staring, expressionless eyes. She must have a sister who works on South African Airways.

We want to go to a community hall in Rondebosch East and need a route spelt out for us.

The ginger Rottweiler purses her lips and gets the map out.

'See here, you can go up here, then branch left here, and

then you go along here and get off here. But whatever you do, don't go there, because you could end up in Mitchell Plains and you don't want to do that.'

Ooh er, missus, what happens there? Ritual sacrifice? Or just a lower class of person, even lower than us, that is?

'Wish me luck,' I call out gaily, having assembled directions, equipment, bottles of water, mobile phones, microphones, recording machines.

'Good luck,' she says with a sort of heavy, flat literalness, devoid of any feeling.

Our only friend in the hotel is the bartender. And this is extraordinary in itself. Because the bartender is the most handsome man in the world. Now that sort of handsomeness does not usually make for friendship material. In fact he was so good-looking that we both took against him at first. How could anyone that good-looking have a sense of humour, or even a brain? He has perfect cheekbones, black glistening hair. All day long he serves drinks. Castle beer, Stellenbosch wine and his own vast range of cocktails. He is in perpetual motion. The hardest working bartender I have ever seen. He shakes, he pours, he wipes and when he's not doing that he's scanning the bar through long eyelashes, his gaze sweeping the room and the verandah like a floodlight, making sure his customers are all right.

'Two beers, please.'

He swivels round. 'What kind would you like?'

'Your finest local brew, please.'

'OK.'

'Is it strong?'

He grins. 'You'll be all right, ladies.'

Aaaah, he's a sweetie. He's called Riccardo and he lives in the dreaded Mitchell Plains.

'Spanish name, Riccardo?'

'My dad was Spanish,' he does one of his checking glances

round the room, 'but I never knew him. He left when I was small.'

'So your mum brought you up on her own?'

'No – she married. I have a stepdad and he's been a real father to me.'

'Your mum Spanish?'

'No, Coloured.' The old racial classifications persist.

Riccardo is twenty-three, but time is distorted in South Africa. He may seem young but it feels like he was born in another era. When he was born in 1975, the Immorality Amendment Act no. 23 of 1957 was still in force. It forbade 'unlawful carnal intercourse or any immoral or indecent act' between a white person and an African, Indian or Coloured. Non South Africans were exempt if both parties were foreign. Nine years later the Immorality Act was scrapped. President Botha stressed at the time that he personally was not in favour of mixed marriages, but the laws had made enemies for South Africa.

And destroyed lives, he might have added. Between 1950 and 1980 11,500 people were charged with contravening the Immorality Act. The penalty for interracial sex was up to seven years' hard labour, and a maximum of ten lashes if the man involved was under fifty.

I guess Riccardo's mum must have loved his bio-dad since she gave her son a Spanish name. But they were not allowed to be together. There are times when love cannot conquer law and prejudice.

The actors I've been working with want to show us what the other Cape Town looks like. We go far beyond Rondebosch East. We head towards Mitchell Plains. It's a hell of a journey. It's a journey Riccardo makes every day to come to work, and cannot make at the end of his shift because there is no transport at night; the hotel, for all its curtain swags,

200

home-made chocolate cake and whipped cream, cannot provide its employees somewhere to kip until daybreak, nor will it pay for them to take taxis home. As we speed along the highway, high-spirited with the actors, the landscape becomes flat, the symmetrical buildings stretched in rows for miles. Memories of Windhoek townships. Everywhere we stop we get out and say hello, and are greeted with excitement – we are trophy whites, a form of entertainment for people who *see* plenty of whites but not to talk to, not at close quarters. They tell us bits and pieces about the different standards of the housing estates and buildings. One area is controlled by a drug gang. Round the corner this area is very quiet. That area can be rough. You want to go into a shebeen? All right.

We go in; there are pool tables and two sweet girls dancing round their handbags. They giggle when they see us and then resume their dancing with the extra swagger of the observed. We visit Raymond's house. It's actually his sister's, and it consists of two rooms the size of a railway couchette and a kitchen. There's electricity and a phone, but it's cramped. His relatives greet us warmly and shyly.

Back at the hotel all is quiet. The cocktail hour is sliding very slowly towards us. We are keen to take up our positions with the most handsome bartender in the world. But someone has pipped us to the post. A white woman in her fifties is perched on a stool, blonde, rather too much foundation and blue eyeshadow, slacks, suede loafers. Bit like one of those women who feature in magazines for sale at British supermarket checkouts, say *Family Circle*: 'Marge wanted a makeover to give her a headstart for her new job as a personal assistant. We got her together with hairdresser Flick Spillane and stylist Sid Smith. First they . . . then they . . . then finally . . . She is thrilled with her new look.'

'Hi, Riccardo.'

Her tone's a bit familiar, I think sniffily. These women!

'Hi there. What can I get you?'

I notice he does not look her in the eye. He's low key. She's moving her head round trying to catch his eye.

'Gin and tonic.'

The sound recordist gives a groan.

'You all right?'

'Let's go outside.'

We go out on the verandah. 'What's the matter?'

'That woman is the matter. She's a cow.'

'Why?'

'That's the woman who started talking to me yesterday about Zimbabwe going down the plug and her son being on drugs. Then she looks at me and says, "Yur very young to be so over wite."'

It's an excellent impersonation.

'So what did you say?'

'Oh I just got up and walked away.'

'Well done.' Mrs Makeover becomes Queen Bitch.

We finish our beer watching the posh and the poor saunter past the hotel. The sun is setting. Oh good, 'she' has left her perch. We surge back into the bar for more idle conversation.

'We don't like her. She was rude to me,' says the sound recordist.

Riccardo scans the room, polishing a glass and muttering something.

'What?' We lean over simultaneously, spreading our breasts generously around his counter.

'She's a p*r*s*t.'

The key word is still hard to understand. We both lean forward at the bar until we're practically in the sink. He says it again.

'A prostitute!' we both yell, truly amazed.

'Ssh.'

'What? She go after you?'

'Yeah – with her, anyone will do.' Riccardo narrows his eyes and looks into the distance contemptuously.

How puzzling. It's not that I think prostitutes should look tarty . . . it's just that they ought to have a bit of glamour and *not* look straight out of *Family Circle*. But it sets me thinking about the whole business of predatory women.

'I suppose you get a lot of women after you, Riccardo.'

'Yeah.'

'I mean, is it a problem?'

'Yeah, man – it's a big problem.' He gives a little rueful chuckle. I resolve to put aside all base desire and be a good aunty to him.

'Have you got a girlfriend?'

'No – I can't find the right girl.' He looks so sad.

I'm reminded of the Five Children and It who were granted their wish of being as beautiful as the day, and then had a perfectly beastly time being treated like strangers. To be very beautiful is to be not quite human as far as others are concerned.

'What do you want to do, Riccardo – stay with hotels and catering?'

'No, no. I sing a bit, play the guitar . . . I'd like to do some of that stuff you've been doing.'

'What, directing? Acting?'

'Yeah – acting. That's it. I'd like to act.'

Somehow he seems too shy and dreamy for that. The actors we are working with are so loud, brash and funny. Controlled and focused only when they need to be for their acting, the rest of the time they are fire-crackers.

Three days later we finish the play early. Time to celebrate with a small drink.

'Martini Bianco and tonic please.'

'Why don't you try a cocktail?' says Riccardo sweetly.

'Oh no.'

'Go on, man – you'll like it.'

'All right – one cocktail won't hurt.' Now this is true. One cocktail won't hurt, but twelve will. Twelve, especially if they incorporate a sample of every single thing on the spirits and liqueur shelf, will hurt all right. The evening begins with easy-to-down Long Island Teas and ends with Traffic Lights – a cocktail Riccardo invented on the spur of the moment made up of layers of grenadine, Galliano and Cassis. In between there's a Smoking Rasta, a couple of B52s, one Between the Sheets and an After Eight, not to mention the Flaming Sambucos and the champagne.

I know I wasn't sick, and I didn't take my clothes off or make stupid remarks. I can remember getting off my bar stool at one o'clock in the morning with the studied carefulness of a very drunk person, and I can remember turning the key in my door. Then: nothing. Until the next morning. A time for self-reproach. What had got into me? I haven't drunk such a bizarre mixture of alcoholic drinks since I was sixteen; the weekend my parents were away and my friends and I took a bit from every bottle on their drinks tray. Twenty-six years later I travel to the opposite end of the world on an important job and end up behaving like a teenager who's trying booze for the first time. I'm a mother, for God's sake. Perhaps all the wealth and order of Cape Town has brought out the worst in me. Perhaps it's the sight of Riccardo's very clever mixing and pouring. How much more grown-up I am in Ghana, Nigeria, Zambia, Los Angeles.

I wake up fully clothed. I must have fallen on the bed because I find my sunglasses crushed beneath me. I feel poisoned. In fact I feel I am going to die. I don't say this

204

lightly. Having broken a shoulder, succumbed to malaria and had a baby (eighteen-hour labour ending in a Caesarean), I have a fairly decent spectrum of discomfort to refer to. Yes, I lay there numb faced, unable to move, the Seapoint traffic thrumming past, light peeping through the very heavy curtains, and I thought I was going to die. Riccardo, my nemesis, the boatman plying his craft across a river Styx of cocktails, has finished me off. In the afternoon my colleague appears, concerned, with grapes and Earl Grey tea.

'You'll be all right.'

'Erghm.'

'You just need to drink a lot of liquids.'

'Gonnadie.'

'No, you're not.'

'Errrrr – mmmff.'

'I'm going to make you a cup of tea.'

My guardian angel and the sound recordist look after me well that day. Somehow the poison drains away. I live.

It is six o'clock. I spring out of bed, look out of the window and there's Robben Island still floating on the horizon. The sky is blue with only a whisper of haze. The sea is calm. It's hard to imagine the weather is so bad sometimes that boats can't cross. In the old days prison visitors would then have their visiting passes cancelled. Instead of just waiting for the weather to improve, they would have to begin their application all over again. Each application took six months to be processed. By contrast, a cosy detail of prison warden life: when a prison warden had a baby, a flag was flown on the island – blue for boys, pink for girls.

I go to the bar to look for the sound recordist. I shall never drink another drop of alcohol again. Riccardo watches me very carefully as I approach. He smiles. I smile. I get on one of the stools.

'Long Island Tea?' he whispers.

'Tonic water.'

He doesn't argue. He gets the tonic water and I admire his skill at pouring again.

'You nearly killed me last night, you know.'

'No, man, you were all right. I poured small shots. I was careful.'

ELEVEN

The Entertainers

&~&

IN CONCERT IN ACCRA

'We had many girls who liked comedians,' says Opia. He is spry and neat for his age, with good cheekbones, a handsome face. He has agreed to talk to me about his life as an entertainer on the recommendation of a kind scholar-musician, John Collins, who has lived in Ghana for thirty years. Opia's house is in the compound of John Collins's stepmother.

There is a little bit of cruelty in Opia, common in comics, a splash of heartlessness to his ha-ha-ha. His voice sounds hard, self-satisfied and bullying as he continues to talk about his success with the ladies. 'When any girl approaches you, because she loves you, you say, "Come on, bring me some food." And in the night she bring you some fine food. They love us. Even if they fight over us: "Opia is my friend", "No, you lie – he is my friend."' He stops suddenly and looks wary. 'Anything else?' he asks sharply as though the interview is a sort of torture. But I think he's enjoying it. He is a proud man. All around him is evidence of his glory days as founder of the Jaguar Jokers. They were a Concert Party group formed in 1954 – performing sketches, singing songs. They are descendants of vaudeville entertainers who came from America in the early part of the twentieth century.

Then Concert Party was a posh affair, performed in English and thus catering for the elite. Besides the American influence, it is nourished by local tradition, and also owes something to the British – the word 'Concert' comes from the end-of-term concerts performed in Gold Coast schools to mark Empire Day.

Opia's group was originally called the Jovial Jokers, but that was changed soon after to the Jaguar Jokers. Opia looks grave as he gives the reason in his idiosyncratic but expressive English: 'The jaguar is a wild animal, but we can joke it not to cause any harm to us.'

And there they are, framed on Opia's wall, not looking very joky but rather dapper in double-breasted suits. These days the Concert Party is under siege from other forms of entertainment: videos, and night clubs with their DJs, or spinners as they are called.

'What do you think about Concert Party today?'

Mr Bampoe – for that is his real name – makes a contemptuous noise. 'It has declined, very seriously declined. You see,' he says warming to his theme, 'It is now very vulgar. There are too many scenes with men and women in them, and the man come up behind and pretends to poke the woman. Poking here, poking there. Too much poking.'

Opia obviously relishes this p— word. Time to move on.

'Would you perform for me, from the early days of the Jaguar Jokers?' Opia's eyes swivel round the room as if somebody was listening to our conversation. I feel sure he will say no.

But he stares at me solemnly: 'When?'

Opia's partner of forty years' standing is Mr Hammond. He is tall and rangy, a gentle spirit, fond of striking comic attitudes of despair, back of wrist held to forehead. Everyone knows Bampoe and Hammond, and people have their favourites. Some prefer the pepper and spice of Mr Bampoe to the creamy fresh palmwine of Mr Hammond. Some say Opia is sly; he is certainly the organizer, the senior partner, but as far as I am concerned Mr Bampoe is tops, not just because he sings Al Jolson's 'About a Quarter to Nine' like a dream but because he was kind to me when my body unexpectedly made its monthly protest. I saw the crimson mark on his white armchair cushion as I was getting up. Instantly I thought, that'll put paid to the recording.

'Oh God, I'm so sorry – please forgive me. Can I give you money to get it cleaned?'

He picks up the lurid cushion and with a deft flick of his wrist turns it over. 'No problem.' He smiles – not a sly or cruel one, but a kind one. Yes, Mr Bampoe, like Mohamed, the taxi driver in Zanzibar, knows all about women.

We arrange to meet Mr Bampoe and Mr Hammond the following day. It is more of an assignation than a meeting. The partners appear with a large old suitcase. 'We must be discreet,' Mr Bampoe whispers. We follow him through the village, round palm trees, houses, stagnant pools and bread ovens, until we are on the outskirts, in an open area which looks as though it is used for debates and public meetings. A small boy has followed us. Mr Bampoe gives him a ferocious scowl and he scuttles off.

The suitcase is opened very carefully, and the following items taken out: two pairs of striped trousers, two white fezes, two waistcoats with large white flowers on them, edged at the bottom with copious gold fringes, then two pink shirts, two large, white floppy bow ties; and finally, one fly whisk. And I think I know who's going to be holding that. The two men dress carefully, and then produce sticks of charcoal which they crush in their hand and mix with water from a small bottle. 'I'm now trying to disguise my face to create laughter for people,' says Mr Bampoe. 'This is charcoal, see. Black powder.' He rubs it all over his already dark face. 'And now I'm going to paint my mouth to be very big.' He gives me a big smile. I notice he leaves his eyes untouched. 'This, white clay – never chalk,' he adds severely. 'And now I've treated my face, I wash my hands.'

Mr Bampoe and Mr Hammond have finished making up. They stand side by side and look at me triumphantly through their blacking, swaggering in their costumes. And yes, the blacking does make them look different; their skin is now not just dark brown but matt black, reflecting no light. Their mouths have become huge and expressive.

Their minstrelsy stands at the end of a twisted path which doubles back on itself, leading from Africa to the slave plantations of the South. There oppression gave birth to a minstrelsy fuelled by satire and irony. This burlesque form of entertainment is first misunderstood by white Americans as foolishness, then copied and used as a way of ridiculing the Negro while entertaining fellow whites. For one white American, Al Jolson, minstrelsy led to stardom and riches. How frightful! But hang on – Al Jolson became a huge hit in West Africa as well as America. Transformed by his costumes, Mr Bampoe launches unbidden into Al Jolson's 'About a Quarter to Nine'. When I return to England, I dig out the original Al Jolson recording – Mr Bampoe is singing in exactly the same key as Al.

I wonder what African-American tourists coming to Ghana in search of their roots would make of this black-up.

QUEEN GRACE

According to John Collins the classic pre-war Concert Party set-up consisted of a few musicians, usually with a banjo and clarinet, always with a trap drum, and three actors, who generally took three distinct roles: the Gentleman or Dandy, the Trickster (together these were often known as the two bobs) and the Lady. Back in 1932, on 2 July, an unworldly contributor to the *Gold Coast Spectator* was in for a surprise when he made his first foray into the world of the Concert Party. The performance went by the title of The Two Bobs and their Carolina Girl.

> *I must confess this is my first time of seeing a theatrical entertainment; therefore having seen only two masked men with handsome brown lady I became fidgety in my seat, my mouth widely open. Now after the very first item on the programme, a lady behind me said: 'The one who just appeared on the stage as a lady is not a lady, but a man.' To appease my surprise I rose up from my seat and walked straight in to their dressing room. Having gone there I saw three gentlemen instead of one lady and two gentlemen. I asked for the lady. He smiled and said, 'Here I am. Anything?' I asked him to see me after the show, because they were very busy changing their dresses for their next item. I resumed my seat quietly with an expression of wonder, and listened to their beautiful sweet items to the last.*

The contributor becomes enchanted with this transvestite vision. Magnetically drawn, it seems, he goes to the actor's house.

> *The following day, I went to his house and saw him sleeping. I asked the lady of the house for a chair and waited till he rose from bed. I looked at his womanish face, when he had cleared it with water, and said, 'Look here! Were you born a woman?' He smiled. 'It was God who made me so; for he knows I have a poor family.' I asked his name as well as the names of the other two gentlemen, and he said, 'My name is Charles B. Horton.' On the stage artists are like angels, who never err, never eat. At least we expect them so. What a wide difference there is sometimes between the man in the street and the artist on the stage. It is said Mr Charles Horton is the grandson of the late Dr Horton of Sierra Leone, who through his laborious work in*

the army won a reward in His Majesty's service at Cape Coast about 50 years ago.

The writer is obviously enchanted by Charles B. Horton. His piece ends with a fervent appeal for funds to further Horton's career.

Of course Concert Party is irresistible. It's funny, burlesque, cruel, funky and hugely long in running time. It is also, as Mr Bampoe says, very vulgar. And I suspect it was so in the past. At any rate, once it stopped being performed in the King's English, it was never considered genteel.

'In those days any woman joining was unfortunately seen as a prostitute, but definitely a show needed a woman. So in the absence of a woman, a man has to impersonate,' says Jo Eyison. He and fellow Concert Party performers have been asked to perform at the newly built National Theatre, as part of the cultural festival Panafest. The only snag: there's no money to pay them. Concert Party has gone in and out of fashion. It was first for the elite, and then for the mob. It continues to be a poor person's entertainment, but has been given respectability by academics. The Concert Party union meets to discuss the matter at the old arts centre. Rows and rows of mainly middle-aged, very straight-backed men with a few women. Mr Addo from the theatre administration appears, flustered and anxious. They look at him grumpily. 'I'm begging you. For the sake of Ghana. It will be a showpiece. We wanted every one of you represented. What is Ghanaian drama without Concert Party? There will be a lot of foreigners coming.' He looks at me. I want to fall into a hole in the ground. He persists. 'It will lead to more work.' There's a lot of harrumphing. This calling on people for the sake of the nation or government has been going on now for over thirty years. When everyone was richer it was an honour, now it's exploitation.

When I leave, the meeting is in a stalemate. One leading light in the Concert Party scene is absent and I want to track her down. Her name is Grace Omaboe and she has no need to haggle over small change. There's no question of her doing jobs to subsidize her acting. Theatre is a business for her as well as an art. Her group is one of the most successful in the country, making thousands of dollars in the festive season, spending months touring the mining areas. Besides directing, managing her group and acting in it, she writes, appears on the television regularly and makes films. She has agreed to meet me for an interview at a small drinking place where her group will later be rehearsing. We wait and wait. I grow nervous. A young man arrives at the entrance to the compound: 'She's coming.' A few seconds later a lady dwarf appears, marching purposefully forward carrying a very large briefcase. She is Grace's personal assistant. She must have seen us but she ignores us. She drops the briefcase and goes out to come back again with stacks of papers and files. She makes a third journey, returning this time with bottles of water. She starts sorting the baggage. Suddenly there is Grace herself, empty-handed and magnificent. She is tall, slim but quite broad-shouldered, handsome-beautiful, long-haired, in a very smart oyster-grey businesswoman's suit. She strides across the courtyard.

'So, so, so – hello.'

We shake hands; her voice is deep. She is reputed to be a very tough boss, a hard operator. I am conscious she is weighing me up, and I begin to gush.

'Oh hello . . . thanks so much for coming. I hope we haven't—'

'What do you want?' she asks abruptly.

My heart sinks a bit. This meeting was all agreed and negotiated through an intermediary, an arrangement ripe for misunderstanding.

'Well, we'd like to do an interview and then record some of the group in action.'

There's a pause.

'OK.'

Grace is tough. But I soon discover she likes talking about herself.

'I'm forty-four. My father is the Osiana, the king of Osu. I didn't even think of becoming an actress, apart from admiring them. People look down on an actor as a drunkard. But there was this girlfriend at training college, St Monica's. She came home from college in the holidays and acted and danced in front of me. I thought, "I want to do that." My uncle and mother didn't like it at all.' She smiles at the memory. 'They wanted me to study medicine or be a lawyer ... something like that – not a concert person, not a joker.' She hits the word 'joker' hard, and laughs. She has four children. She's been married, but has now given up on men.

'Right now I'm not bothered about men. They cause too much heartbreak.' She looks at me. I look at her. We know what she's talking about.

KNICKERAMA

The following night we go to a Grace Omaboe production: The Tagoe Sisters. It's a story of lust, deception and witch-craft. A poor young girl is given to a horny rich man by her family to settle a debt. Grace plays the sister of the rich man, a sort of wise woman with glamour. The girl is already betrothed to a young man, who is now pining for her. He settles on the wheeze of dressing-up as a woman with another friend, so that they can visit his fiancée masquerading as sisters.

The show begins at eleven at night in a large courtyard, at a place called the Cottage Hotel. It is packed by the time I arrive. The drama will start at midnight. Before that there's sexy dancing and music which is massively amplified. Men are dragged on stage by Omaboe's ladies; one specializes in pelvic gyrations which pin down every half-excited, half-terrified spectator she gets hold of. After twenty minutes or so, the general hubbub and heckling swell into a roar, the dwarf lady is making her entrance. She has abandoned her brisk image of personal assistant, and is now shaking her bits most vigorously to the beat. She marches around and then shakes; march, shake, wiggle; march, shake, wiggle. And then begins the striptease. She is very small – not more than three foot six – her legs are two barrels, and yet she manages to get the most extraordinary movement out of her hips. Off comes her blouse, off comes her skirt, and then she bends over, bottom in the air, and – no, this cannot be – but yes, off come her knickers!

Actually she's got another pair underneath, but with this act of apparent lewdness she has sent the crowd completely wild. Now with her back to the audience she has hooked the knickers around her finger and is swinging them round and round over her head, then she lets them go, and *wheee* they fly over the first few rows of the audience to land somewhere in the middle of the crowd. If the place had had a roof, it would be off by now. With one last defiant wiggle she leaves the stage, not, I notice, wearing much less than when she first appeared.

Later I was told that the knicker-flinging stunt had nearly cost the group's livelihood. It was a command performance for President Jerry Rawlings at the swanky new National Theatre. On came the dwarf lady to strut her stuff, off went the knickers – whirly, whirly and *wheeeeeeeee*. They flew effortlessly through the air, only to land on the President's head. Now this was a sensation he apparently enjoyed at the time. He was seen to remove the knickers and laugh. But the sensibilities of a leader are not the exclusive preserve of the man in question, they are fuelled and defined by a gaggle of aides and advisers, not to mention the hangers-on and troublemakers. Indignant letters were penned to the press. The Ministry of Information made an announcement about the dignity of the office of the President being undermined. Grace's group was banned from appearing at the National Theatre ever again, although with the cultural festival coming up that ban was quietly rescinded.

TERRIFIC STYLE

The Tagoe Sisters ends at five a.m. Large chunks of the drama passed me by because I fell asleep. I did wake up to hear the young girl shout hysterically, 'I'm going back to my village.' Then the rich man responds with terrific style: intimate, close up to the microphone and slowly, 'My dear sweetheart,' he says pausing for effect, 'take it easy, eh?' The crowd roars, and it makes me chuckle even though I am half asleep. What a rogue! The rich man then gets down on one knee and goes into a sort of rock'n'roll riff: 'Don't let me down, don't let me down, don't let me dow-owa-dow-owa-down, don't let me down.' Even the actress playing the young girl giggles. I fall asleep again soon after the girl's boyfriend arrives dressed as a woman. I just catch the rich man saying lasciviously, 'I like lady visitors – if it were to be a man I would sack him right now.' Then I slumber on until I am woken by frantic drumming; the rich man is taking the girl and her fiancée to the fetish priest to be sacrificed. The stage is dark, but the scenery is painted in lurid fluorescent paint which is now being picked out by ultraviolet and manically flashing strobe lights. We never see the fetish priest, but hear his voice from behind a six-foot-high mask. It scares me. The rich man turns to the audience and says, 'My fetish priest needs human blood, so he can make me rich.' The audience is now very quiet – maybe they are a little scared too. There are a few bass growly sounds close to mike from the fetish priest, and then, rather in the urbane style of a chat show host, the fetish priest says, 'Thank you very much, thank you very much. Today's a very happy day for Nana Jigaji, because today we have human blood.' The trap drum goes boom-boom in the vaudeville manner.

Of course, in the end nobody is sacrificed. A Christian priest comes on in the nick of time to save them all. Grace belts out the closing number of the show, fresh as a daisy. I totter off to get some sleep, ashamed of my lack of stamina.

No baby no song

To be a successful woman you have to be a bit of a goddess – standing above base appetites, above the eroding irritations of everyday domestic life, infinitely beautiful and strong, and if you can't manage all of that at least you must be mysterious and good at hiding what does go wrong. If the least mishap in your personal life gets out, it could be curtains in the power and success department. I never met Venetia, but she was by all accounts a brilliantly successful singer who earned a decent whack on the hotel circuit in Zambia. I heard her story from her erstwhile partner Violet. At the time I was with the Very Clever Man, a few days before the terrible cracker day. We had gone to Livingstone for the weekend and it wasn't working out very well. We weren't rowing, but then again we weren't talking. We sat next to the pool in silence. He was leafing through a sheaf of poems given to him by a young student anxious for advice. I was wistfully watching a young couple gambolling in the pool, obviously in love. And then like a vision Violet appeared, slim, tall but with sweet little plump breasts, long legs, make-up to perfection.

'How's it?' Her voice was throaty and soft.

The Very Clever Man perked up, put his papers down, stood up and kissed her on the cheek, touching her shoulder a fraction too long for my comfort. I said hello in a thin voice. And Violet gave me a curious look.

'Please, Violet, join us.'

Oh please don't, I thought meanly.

'Thanks,' she smirked and lowered herself elegantly into a wonky poolside chair, crossing her legs like a model.

'Would you like a drink?'

Violet pulls a ladylike expression as though alcohol was the last thing on her mind. Then she pouts a little and asks for a beer. The Very Clever Man gestures with a languid hand to the waiter and then returns his gaze to the lovely Violet. 'So where's Venetia?'

'Didn't you hear?'

He stares, waiting for more.

'She had a baby.'

'But I saw her at the Pamodzi only last month, she wasn't pregnant . . .'

'She was pregnant. But she was tying herself up, every time she went on stage she was corseted up so tight she could not breathe, I swear it. She never wanted that baby. And she didn't want anyone to know about it. I knew but no one else knew. And she was leaping around on the stage. You know how she was in our act – she was the wild one, I was the quiet one. I said, "Venetia honey, you shouldn't be doing that in your condition," but she didn't care.'

The Very Clever Man taps me on the arm. 'She was a fantastic singer, fantastic voice. She had at least one American record producer interested in her.'

Violet shakes her head in concurrence, and smiles a pitying smile. She recrosses her legs, leaning forward confidentially.

'And the way she had that baby – I knew it wouldn't live long. She didn't want to go into hospital. She want to have it on her own so she could do away with it, but the neighbours heard her screams and came in so she couldn't do what she wanted to do. So she had the baby, but she didn't want to care for it. The day after she had it, she brought in some ten-year-old brat to look after it, while she was out drinking. Over a week goes by – the baby screaming, not taking its milk properly, and Venetia down some shebeen. She wasn't singing, she was drinking. Then one day she comes to me at the club crying and weeping, her eyes all crazy. At first I couldn't understand what was the problem, then she say she woke up that morning and found the baby dead next to her. So Tony say – you know Tony, is it? – Tony say, "That is it, you are out. I don't want you here no more." She cannot work anywhere now. Well maybe she can sing in a shebeen but hotels ... They all know ... she smothered that child, she was drunk and she smothered that child. It was buried last week.'

Violet tosses back her hair revealing her beautiful throat. She takes a sip of beer, well pleased with the effect her story has had on us.

'Oh well, got to do a sound check. Tonight's my first night without Venetia.' Off she sashays, slips across the checkered flagstones on high-heeled shoes, clack clack, swively hips. She is singing tonight with the resident band. The Very Clever Man and I fall back into silent misery. Dimly from inside the hotel's dance room, I hear tapping of microphones, guitar notes twanging, self-important 'one, two, threes' repeated again and again. Then the musicians slip into a lazy rumba.

A quavery voice half chants, half sings 'The Green Leaves of Summer'. Not a note is in tune. I nudge the Very Clever Man.

'She can't sing. She can't sing.' I am horribly pleased with the discovery. 'Won't she make a complete fool of herself? She obviously doesn't realize how awful she is.'

He puts down his poems. 'No, she can't sing.'

'But how did she ever get to perform . . .?'

'You couldn't tell how bad her voice was when Venetia was there; she covered up for Violet.'

'But how can she perform in public if she can't sing?'

'She's beautiful, she's sexy. You can see that. Who cares if she can't sing?' He picks up a poem and starts to read it studiously.

I notice a heat rash spreading across my arm. The pool is now empty. The young lovers have gone. 'Time to be reaping, time to be sowing, the green leaves of summer are calling me home . . .' Violet warbles on tunelessly.

Exposed

Felicity took a risk and just about got away with it.

'If they could have stoned me, they would have done,' she says solemnly, looking me straight in the eye. Felicity is the first woman in Namibian history to have appeared bare-breasted on stage. There she is in a poster with an 'I-dare-you' look on her face, bare to the waist but with tasteful stars over her nipples added later by a layout artist. The play was written by Frederick Philander, and was called *The Beauty Contest*. 'Freddie always writes great parts for women,' she says. 'And the business of me baring my breasts was essential to the play. It was to show that women are exploited in these beauty competitions. In that sense it was a very moral play.' Felicity is working as a senior administrator in a bank. She is confident, plump and beautiful. She works over eight hours a day and then up to six hours afterwards at the theatre. Her job and her acting are her twin passions. She grew up classified Coloured. To me she looks Mediterranean, and in fact is part Italian; she also has relatives in Lesotho. 'I'm very proud of my Sotho aunties,' she says. She knew her exposure on stage would create a reaction among the staid theatregoers in Windhoek, but she was surprised at the extent of their anger. 'I had people phoning up making nasty remarks, saying I should be ashamed of myself. But why? I like my body. It shouldn't be hidden away. My body is a work of art. People are very narrow-minded. If you play the character of a good woman on stage that's not too bad. But don't you dare do the role of a bad woman. They will confuse that role with reality and say, "She's this sort of person, or that sort of person." But you see, people judge you very harshly being in the acting business if you are a woman.'

Felicity felt exposed with nothing on. When I agreed to go on stage in Mombasa I felt exposed full stop.

FADED GLAMOUR

'Hold it there and pout,' says my very good friend Zengle.

'Oh, this is ridiculous.' The grass is tickling my legs.

'No it's not.'

I really shouldn't be so ungrateful. She knows a thing or two about acting – she went to drama school, she can sing the Blues and she is dead glamorous, and now she has very kindly lent me a dress and some jewellery in an attempt to make *me* look dead glamorous, but the words 'mutton' and 'pig's ear' come to mind rather than 'Hollywood' or 'starlet'.

'Come on – toss your head. Make love to the camera.' We pause to laugh and then she's off again, quite ruthless.

'Tease me, pout some more. No, no, now you're squinting.'

'I think your mum's friend looks a bit strange,' says Zengle's nephew to her daughter.

'Do you want to try out the wigs?' says her daughter tactfully, and off they scuttle indoors.

'Do you want a wig, Fiona darling?'

'Um . . . I don't think so.'

'Not that there's anything wrong with your . . .' she says, noticing my anxiety.

'No, thanks – just get on with it.'

'OK, OK – we've got to get this right. Now I want you to look like a startled nymph. Hover behind that branch of forsythia.'

'It's no good, I can't . . . I just . . .'

'You must – publicity photos are very important. Mind you, I don't know if they'll come out because I haven't a clue how this camera works. Now let's see, what next? I know, let's have a smoulder over the shoulder, holding . . . hold a piece of forsythia.'

And so it goes on. The film is used up, developed, and the photos are dispatched to Mombasa. They are in focus, vaguely glamorous in a Norma Desmond kind of way, and as I said to Zengle, you would never guess that they had been taken in a backyard in Harlesden.

'So what's wrong with guessing that they were taken in a backyard in Harlesden?' One of her eyebrows is arching horribly.

'Um, nothing really.'

As the plane takes off I have to ask myself this question: what am I doing? I'm jobless, forty-one, at least one stone overweight and I haven't acted in twenty-two years, and now

I've agreed to take a big part in a stage production on the east coast of Africa.

Perhaps this is revenge. For seventeen years I've been crawling over the continent like a juice-sucking bug, recording, writing, talking, analysing, judging. And now I'm putting myself up for show. Maybe it's a bloodless form of ritual sacrifice – I am atoning for 120 years of colonialism, neo-colonialism, 120 years of telling people what to do. Now I'm going to be judged – in public – on stage – performing live – learning 250 lines by heart and standing up in front of hundreds of people who'll buy tickets thinking, 'I suppose she's good because she's come from London.' And then when it comes to it they'll be thinking, 'Why is her voice so quiet? Why's she forgotten her lines? She's not very good at acting.'

Oh, it'll be all right. It'll be fun.

DEVELOP A POWERFUL MEMORY!

We're on the train now heading south to the coast. And that's one of the most delightful things you can do in Kenya. Get on the night train and leave the arching colonial columns of Nairobi station. Everything getting dark, with the echo of goodbyes and music on the loudspeakers and rueful porters leaning on their trolleys wishing their tips had been larger. The long train clanks off awkwardly, leaving the livestock and horses, the vegetable farms, the winter fires of the highlands behind, heading downhill to another world by the Indian Ocean: white beaches, palm trees, old stone houses, carved doors, remnants of Omani rule, and loads of tourists. We are travelling first class which means we have two bunks, a cupboard and our own washbasin with a lid which doubles as a table. The compartment has the stale smell of a place that's been casually wiped on a regular basis, but never properly scrubbed. We've purchased our dinner vouchers but have half an hour to kill before supper. My daughter, Rebecca, gives me a stern look. She is holding the script.

'Go on then, "I have a small shop in Frankfurt and . . ."'

'Right, "I have a small shop in Frankfurt and also sell curios and artefacts and . . ."' My brain goes blank.

'And?' Rebecca looks very severe now. It's funny what an appetite children have for power.

'"And, and . . ." Oh, I can't remember.'

'Mummy, you're hopeless. We've done this bit about five times.'

A terrible fear is welling up inside me. My acting career ended at a drunken student ball in 1978, and since that time I have never had to memorize anything . . . not anything of any length. And since that time I've had a baby. I've had loads of bottles of wine – I mean, I'm not a drinker but still . . . Maybe the memory cells are simply not there, have disappeared. Wear and tear. If only I'd paid more attention to Dr Bruno Furst's advertisement about developing a powerful memory. 'How I Improved My Memory in One Evening' – ha! – I thought that was one for the trainspotters.

I am to play the part of Helga. She is described in the script as 'a sexually active, middle-aged German tourist'. It sounds terrifying, and I don't feel up to the mark. And suppose nobody says, 'But you're really too young to be playing the part of a middle-aged woman'?

The porter comes down the corridor with dignity and a small xylophone. *Ting a-ling ling* – he picks out three notes on the xylophone with a little hammer. Dinner is served.

'Do you have to do this play, Mummy?'

'Yes, I'm doing the play in exchange for a nice holiday –

that's the deal: free hotel accommodation for me performing in the play. Lovely swimming pool for you, sunshine, fun.'

It seemed such a brilliant idea: barter, a new form of economic survival. The author of the play owns a nice five-star hotel with yummy food and swimming pools and everything. I went there six months ago to direct his play for radio and had to step in at the last minute to play the dreaded Helgá. He thought I sounded like Meryl Streep. But with radio you don't have to learn your lines. You just hold your script and act off the page, trying as hard as possible not to make any rustling sounds.

We take our seats in the dining car with its phalanx of ceiling fans to keep us cool, and have our strange semi-colonial three-course meal of brown Windsor soup, lamb chops (not in Bisto gravy but served with onions and peppers) followed by comforting steamed pudding and custard. The waiters, dressed in starched white uniform, advance with strained expressions, bowls of soup on splayed hands, swaying in time with the train. Not a drop is spilt. The tables are laid with starched white tablecloths and heavy silver service. I find I have only fifty shillings, not even enough for a beer. I long for wine. The man sitting opposite us, an unfriendly Englishman with a prissy manner, orders a bottle of wine. I will him to offer me a glass, but to no avail. Rebecca hates most of the food but likes the pudding.

'And when you wake up we'll be by the sea,' I say to her, trying to jolly her along. I am conscious that travelling in old trains is a rather adult taste. But when we get back to our neatly made up couchettes, it's she who falls asleep straight away as I lie there fretting, and smelling strange old smells in the crevices of the compartment. The air grows colder, the cockroaches bolder. On we rattle and gallop, sometimes stopping at tiny stations for no apparent reason.

A terrible homesickness sets in, such as I never usually feel. Oh, I want to be back in Harlesden, pouting, smouldering, making love to the camera with Zengle's rabbit hutch just out of shot. Too late, mate.

The sun rises, and so do my spirits. Breakfast of bacon and eggs, toast with real butter, Camp coffee and old-fashioned Libby's orange juice. All this with the dewy scrubland of the Dika plains sliding past, and children waving hello on their way back from fetching water. There's nothing quite like making a long journey by train even if you haven't slept a wink.

We are met at the station by the blond German hotel manager – big, flirtatious, insolent. He was Mister Fixit when we recorded the play for radio, getting us up early on location; as in Namibia there is wind, but also incoming tides, all of which get louder as the day unfurls. So good at timetables and locations is he that the sound recordist and I called him the Tidemaster. He gives Rebecca and me a friendly poke in the ribs and loads our luggage in the car: 'So you have two hours to wash and rest. Then you must be ready to go to the Little Theatre Club for rehearsal.' My joyous feeling is ebbing away.

'You're joking.'

'Zis is no joke. Listen, we have already rehearsed one week, we have only five days and then we have the performance.'

'So are you in it too?'

'Yah.' He fires me a furious stare through blond eyelashes.

'Are you any good?'

'Of course.'

'Have you learned your lines?'

'Of course.'

'What part do you play?'

'The part of the German hotel manager.'

226

The play is set in Mombasa with the middle-aged Helga buying the love of a young beach boy. This is actually a sub-plot. The main plot is about a piece of land on the coast being sold for development. The path leading to the beach running through the land is illegally blocked off, stopping the beach boys from having easy access to the beach and their tourist clientele. It's a hot topic in Mombasa and makes a change from the diet of South African and Nigerian plays served up by African members of the Theatre Club.

We arrive at the hotel. Our room is large and airy. And there's the Indian Ocean – a vista of blue dissipating my fears. There are two swimming pools, very blue and still; the heat is nurturing. Rebecca is excited.

'I want to swim now.'

'Oh please test me again,' I beg.

'Do I have to?'

'Yes, please. Go on, give me Hamisi's line at the top of page fifty-one. Here's the script.'

' "For you two thousand shillings," ' says my daughter wearily.

' "Well I could sell it for—" '

'No, Mum, you've missed a bit – "Now how much is that in marks. Let's see, yes, about seventy marks." *Then* you say, "Well I could sell it for blaa blaa blaa!" '

'Oh bugger.'

'You shouldn't say that word.'

'Sorry . . . well, anyway the hotel's nice, isn't it?'

'Suppose so,' she says grumpily, playing on my anxiety.

The phone rings. It's the playwright's secretary. He wants to see me.

He sits behind his desk, neat, clever, a thoughtful Indian Kenyan in his sixties, who can make a quick decision if it's needed but is careful and meticulous in his judgements. He owns several businesses, but gets up every morning at six o'clock to do creative writing before beginning on the commercial demands of the day.

He looks at me keenly. 'So everything all right?'

'Brilliant, lovely room,' and I mean it.

'Now Markus will take you to the theatre in one hour. You know your lines?'

'Um, yes, well I've gone over them all . . . almost.'

'Here, take a look at this,' he says, twinkling with pleasure. It's the *Coast Weekly* newspaper and there's a photo of me smouldering, face on. The caption reads: *Fiona Ledger has been specially flown from London to take the part of Helga . . .*

'We're pleased to have you here,' he says solemnly.

'Thank you.'

Oh why have I done this? *Specially flown in . . .* Never mind that I paid my own air fare and I'm not getting a fee, it sounds so extravagant, and it promises so much.

The Little Theatre Club sits on the outskirts of Mombasa opposite a well-tended graveyard. The stones bear the names of white Kenyans dating from the 1920s, but most are dedicated to those killed in action in the Second World War. It's supposed to be a favourite habitat for snakes.

The main vestibule of the theatre is in the open air, built round a fountain and octagonal in shape. The fountain does not work and the pool is now stagnant, a lure to mosquitoes. The bar has some nice wicker chairs in it. It's one of those institutions that was only gradually forfeited by the white Kenyans after independence. The bar once played host to boozy Europeans and now plays host to boozy Africans, making the Europeans grumble. The theatre is small but enchanting. Everything is decaying, of course. The dressing rooms are particularly mouldy, with ceilings about to collapse. Today the rehearsal is being held in the dance room. I walk in, rigid with nerves. The director bounces up with lowered head – he has a nervy manner, over-charged, and this makes it very hard for me to understand what he says. I know he loves theatre. Everyone turns to looks at me as I come in – curious, interested. At last Helga is here.

'Fantastic, fantastic. We have Helga here now. Let's do scene eleven. Come on, everyone – no scripts now.'

'If you don't mind, I've just come off the train, I didn't get much sleep and I think I still need my script for reference.' My voice is low, streaked with self-pity and gloom. I could let these people down so easily. They think I'm going to be brilliant and I shall be manifestly awful. I know quite a few of them because they acted in the short radio version. The last time they saw me I was in charge, directing, on top, so sure of myself, so quick to pounce on their shortcomings, iron out hesitation, confusion. And here I am now, hesitant, confused.

'OK, from the top.'

This room is used for ballet lessons for the children of the Mombasa bourgeoisie – European, African and Asian. To inspire them, on the walls are posters of young ballerinas – mainly white – striking various poses, in soft focus, softly lit.

'"Jambo, Mama,"' says Gilbert, who plays my toyboy lover.

I parry, alarmed at my complete ignorance as to where I am supposed to be in the acting space.

'Hang on – where do you want me? Over here? Right. So I'm coming in here from the left and . . .'

'Yes, yes,' says the director, eyes sparkling. His day job is marine biology; his passion is the theatre.

'"Jambo, Mama."' Gilbert gives me my line again.

'"Jambo, young man. Young man, you usually open earlier than this . . ."' My voice sounds flat and tinny. The so-called German accent, vaguely modelled on Marlene Dietrich, has lost its bite.

' "Yes, Mama – we had a problem." '

' "Oh, what problem is that?" ' The question is meant to be kittenish, curiosity wrapped in insouciance, all delivered with one arched eyebrow.

But I hit the first note of the sentence too high; a slightly strangled sound comes out. I slide down the scale, reaching an unintended basso profundo on the last word of the sentence. Had it been appropriate I could have launched into 'Falling in Love Again', but it was not. I feel sadly bereft of that natural authority and dazzling talent that comes with being *flown in specially*.

Day three. Most people have learned all their lines, except the man playing the inspector. I am still going blank. Today the author is coming in to see the rehearsal on stage.

The dressing rooms are decrepit, with no chairs and speckled mirrors. Notes from an old production of *Joseph and His Amazing Technicolor Dreamcoat* are still on the wall. There are huge cobwebs in the corners and mosquitoes dancing in the doorways. It's pretty much like dressing rooms in small community theatres in London, leaving aside the insect population.

We are rehearsing my second entry.

' "Here, let me put a cloth on the sand for you." ' Gilbert is generous and sure in his acting, even though he hasn't quite learned all his lines.

' "No, that's all right." ' I sit down, and the act of sitting down drives the rest of my lines out of my head. Gilbert covers up by moving on.

' "You like this beach, Mama?" '

Again nothing. My brain is blank. The playwright prompts, ' "Yes, but there are—" '

I leap in wildly, ' "Yes, but there are too many tourists. It's getting crowded." '

The scene goes on, sluggishly. It stops and starts, there's very little dash on my part. I can see I'm dragging Gilbert down, and I'm certainly not giving off any sexual promise. We finish. The playwright comes up to me with a slight frown on his face – no more than that – but he looks disappointed. He speaks quietly.

'Listen – you should know your lines by now.'

The rebuke stings for its mildness. He is a decent man who all his life has believed in doing a job well.

'I'm nearly there, nearly,' I say with forced jollity.

'The thing is,' he says pursuing my inadequacies, 'if you forget a line, can't you say *something*? I mean, when it comes to the real thing you can't just stand there if you forget a line.'

Well, there'll be a prompt, I nearly say, but actually that's not the point. The point is either you're in character or you're a marionette, and acting has to be more than a line-learning exercise. I know I'm being under-directed, because the director is nervous of me; he remembers me directing him in January and doesn't feel comfortable bossing me round. Whatever the explanations, the circumstances, I want to run away. This isn't anxiety, it's panic. But what right do I have to indulge a panic that is without true foundation? It may be appropriate in North London, but here where life is on the margins for most, and even the stinking rich live daily with the prospect of all their investments being swept away by mass revolt, and have to duck and dive to keep the good will of the ruling group – in this situation panic is not appropriate. I have to deal with the problem. I remember the words of a dancer friend – the body, the muscles have their own memory. I go back to the script and plot every word.

'"What you have is very good."' (*pause after 'is' to look at his body*)

'"Thank you, Mama. See this giraffe? It's well carved, isn't it?"'

'"Yes, (*cock head to one side*) it's well carved (*pick up giraffe, put it down*). You have many things to offer (*smoulder at Hamisi*) and I (*step back a pace*) like what I see."' (*look at body admiringly*)

And so it went on, line after line, page after page. Nothing is left to chance. Thus my poor old brain cells were relieved of much of the work, and my body became my prompt. And while I have the luxury of doing this on the veranda of my five-star bedroom, with an Indian Ocean breeze in my hair, most of my fellow actors must leave learning lines to after hours, having done a ten-hour working day in some cases coming home to an airless, dark tenement.

Rebecca is fed up. She has learned not only my lines but everyone else's as well. She has made friends at the hotel but sometimes they go out; sometimes she is invited and sometimes she isn't. On day four she says she is homesick. But there's little I can do, propelled as I am towards the big night. Not a motherly figure. It's the last rehearsal. I'm waiting to be called on.

Our counterparts from long ago

I kill the time looking at the memorabilia of past productions on the wall – faded photos and programmes documenting tragedies, farces, and whodunnits. Europeans having fun. In the lobby in front of the actual theatre hangs a big framed assortment of ageing photos and cuttings and an old programme. One is a cutting of an article from an unnamed newspaper, dated Saturday, 3 November 1917. It is accompanied by a photo of a European couple gazing at each other romantically in front of the painted backdrop of a sea and palm trees. The heading of the article reads:

Pili Pili
Mombasa Revue – Tremendous Success.
We are at a loss to find superlatives big enough and expensive enough to adequately describe the pleasure that the two and a half hours of Mombasa's first revue gave us; and judging by the repeated and spontaneous applause the packed house was also having the time of its life.

The young woman in the photo is wearing a muslin dress, the young man is in blazer and boater: the 'Pili Pili' crowd are all Europeans. In our cast of eleven we are: seven African Kenyans, three Indian Kenyans, one Indian English (from Ashby-de-la-Zouch in Leicestershire), one German and me. We comprise three unemployed, one hotel manager, one lawyer, a warehouse manager, a teacher, a tea broker, a hatmaker, an accountant, a nursing mother and me. The multi-racial nature of the cast is a selling point of the play. We are hoping to pull in a multi-racial audience, which will mean big audiences over seven nights. Seventy years ago, multi-racial was not a selling point. The Europeans were self-contained. Well, almost – I notice that at the end of the 'Pili Pili' article, there are credits to a Mr Singh for generously loaning his theatre and Lalichard Moochard and Souza Dias for donating materials and costumes. And all of this back in 1917. Another thought strikes me: strange that they could find the men to act in the revue, considering they were in the last stretch of a world war. My reverie is interrupted by the props and make-up girls advancing on me. They are smirking frightfully. They always arrive very late for rehearsals and have contributed little in terms of materials so far, but both are terrifically turned out – ready, it seems, if necessary, to appear on stage.

'Hello, Fiona.'

'Hello.' I greet them absent-mindedly, as I am now

wondering whether the 'Pili Pili' crowd were as bothered as I am over what to wear: should it be a top and trousers in ethnic print? Or a swimming costume with wrap-around kanga?

'Fiona, we want to say something about your acting.'

'Oh, what's that?' I reply good-humouredly, ready for a compliment.

'You're not really sexy enough,' the tall one says. They burst into giggles.

'You have to be really sexy,' says the short one. 'It will be bad if you are too serious.' They laugh again in a maddening way.

'Right. Well, thanks. But the thing is, I'm not going to waste my sexiness on rehearsals,' I say thinking on my feet, 'I'm saving it for the real thing.' And with that I sweep off. Yes, I'm learning to be a real primadonna. But of course they are right. I've got the lines, and the movements, but I'm about as sexually charged as a nursery nightlight, especially in the cave scene, which is supposed to lead to passionate lovemaking (we've agreed on a blackout at the strategic moment).

RADICAL LIGHTING

It's time for a technical run-through. It's the last and, technically speaking, most difficult scene, involving the onset of night, a storm, Hamisi's departure up a cliff, and me exiting in a storm-tossed boat only to be drowned.

' "Look, Hamisi, it's growing dark outside . . ." '

The lights are full on. I cough, and repeat the line.

' "Look, Hamisi, it's growing dark outside." '

Nothing happens.

'Hello, anyone there? Can we have a bit of "growing dark"?'

'No,' barks the lighting man from his eyrie.

'What do you mean, "no"?'

'You got blackout and moon next page.'

'Yes, but on this page it says "It's growing dark outside", so please can it grow dark? Or I shall look very silly.'

'No, wait until next page.'

'Look, either it grows dark or we cut the line, but I shall have to tell Mr S. if we cut the line and he might not be very happy.'

There's a pause.

'I try,' comes the muffled response.

The lighting man is small, furrow-browed, young and hard to understand. He's always clutching a book and conducts his work on the lights rather as the spirit moves him. The lights dim. I am now standing in a puddle of moonlight.

'"Dunda is waiting to take you back in the canoe. There he is,"' says Gilbert.

'"Yes, I see him."' I move on my line to bid farewell to my lover.

A voice from on high crashes in on the tender love scene: 'Hey, you moved out of my light!'

'What? What do you mean, *your* light?' He's trying to drive me mad.

'I said, stay where you are – you gotta be on spotlight.'

'Yes, but I've got to move on the line. I'm saying goodbye to him and he's exiting right.'

'Don't move.'

'Don't be ridiculous.'

He sniggers. I give up.

We move on to my final scene. Our argument remains unresolved. I pack my costume and wait for a lift back to the hotel. Tomorrow will be the real thing. I linger by the 'Pili Pili' picture. It seems that back in 1917, it was the actors causing the stagehands grief:

*We liked Mr Pagden in this, although he only had a few words.
But one can only imagine the ire of a stage manager when the
heroine is waiting for her life to be saved and the hero strolls in
late and says he's awfully beastly sorry what!*

Where had he been? I wonder. Drinking a G & T? Or a
whisky? And why wasn't Mr Pagden fighting? TB? Invalided
out? Maybe that's it: he was invalided out after sustaining
some shocking war wound, which leaves him in constant
pain, so he consumes large quantities of whisky and subsequently loses track of time, missing his cue on stage and
leaving the stage manager in a state of high anxiety.

We have no war wounded in our cast, but one is down
with malaria.

'He will be fine,' says the director. 'He only has to
come on and shout at the area chief a bit, then he can lie
down.'

The day of the performance. It is six o'clock and the
playwright's nephew notices that I am nervous. He has been
educated in America and Britain. 'She needs tea and scrambled eggs,' he says. I want to kiss him for his kindness. The
playwright and his wife take me back to their big airy house
overlooking the lagoon and feed me. We return to an empty
theatre. Only Gilbert is there. Anxiety wells up – we're
starting in forty-five minutes. Where is everyone? No, no,
says Gilbert, we won't start until eight.

'But it says seven thirty on the posters.'

'It always says that. But nobody will come until eight.' At
seven fifteen people begin to drift in casually. At seven thirty
the audience begins to take its seats. At seven forty-five Mr
S. gathers us on stage behind the curtain. 'Let's pray.' We all
hold hands. Mr S. is a Hindu, his cast is a mixture of Hindu,
Muslim and Christian. And every night from now on, a
different person says prayers. 'Oh God,' says Mr S., 'please

help us to do our best and support us in this collective endeavour. Thank you for bringing us all together to entertain the audience in this theatre.' And it's a big audience, a big, good-tempered audience.

I have opted for the swimming costume and kanga. I've made every effort to be sexy: loads of make-up, big hair (with the aid of clouds of hairspray), I hold my tummy in, stick my bust out and breathe deeply – big breasts and big breaths. Rebecca pops her head round the door before taking her seat.

'You look revolting,' she says reassuringly.

'That's what I'm meant to look,' I hiss at her.

I pace up and down like a tiger waiting, waiting, adrenaline coursing through my veins. I add more hairspray, more lipstick, tie my kanga tighter and tighter, and suddenly it's time to come on. I slink on with as much pelvic thrust as I can manage. 'Jambo, young man.' My accent is practically Transylvanian. There's a ripple of appreciation from the audience just at the sight of me. They can see I'm a Bad Lot all right. And yes, I'm really enjoying myself, and so is Gilbert. We toss our lines at each other playfully, embroidering them with new stresses, improvised embellishments and comic pauses to bring out the meaning. There are no memory lapses. The spirits of the 'Pili Pili' crowd have given us their blessing. In the words of that critic, writing back in 1917:

> *It did not take long for these amateurs to show what they could do and soon everything was going with a swing. The artists soon felt that they were on the winning side and the confidence thus gained made them let it rip with the result that each succeeding merry quip and jest was hailed with delight by the appreciative and enthusiastic audience.*

DARLING, YOU WERE WONDERFUL

The performance is a success. The audience roars and claps approval. Even the elderly Indian ladies in the front row seem to have enjoyed themselves. Only the Inspector hasn't learned his lines. The lighting works.

'Well done with the lighting, Alf,' I say warmly to this subversive young man.

He sniggers. 'You know what Malcolm X say?'

'What?'

' "The white man was created a devil, to bring chaos upon this earth." Read Malcolm X.' He sniggers again, and saunters off.

Mr S. appears. He is beaming. 'You did a magnificent job.'

'Thank you – I was a bit worried about what the elderly Indian ladies might think.'

Mr S. inclines his head towards me confidingly. 'You know, these Indian ladies are a good deal more worldly than you would imagine.'

Mr S.'s tough and beautiful daughter, who has come from London for the show, thanks me. 'Well done. You've made him very happy. It was a good show.'

Then the make-up and props girls, who arrived half an hour into the performance, greet me excitedly: 'You were sexy,' says the tall one. 'I didn't think you could be sexy like that, Fiona,' says the short one.

And then there's my daughter in the throng, giving me a reproachful look.

'You were so embarrassing. That stuff in the cave was yuck.'

'We were only holding hands.'

'Yes, but when the lights went out you were meant to be snogging. I know you were.'

'Well, at least I learned my lines – it would have been more embarrassing if I had forgotten my lines.'

'Do you think your mum was good?' asks one of the actors.

'She was all right. I'm going to be in a play in November. It's called *Grizelda Queen of the Bog*, and it's about . . .'

The actor's attention is diverted by an admiring relative. There's a hurt expression on my beloved's face. My heart contracts. 'Where are you going to perform it, Beckyboodle?' I ask, trying to sound interested and make amends for the actor's lapse in interest. Never patronize a child. She spots the pretence immediately.

'You know where we're performing it – Jackson's Lane.'

Her voice is quietly angry. I suppose it's all a bit much seeing your mum done up like a dog's dinner, flirting with a souvenir seller, two thousand miles away from home. Motherhood and celebrity don't mix.

Our third night: I am bitten by mosquitoes, having forgotten to put on the jungle oil. Other people are getting a bit slapdash too. Well, it's often the case, you try very hard first time round, then it stops being difficult and you start to take it easy. Nobody remembers the spare chair for the scene between the area chief and the lawyer. Andrew is the area chief. He reacts to the problem quick as a flash, adapting a line about offering a chair: 'I'd offer you a chair, Mr Hassan, but it's being mended at the moment.' Hassan takes the ball and runs with it: 'That's all right, I'll stand.'

Andrew is twenty-two, and yet manages with total conviction to play a middle-aged corrupt area chief (a sort of head of the council). He weighs about twenty-four stone. He has massive legs and he sweats heavily. Like others in the cast he has a long, complicated journey to the theatre on foot and by bus. I've never seen him eat. I've never heard him complain. Someone says his weight is to do with his thyroid. He is a clever young man, sharp, witty. A very good actor. He tells me he is looking for a job, any kind of job. He is passionate about acting, getting things just right. Every night he gazes from the wings with furrowed brow as the inspector waits for the prompt to give him his lines. The inspector, I am told, has a good job in a bank.

IMPOSTERS

We have two nights off before we perform again, so an evening in at the hotel beckons. It's a Saturday night and that means entertainments followed by a disco. Rebecca is excited. I feel my liberal heart become heavy with gloom. I'd seen those poor Masai dancers the week before, prostituting their talents and traditions for a mess of pottage in front of a gormless load of German tourists.

'Oh come on, Mum, it's fun. You can drink one of those cocktails you like.'

'You come watch the Masai dancers tonight?' asks the blond Tidemaster.

'Oh well, I don't know – I've seen them before.'

'And I have seen them fifty times before – so what? You better come.'

The Saturday evening's entertainments are organized by the animation team; it is the animators' job to make sure that guests are never bored. And all too often the guests do look bored; they are totally incapable of entertaining themselves, making friends or having fun.

A bumptious animator called Max is the DJ. 'And now, ladies and gentlemen, all the way from their villages in the interior, coming to you special tonight to share their traditions please give a big applause, Hände zusammen bitte und grosse Willkommen für die grossen Masai Tänzer, the Masai dancers. Their first number is the dance of manhood.'

And on they come – conferring in a circle, turning round to face the audience and giving a series of great orchestrated exclamations and groans. Then they do the traditional Masai leaping, some better than others. In fact one at the end is more of a jumper than a leaper.

'And for their next number the Masai fighters will do a war dance.'

A very slight frisson runs through the pina-colada-drinking tourists, particularly the ladies, and even me. I'm actually on my second pina colada. And I have fallen in love with the very tall one with ochred fringe and waist-length plaits. Off they go again. This involves more knee bending. Again, the one at the end looks some degrees off being lithe as a panther. His outfit does not match the others. He looks vaguely familiar.

'And for their third and last number the Masai will sing a song to celebrate wedding.'

Their faces are as impassive as they were in numbers one and two, except for the chap at the end. He is beaming from ear to ear. A closer examination of his costume followed by a glance at the tables in the bistro confirms that he is wearing one of the tablecloths. How can the others tolerate this cruel parody of their culture? I wonder. Will they beat him up outside afterwards? I tackle the Tidemaster about it the next day.

'They are not Masai – well, some may be but many are just coastal people. They know that's what the tourists want, so they dress up.'

'And what about the chap at the end with the tablecloth?'

'Did you not recognize him? That is Francis, the children's entertainer. He always dances with them.'

'Do they mind?'

'Excuse me?'

'Do they not get angry with him?'

'No. Why should they be angry?'

It's our last but one night. I complain to the director about the inspector. A shadow flits across his face. 'Oh dear,' he says. 'Yes, it is a problem.'

I'm practically breathless with anger. 'You must do something. It's horrible to see him mess things up every night. He must know his lines by now – everybody else does.'

The director looks pained, and suddenly I am aware that I am treading on something so fine, delicate and painful that it would be cruel to pursue it any further.

'Oh well . . . apart from the inspector, it's going well, isn't it?'

The director's face is wreathed in smiles again. 'Very well. Oh, very well.'

I am now in the swing of things. Hey ho for the life of an entertainer. Rebecca has made new friends, small and big; she's become a character in the hotel. And I know my lines, as well as everyone else's. Like a drug addict I look forward every night to the charge I get from the audience. I'm rather hoping that it will all go on for ever. But sure enough the last night comes. We throw everything we have at the audience, which by now includes a few whites. We get a stonking applause at the end. I feel fantastic. I have looked fear in the face and triumphed.

THE COBRA

Perhaps all this makes me a little too brave, as I pack up my bracelets, my lipstick and hairspray (nearly empty), fold my kanga, and tenderly collate my battered script. The inspector has walked into the dressing room to get his kit. There's me and two other actors packing up. I take a deep breath. 'So how come you couldn't be bothered to learn your lines? The rest of us did.'

He turns round to look at me. He's a burly man, a man you wouldn't pick a physical fight with. His eyes are blazing like a cobra's.

'What did you say?'

'I said, why couldn't you learn your lines like the rest of us?'

'I learned my lines. What are you talking about?'

The big lie momentarily disturbs my equilibrium. I look round hoping for support from the others. But they have silently turned their backs to me and are packing quickly with lowered heads. I have the feeling, though, that they are listening.

I persist, 'You didn't learn them – you used the prompt every night.'

His eyes are tawny and glittering dangerously.

'Who do you think you are, coming here, telling people what to do?'

Specially flown in I suppose is what he means.

'Oh, there's nothing special about me, I just believe it's important to do your best for the sake of others.'

'This is amateur theatre, you know.' The contempt in his voice is quite unnerving.

'Just because it's amateur doesn't mean we don't try our best.'

'If you're so marvellous why don't you go to Hollywood?'

It's such a ridiculous riposte that I want to laugh, but am stopped by the venomous look in his eyes. Hatred. He hates me because I won't accept he's the big man, he hates me because I'm the carping European who thinks she can defy the local order.

'Mummy, they want you to come for the dancing.'

Rebecca rescues me. He turns his stare on her. My heart lurches. I can take any amount of ill will, but leave my child alone. She notices nothing. 'Come on, Mum.'

The rest of the evening – the dancing, the lovely food and speeches – is overshadowed by this bully. I now have an inkling why the man gets his own way, why it takes an outsider to criticize him. An outsider can come and go. The others have to live with his menacing behaviour.

Later on in the evening someone explains he is after the presidency of the drama club. The director is standing in his way. The two men are from different parts of the country. 'Are you saying he's willing to sacrifice the success of a production in order to become a leading light on the committee? He can't be very interested in drama, can he?'

'This isn't about drama – he's not interested in drama – it's about power,' says my informant.

I seek comfort in the past and those colonial entertainments of seventy years ago.

Another scene in 'Pili Pili' that appealed was set in the interior of the Hun submarine, in which the Kaiser (Mr Overman) was holding a council of war. We adored Mr Pickering's whiskers and his acting as Admiral Tirpitz – what a villain he was, and we are open to bet in this character he would put ground glass in his dearest pal's whisky and soda.

EATING HER OWN

Ten days later with a bout of malaria cured (those mosquitoes enjoyed me as well as the show) we make our goodbyes and head north on a ropy old train that breaks down within two hours of Nairobi. I feel impelled to ring Mr S. as soon as I arrive to thank him again for putting me on the stage.

'How's it down there? It's so cloudy and cold up here.'

His voice is strained. 'Haven't you heard?'

'No. What?'

'It's been terrible here. There was a terrible massacre at Likoni. A lot of people killed. The police station was attacked.'

As our train clanked out of the station, unknown to us the killing began. First a policewoman was disembowelled at the police station next to the Likoni ferry route, which links Mombasa across the lagoon to the coastal road going south. Then five policemen were killed. This was the beginning of a ten-day reign of terror. The victims seemed broadly to be people from up-country, who had moved to the coast to take advantage of the tourist economy. Two days after the Likoni incident 2,500 people seeking refuge in Likoni Catholic Church are attacked. The police do nothing to defend them. A week later stallholders in Malindi, a popular resort with Italians, have all their kiosks burnt to the ground, destroying hundreds and thousands of dollars worth of goods. The death toll now stands at thirty-nine.

'As Kenyans count their loss after what has been the most brutal peacetime killing in the country, the question is on everyone's mind: how did it happen?' says the editorial of a national paper. There's been tension between coastal people and up-country folk for some years, but there was no buzz, no rumour in the shanties or poor housing estates, that this was on the cards. Just the shock of it happening.

The verdict is, the massacre was organized by the government, anxious about the forthcoming elections and the unreliability of the vote of up-country people. This is an intimidation tactic to warn those people to get out of KANU safe constituencies. The price is a high one to pay: over forty dead, tourists cancelling their holidays in their droves.

Mr S.'s hotel will surely suffer. If the bookings go below a certain level he will have to start laying off staff. So more young men will be kicking their heels. At Nairobi station we see the bedraggled victims of intimidation and violence newly arrived from Mombasa, sitting on their suitcases, wondering what next. Power has no heart – anything or nothing could happen.

TWELVE

Taming the Tiger

∽ல்லை

Cold war orphan

In November 1989 the Berlin Wall collapses, and one month later a man called Charles Taylor, on the run from the FBI, freshly trained by Colonel Gaddafi, enters the northern part of Liberia. I cannot say the two things are directly connected. But with the collapse of communism Liberia becomes what one American analyst cutely describes as 'a cold war orphan'; its strategic importance to America has declined with the end of the cold war. And strategic it had been. The two countries had a mutual defence pact. America was behind the Liberian ship registry – useful in times of war for quick naval mobilization. When it saw the Germans sniffing around its mines, America built a port so that Liberian iron ore could head west, not north. America built listening stations in Liberia to monitor what diplomats and security agencies were saying in the region, what radio stations were broadcasting; America built an Omega navigational station, one of only eight in the world, to guide ships in the Atlantic. And in return Liberia got the biggest tranche of American aid on the continent. Most of it was salted away by corrupt government officials.

Then from 1990 on, with its old Soviet sparring partner on the ropes, America didn't need to care quite so much about its sphere of influence. Along comes Charles Taylor. A graduate in economics, he takes a job as a senior administrator in the government department of procurement. He flees to America, having allegedly embezzled a million dollars; under an extradition treaty between the two countries he is jailed in Massachusetts. He escapes from jail. Somehow he crosses the Atlantic and lurks in Sierra Leone and Ghana, then goes to Libya to prepare himself for an invasion. This is a man with a mission. He is clever and ruthless. He creeps into the country on Christmas Eve 1989 to start a war which goes on and on and on. America dithers, discusses and decides it would be too messy to get involved. After slugging it out with nineteen other factions, Charles Taylor gets his official recognition. In the end he does this not through the barrel of a gun but through a fair and free, internationally monitored election, during which he displays a truly American mastery of the media; but the subtext is 'vote for me or I'll take up my gun again'. With chilling wit the electorate dreamed up the following slogan: 'You kill my ma, you kill my pa – I go vote for you, Charles Taylor.'

Now the theory is, the tiger has got what he wants, so he can be tamed with treats of trade and aid. Then Liberia will be a reliable voting ally at the UN and will have no need for the support of Colonel Gaddafi.

IVORIAN ESCAPE

I'm on the runway at Abidjan airport. Russian pilots stand around the plane I shall soon be flying in; I think they're smiling, but it's hard to tell because they sport large walrus moustaches. I make an attempt at conversation with one of them.

'What kind of plane is this?'

'Antonov 40, very good.' His tone is slightly defensive and irritable. He saunters off round the other side to the cockpit. As I climb up the shaky steps, there's a cheeping sound. For a moment I think this signals some obscure mechanical fault. Then I realize that it's an animal noise. To my mind livestock belongs in lorries or trains, not in planes, but this plane is taking six boxes of five-day-old chicks to Liberia. They cheep, and they give off a slightly cloying, sweet smell. In keeping with the farmyard feel of the plane, planks of wood extend the entire length of the aisle. The seats are not very comforting; they flop forwards and backwards, but they are covered in an ancient pale green tweed of what looks like fine quality. Luggage occupies the first three rows in a terrifying mountain, which threatens to turn into an avalanche. The walls of the plane are painted in a pastel blue gloss paint. In places it is cracked; in places it is patched with inch-wide gaffer tape. I've moved down the aisle, escaping the worst of the cheeping and the smell. I am very nervous and choose a seat next to a solid-looking man. I gaze around the plane. I remember Angola, I remember Moscow. And now a different sort of smell invades my nostrils – a smell from the past – the glorious Soviet past, no spicy frivolous capitalist hint to it but a very serious smell of ink, paper and cheap books, heavy red plastic phones, bureaucrats who wash in plain soap and eat pickled vegetables; even the booze, the vodka, is a plain-smelling spirit.

My reverie is disturbed by the engines starting up. Clouds of evaporated water begin to seep out of one side of the plane, forming condensation on the roof. I pretend to be alarmed to amuse myself, but I'm not really. The main thing is I've got a seat on a plane, which is more than Ghana Airways was offering, despite the fact I had a proper OK'd ticket. There I was, at their counter, a hair's breadth from getting my boarding card, and I was elbowed out of the way by a Liberian claiming to have tickets for ministers (which ones, I never found out).

This was the second time I had failed to get on a Ghana Airways plane. And now the Russians have come to my rescue to take me from Abidjan to Monrovia, the capital of Liberia. Take me away from hours of sitting around in the airport, harassed by young men masquerading as porters, and me trying unsuccessfully to make conversation with other passengers. They include a large number of European aid workers on their way to Sierra Leone. I try to start a conversation to kill the time. After all, we are all stuck in the same airport. My immediate neighbour is a birdlike French-woman who is working in Freetown.

'So there's a curfew?'

'Yes.'

'So where are you all staying?'

'Hotels.'

'Is Brookfields still there?' I ask, trying to get the conversation flowing a bit more.

'It's still in a high security risk area,' she replies dismissively.

'And do you feel frightened?'

The coup launched by the military junta against President Kabbah resulted in most of Freetown going up in flames. Meanwhile West African peacekeeping soldiers, the ECOMOG force, try to hold the fragile truce. So 'do you feel frightened?' is a fair enough question; perhaps too personal for her – she shrugs it off with Gallic froideur.

'It's OK. I've known worse.'

'But what's it like walking outside? I mean . . .'

'I work ten hours in the office every day. I don't have time to walk around very much.'

'Ten hours. My goodness. That's a long time just sitting in an office. What do you do?'

She darts me a mean look, as though I've asked her what colour her knickers are. 'I am working on a health and development programme for UNICEF.'

It puzzles me, this. How can she possibly know what the state of health and development is in Sierra Leone if she's stuck in the office for ten hours every day? I think better of asking her that. So far she has not asked me a single question. I try to steer the conversation round to the pleasantly general, even philosophical.

'So what went wrong with Sierra Leone, eh? For years it was a stagnant backwater, trundling along. Top hats and tails, church on Sunday, great newspaper tradition, dough-nuts, sleepy, safe . . .' I am beginning to run out of adjectives summing up the cosy Krio Sierra Leone of the past. My words are swallowed by a huge silence, which the hum of the airport air-conditioner gradually reclaims. I persist like the bore at the bus stop.

'. . . then there's soldiers on the rampage, rape, killing. So what happened *there* then?' I am conscious of my voice taking on a hectoring note. But I'm on the West African coast and I want to enjoy myself, I want to chat about the history and the politics – after all, this is one of my favourite parts of the world, full of bustle, trade, clever tricks, gossip, skyscrapers defying a backdrop of grey billowing clouds, ragged dark green horizons. Heat, damp. And going back in time, say a century: palm oil ruffians, down-river raids, 'The Bight of Benin, the Bight of Benin, one comes out, ten went in.' Europeans defeated by what were described as sickly humours hovering in the air a mile out to sea.

'So what happened *there* then?'

Eventually the Frenchwoman answers my question. She

purses her lips. 'Well, I don't know what it was like before the emergency.' She pauses. 'But you know, in the hinterland the people were very poor. The young men didn't have enough to do.' She turns away and is silent. This conversational impasse allows me to set about reconsidering my great romance with the West African coast. I marshall a few events from the last thirteen years or so. Nigeria is at the mercy of insecure, unpredictable soldiers, their drug baron friends and a vicious security service, its press stifled. For seven years Liberia has been torn apart by a civil war. Sierra Leone has only just fought off the rampaging soldiers, and up-country crazed gunmen still lurk. More recently, Guinea Bissau has collapsed into fighting. Ghana remains virtuous, pet of the World Bank and IMF, although there are those who will never forget Jerry Rawlings's bloody rise to power. But . . . but people still give birth, fall in love, write, act, sing and trade. I make up my mind to stand by that; particularly after my encounter last night with the man from the twilight zone.

He was in his late twenties or early thirties. A tall and very overweight American. His lips are thin but cherry red. His eyes turn up at the corners slightly. I met him in the flat of a friend of a friend, while killing time. He makes tidy sums of money as a consultant. I meet him in Abidjan for just a few hours before he flies back to America with his swag. He smirks most dreadfully when he hears I'm going to Liberia. 'You know those Stephen King novels,' he says in a quiet twilight-zone voice, 'the ones where you're in a small town or village and everything seems normal? Then you realize that there's something terrible wrong; there's something weird going on. People look ordinary, but deep down inside they are weird. Well, that's Monrovia. The people there are sick.' He pronounces the last word with unnecessary sibilance.

'Oh,' is all I can think to say.

He smiles, pleased at the effect of his words. His large brown eyes gaze wetly through glinting glasses, one eyebrow raised as though to say, so that's the score, pal. I return his gaze: nothing can be quite as weird as you, I think.

This is not what I say. What I actually say is, 'So how long were you there?'

'One and a half years – quite long enough. How long are you staying?'

'Oh, just three and a half weeks. Training at the radio station.'

'Good luck,' he says in a doomy voice.

THE LONGEST RUNWAY IN AFRICA

Now the two days of purgatory in Abidjan are over – meeting the weird consultant, struggling to understand French, fighting off the porters and missing planes – it's all behind me. The Antonov is rumbling down the runway. And just as I think it will never take off, there's a tilting sensation, and we're up. Gravity has released its hold. There's a crackle on the intercom. It's the Russian pilot. 'Ladies and gentlemen, welcome to this-er floyt to Monrovia from-er . . . Abidjan.' He sounds as though he's doing something else while talking to us; flying the plane, I hope, rather than getting the seal off a bottle of vodka. 'Fasten your seffty belts. We hope you-er enjoy-this-flight.' He rushes the end of his announcement, then it's *crackle-crackle* and *click*.

We're just beginning to pierce a thick blanket of cloud, but I can still see the lagoons and mangrove swamps and jungle of West Africa. My neighbour is a sombre Liberian who runs a cold storage business – he's been looted twice, lost everything both times within the space of eight years.

253

He makes this trip regularly to buy spare parts. He puts up with my nervous prattle. I feel ashamed of my panic. The plane is as smooth as a dragonfly. Rather amazingly, a man comes round with light refreshments: a very nice tin of fizzy drink and some perfectly edible Ivorian biscuits. The condensation begins to collect on the ceiling into great drops which fall on the suitcases. Still the plane works. And it always flies on time, and is probably better maintained than the Ghana Airways plane as it is the property and livelihood of one man, a Spaniard who has lived in West Africa for forty years.

Our landing is perfect. Robertsfield has the longest runway in Africa. It was built as a major transit point for the Americans and Allies during the Second World War, and its runway is long enough to land an American B47 bomber with ease; so much safer than Heathrow. The longest runway maybe, but now the smallest airport building. It's a sort of small brick bungalow, newly built in the past six months. As I enter it, trying to look purposeful, I am enveloped in a scrum of people and officials. A tough-looking woman in khaki uniform asks for my passport and leafs through it looking grave. Women in uniform: the worst. But then I spot a chink in her armour. She has spectacularly long fingernails painted with a red, white and blue motif based on the Liberian flag. Ruthlessly I appeal to her vanity. After all, a dame's a dame, even if she is in uniform.

'I like your nails, they're fantastic.'

'Well, thank you.' Her serious expression melts away.

'No, they really are amazing, beautiful.'

'OK. So where you stayin'?'

'Star Radio.'

'I'll come round and do yours.'

'Ooh, yes please.'

My passport is handed back. But just as a smug feeling is

making itself at home, a tall young man approaches. He is very keen to do his job properly. That's always a bad sign at an airport. He gives me precise instructions in a slow Liberian-American drawl.

'You must now fill in this form. OK? Now what you do is, here, jus' here, put your name, OK? Your name, your full name. OK, go on then . . . put your name in the box.' I write my name very slowly. 'Right, OK. Now you put your status in this box here. That is to say, you must declare if you are single or married, OK? So what are you? Single? OK, write it there . . . there in that box, just there – single.' He then spells out 'S-I-N-G-L-E.'

'Ooh, I wish they had one of you at every airport.' Even I'm not sure whether I'm being ironic or complimentary. Anyway, he is not bothered; he's intent on getting the job done. I finish the form, fairly well infantilized by his treatment ('Should I sign here? And the date? Is that all right? And do you want my passport again?')

He studies the form carefully and then looks up. 'Well, in Liberia it is against the law to bribe, but a tip is sure appreciated.' He laughs, I laugh, but I can't accommodate his wishes.

'Um, I'm afraid I don't have any Liberian dollars.' I'm certainly not parting with my twenty-dollar American notes.

He stops smiling. Just as I start to feel wobbly, a man even bigger than him in a very bright shirt calls out my name.

'Fiona, follow me.'

This is, I later learn, William, the accountant. He knows everybody, greetings are exchanged, notes are discreetly flashed, and my luggage is found. We leave the airport behind us, and a hapless Ivorian who has not been met by anyone. Like a pack of hyenas, taxi drivers descend on him, sensing his vulnerability, his ignorance.

255

'Probably charge him a few hundred American dollars to get into town,' says William.

It's a long journey to town. The airport was built for the convenience of the management of the Firestone Rubber plantation. It's way out in the middle of nowhere – there's none of the bleak airport scenery you find in most countries: no hoardings, no flyovers, no high-rise buildings, no warehouses, no industrial units, just miles of verdant countryside, occasionally punctuated by damaged cars and buildings. Everything is damaged, spoilt, burnt. The old airport is a breathtaking example of destruction. I suppose that once it looked like any other vaguely modern minor international airport. Now it looks like a giant mattress that has been incinerated; the slipformed load-bearing pillars are still there and one level of flooring, the rest is a mad tangle of metal and wires silhouetted against the sky. There is no fabric to the building left.

'Flight all right?' asks the English station manager as I gaze at all this. For the next three and a half weeks he is my boss. He was my boss many years ago in the BBC, a source of some apprehension for me. Tall, aloof – he was variously thought to be eccentric, easy going, difficult, peculiar, clever, bored and ordinary. Which will predominate over the next three weeks? I wonder. I can already detect he's more mellow than I remember; perhaps I am more detached, perhaps I am more likeable than I was fifteen years ago – less pretty but more likeable. I try to make light of the flight. I don't want him to think I'm a weed.

'Yeah, the flight was fine. I mean, the plane's a bit old but it was a good flight.'

'It's only crashed twice.'

'Oh really?' I try to sound not very interested.

'Yes, and the second time was at the old airport. Short landing strip and straight into the swamp, which was full of bodies; there'd been a massacre. So as the plane went in the bones flew out, and passengers had to wade through the whole thing. Everyone survived.' He gives a little murmur and smiles into the distance.

Yes, well, quite funny; absurd really, to nearly die by plunging at speed into a mass grave, but I feel uncomfortable with the image of the bones and flesh disintegrating in the swamp. Of course, British soil has been fertilized by the bones of massacred soldiers and innocents countless times, but you have to dig down deep to find them. Not so deep in France; the Somme, 21 March 1918: 150,000 men slaughtered in one day. That's almost the total estimated number of Liberians killed during the seven years of civil war. And today there's Bosnia. But what makes Bosnia and Liberia different from the First World War is the blurring of lines between civilians and soldiers. World War One was a soldiers' war. Civilians – bar a few nurses – stayed at home. There was no hiding in Liberia, no hiding in Bosnia, no front line.

Bienvenue à Gîte Taylor

'I think you'll have a good time here. Everyone's really looking forward to you coming,' says the station manager, perhaps concerned at my silence. We are now passing the President's home. It looks a bit like a motorway inn or a French *gîte*. It is a large building but in a domestic style, set flush against the edge of the road. In front, a row of shiny metallic four-wheel-drive cars are parked. It's nicely painted a pale cream colour. I half expect to see a Routiers plaque or an AA recommendation on the wall. And there are lots of flags flying above the parapet. But what would Egon Ronay say about the sandbags and the soldier manning the machine gun on the roof? The Executive Mansion in town is supposed to be the official residence of Liberian presidents. It's an early sixties monstrosity built by the expansive William V. S. Tubman. The President has refused to move in there on the grounds it is haunted by evil spirits. Next week it will be exorcized.

THE DEVIL'S WORK

Thirty miles later we roll into Monrovia. More a town than a city, it looks like the devil has taken a blowtorch to it. The last time I saw so much devastation was in 1992: Los Angeles in the aftermath of the riots. But although it doesn't look like it, I'm seeing Monrovia on the mend. It's 1998 and the last serious violence was in April 1996, when the city was pulled apart by two raging factions. The episode is still vivid in people's minds and earned the nickname 'Octopus'. Look carefully now and you can see licks of paint springing up here and there. Blocks of flats are being spruced up all over town. Men on ladders in Liberian Electricity Board uniform try to mend bazooka'd cables. But their efforts have little impact. Mains electricity hardly works and everywhere generators throb and pound, making Monrovia one of the noisiest cities in the world. And everywhere there are soldiers: Nigerians and Ghanaians at the ECOMOG peace-keeping force checkpoints; unpaid members of the old army – the Armed Forces of Liberia; the President's security men wearing uniforms made out of what an English expatriate describes as the sort of curtain remnants you might buy in a John Lewis sale. So plenty of soldiers and plenty of four-wheel-drive cars, ferrying expatriates and consultants backwards and forwards from offices to conflict mediation workshops, from launch parties to strategy meetings, from field trips to briefings about the field trips, and so it goes on. Most of these foreigners are

Americans now anxious to steady the country which their government watched being wrecked. In the American Embassy the helicopter is ready to be scrambled in case of an emergency evacuation. And of course their wealth and standard of living cause envy and greed.

My first day in Monrovia I spend a morning in the Capitol, in the House of Representatives, listening to the representatives attacking the deputy speaker for having a car when they didn't.

'I say, that's a poor show. How can every member of the House of Representatives have a car when the country's in this state? Besides it's not as though Monrovia is so big.'

The members of the Capitol press office look at me with pity. 'It is right they should have cars. They have much work. The public transport is very bad.'

'What about bicycles?'

They laugh. Their pity for me has increased.

INFORMATION AND ORGANIZATION

The radio station is funded by the Americans. Its mission is to cut a swathe through the forest of frothy music and talk radio stations (including a few owned by the President) with a plain menu of news and current affairs. It's had a lot of money thrown at it but it's got good people, enthusiastic, efficient. For the first time in my life I have my own office. In one of the drawers neatly laid out are pens, dry markers, Sellotape, Post-it notes, a notebook, a hole puncher and a stapler. 'That's our Miss Diggs – she's very organized,' says the manager. And so she is. She could quite well, had she been of another turn of mind, sneaked off with the stationery and sold it for a tidy sum. Nobody would ever have known. But she likes to run a tight ship. During the war she had a gun held to her head. 'Go on, shoot me,' she bellowed at the fighter. He lost his nerve. Aah, Miss Diggs, thank you for my office kit.

The training course is attended by a lively team, the best I've ever held. They are a mixed bunch: there are the quick, the keen, the slow and the dull, but all are bristling with enthusiasm. And eager to talk, to discuss: the war, the President, freedom of speech and the risk of getting beaten up (which happens to a couple of newspaper journalists during my stay). I take a big breath.

'So are you all from different parts of the country, different ethnic groups?'

There's no awkwardness. Several of them answer at once.

'We're all different.'

'Is that hard?'

'No. No. It's fine.'

'What about listeners – do you ever get attacked for coming from where you come from?'

'Well,' says the news editor, 'if you make a mistake, listeners might say, "Oh, he's a typical mmmm . . ."'

Perhaps they are not telling me the truth. But on the whole I think they are.

'I don't know what it is about us Liberians,' volunteers another trainee. 'We had seven years of war but we keep bouncing back. Must be crazy.'

Her colleagues laugh.

Only it wasn't really a war – it was young men who had nothing to lose, on the rampage, stirred up by some ruthless, ambitious men who had lots to gain. Everyone wanted something they could not have. Even the Boy Scouts move- ment managed to mirror the turmoil, dissolving into what the *National Chronicle* described as a *long-standing leadership struggle . . . meanwhile a five-member transitional scout council was set up and charged with the responsibility to plan, organise and supervise a general election for legitimate officers of the Boy Scouts of Liberia in the shortest possible time.* But camping and learning to make a fire without matches are small adventures compared to what for men is the biggest adventure of all: war.

It was a period of improvised violence. Some soldiers took drugs, some wore masks and wigs. They all just went for it. No rules, nothing off-limit. Every cruelty you can imagine, with women and children a prime target.

OUT OF TOWN

Our first weekend we travel out of Monrovia to the Bong mines. These iron ore mines were once the source of huge wealth. They are now so isolated and decaying that the road leading through the mines is covered in washing laid out to dry in the sun. It has to be moved before we can go any further in our four-wheel-drive car. All the way to the mines the trail of destruction is visible from the roadside. Each building is marked not just by gunfire and mortar fire but also by graffiti. Whatever the situation, whatever the place, these boys always seem to get hold of a pot of paint and a brush and leave their mark: 'NPFL HQ', 'ULIMO Now', 'Die Enemy'. What looks like it was once an ordinary house has 'Death Squad NPFL' painted on it. So what happened there? I ask one of the trainee journalists. 'Oh, people were taken there to be shot.' 'Who exactly?' 'Well, anybody could be shot.' And there's occasional retaliatory graffiti: 'No Man No War' it says on one of the walls in the shell of a house.

Two of the trainees grew up in this area, and they remark excitedly at the landmarks of their youth. 'Look – my old school.' And you have to look very hard. The roof has been blown off and vegetation is swallowing it up.

'Was it a primary school?' I ask.

'No, a big boarding school. That's just one bit of it. I don' know where the rest of it is. It was a good school.'

'And there's the hospital,' cries Sao, the youngest of the group.

There *was* the hospital. Sao is a clerk at the radio station. We're taking her to see her grandmother and do some interviewing at the village. Her grandmother doesn't know she's coming. It will be a surprise.

When we arrive I think the surprise will half kill Sao's grandmother. She flaps her leathery hands to her face and moans a little; tears begin to course down the lined cheeks. The shock of seeing her favourite granddaughter without any notice is too much. And there's me in tow, tactlessly taking level, fumbling with my microphone and cassette recorder. I imagine how furious my mother would be if I turned up with friends, not giving her enough notice to rearrange her furniture, plump the cushions and change her dress. The old lady moans again and disappears into her house, leaving the fire she was tending to smoke uncertainly. I notice graffiti on the wall of the house and a scribbled drawing. Someone has tried unsuccessfully to scrub it out. It looks obscene, and I resist the urge to examine it closer.

Haindi is not a village. I am reprimanded for not calling it a town; but that's the way it seems to me: a beautiful, tranquil village. For a start there's no traffic.

'It will be very busy on Tuesday,' says Sao's cousin. 'That's when the lorries come.'

He has returned to start a commercial farm growing vegetables and groundnuts. There's no traffic and it's so lovely to look at – green, peaceful, perhaps too peaceful. I look in vain for gossiping hens and stubborn goats. Along the path by the St Paul River there are high trees, but no chattering monkeys, no birdsong.

'All frightened away by the war,' says Sao. 'So many monkeys when I was a child.'

Back at the village we meet the commissioner of Haindi. He used to be a teacher and now he's a sort of mayor. In the shade of a tree, mopping himself fiercely, he bitterly complains of neglect from the centre of power.

'We here ting from Monrovia. Bu' we no' satisfied, because we cannot see our big-big people. We wanna see them. We wanna see our representative. Since we have elections we have no' received any of them to come and have meeting with us.'

President Tubman in the 1950s, Doe in the 1980s, and now this present incumbent – all came to power with harsh denunciations of Monrovia's neglect of the countryside, of its complacency, its capacity to devour all the wealth of the rest of the nation. Master Sergeant Samuel Doe whipped up a frenzy of hatred against what were seen as those high-mannered Americo-Liberians, the descendants of freed slaves, who spoke no African language and prided themselves on family heirlooms of silver, photo albums and pianos. In his fighting days, before he became President, Charles Taylor burst in from the bush to lay waste to Monrovia, that's how much he thought of the city. Now the city is being rehabilitated – and the countryside is still as neglected as ever. Only this time people are too tired of fighting and killing to do much more than complain to anyone who will listen. 'We appeal to the international community' becomes the catchphrase of the most illiterate, uneducated backwoodsman.

We come across a group of young men digging a pit latrine. It's very deep and the sides are very straight. They are happy to talk, and explain that they are staying here to rebuild the community.

'What about going to Monrovia or Gbanga?'

'No work.'

'But is someone paying you?'

'No, we just doing it free, as the youth.'

'Do the older people appreciate you?'

'Some do, some don' appreciate us at all. They take it to be foolishness.'

'Don't they say, "come and have a drink, well done"?' The very suggestion makes the young man laugh.

'Not at all.'

'It looks good work.'

'We're trying, but we cannot finish.'

'Why not?'

'We need the Red Cross to come and give us materials to finish. We appeal to the international community to help us.'

'But you're practically done. All you need is a bit of wood to make seats and a roof.'

'Precisely. So we appeal to the international community to come here and help us.'

I talk to Sao. She's a little nervous. But she talks very clearly. She has a naturally sharp brain. She watches me with her huge eyes through a fringe of prettily relaxed hair.

'Would you ever come back to live here?'

'Oh no,' she says, a little indignantly.

'Why not?'

'Well, there is nothing to do. It is very boring in Haindi. And I could not find a husband.'

'What about those lads digging the latrine? They seemed nice.'

She gives a half grimace, half smile. 'They are below my class.'

'But didn't you grow up with them?'

'Some, but many in the village come from far away. They are displaced people.'

264

'And the people you did grow up with have gone?'
'Yes.'
'Where are they now?'
Sao shrugs.

TORTURED EUROPEANS

In the evening we go to the launch of a radio soap, an attempt to get to grips with the past and look to a better future. It is being held at the UN complex, safely out of town, looking across to Bushrod Island. There are delicious little canapés, spicy sausages to eat, and good beer to drink. The actors come on and perform a sequence from the soap. They play two women wandering in a forest. They are displaced from their village by the war. A fighter leaps out at them. He wears a strip of cloth across his nose. 'You know why I wear this?' The women cower. The audience, a mixture of Liberians, Americans and Europeans, sip their drinks. 'You know why I wear it?' he bellows. 'Because I was attacked. I was attacked and tortured. They cut off my nose and pushed a bag of red ants into the hole that was left. That is why I wear this strip of cloth. And now I am going to kill you.' The Europeans look uncomfortable. This kind of stuff really happened. But the Liberians laugh. The same laughter I remember from the audience in Mombasa, when one of the characters in the play describes graphically how he was tortured. It is the laughter of recognition and thankfulness that they themselves are now safe. But it is unnerving for us pampered Europeans. We pull long faces through a feat of imagination, not because of any personal experience. While those who suffered, laugh.

SMART TIMES AND ODD BOOTS

The Monrovia museum is in the centre of town. It is built in a mock classical style with great angels at the two corners of the building, a temple to the society created by freed slave settlers who came from America in the early part of the nineteenth century. They arrived on the wettest part of the West African coast, with trunks full of frock coats, winged collars, corsets, hooped skirts and later bustles. They brought not just an American dress sense and plantation manners, but also Christian beliefs and hope for a better world; it would be a world like the one they had come from but without the racial prejudice. The only problem was the locals, the locals with their immodesty, paganism, belligerent ways and refusal to accept the superiority of these American colonizers, or Americo-Liberians as they are called. The quarrel was only settled eight years ago, when civil war broke out and everyone went to hell in a bucket.

Sorsor, the clever driver from the radio station, has managed to arrange for me to visit the museum out of hours – the museum closes at lunchtime. We enter a big empty room festooned with bunting from some past dedication, the only colour in a decaying, shabby space. Sorsor has never been there before but he has a friend, a caretaker, who shows us round. The museum was badly looted in April 1996, mainly by fighters but also by foreign correspondents. So the best and oldest carvings now adorn smart bachelor pads in London and New York.

To the left as you walk into the museum is a huge oil painting. It's an amateurish affair with high Americo-Liberian pretensions; the canvas is slashed but it still clearly shows President Tubman. He was in power a very long time – certainly one of the longest running presidencies in the world – from 1944 to 1971. And there he sits on a grand chair, with two American Presidents standing behind him: one from the past – Abraham Lincoln; and one contemporary – J. F. Kennedy. Tubman holds what looks like a sceptre. A crown would not look out of place. It is a fine example of self-aggrandisement and self-delusion: the Liberian President attended by two American Presidents. Elsewhere there are photographs of the founding fathers and mothers, the house slaves who escaped the field work, took their courage in their hands and crossed the ocean back to the continent of their ancestors, or in some cases of their grandparents, even parents. Here are their photos, still hanging on grimy walls, unwanted by the looters: the women stand in huge, hot bustles and corsets, the men in their frock coats and stiff wing collars, staring out from their frames into a future they could never have imagined. So irrelevant are these grave and formal people, the looters did not even deign to smash their photos up. Here's Z. B. Roberts, nearly a hundred years ago. He's decided to have his photo sitting outside on a wicker chair, young and smart in his suit and wing collar; his legs are crossed, he looks up at the camera from a book he is holding; he is a study in bookishness.

Elsewhere in the museum, there are less historical objects: a battered old office chair and table, a mawkish 1960s print of a muddy, big-eyed crying child, paintings of ships and palm trees in the sunset.

Sorsor has been examining everything very carefully. I thought he might be bored, but I was wrong.

'What do you like best?'

'This is my favourite photo. He reads the caption. '"The inaugural parade along Broad Street in January 1944 at the installation of William V. S. Tubman."' He continues in his low voice. 'Even though I was small when he was in power, I think he is my favourite President.' The photo shows a great motorcade with outriders, the pavements lined with onlookers. The houses look spick and span and hark back to the architecture of the deep South. And one interesting thing: the photo is taken from the roof of this very museum. Thus the scene is framed by the angels' arching wings.

'Why do you like this photo?'

He does not look up, but carries on studying it. 'Everything looked so smart and nice then.'

'Would you like to see it like that again?'

'Very much, very much,' he says softly and sadly.

On the other side of the screen is a photo of the British West Africa Bank, taken some time in the 1930s. The building looks remarkably run down.

Across the room is a huge chair. It is covered in red velvet with gold brocade and tassles. And stretching up from the back is an enormous canopy. All in all it is about seven foot tall – too big to loot. In this chair President Tubman sat in his capacity as patron of the Grand Masonic Lodge. It looks faded and to my mind ridiculously large. Once the source of all influence and power in Monrovia, the Grand Masonic Temple (where this chair came from) was stormed by Samuel Doe in 1980. It was a symbolic act, as much as part of the destruction which went with the *coup d'état*. Not only was the Lodge implicated in corruption and cronyism, but there were stories of the big-big men at the temple commissioning ritual sacrifice. The price for wealth, power and success can be very high – sometimes an eye, a few fingertips, even a whole head. And today it still goes on; only the big-big men do it, I was assured by a journalist. My second week in Liberia the *Human Rights Review* ran a report on the murder of an eleven-year-old boy. His mutilated body was found by the parents near their home – an eye, two teeth, a piece of an ear and his lips had been removed. The police were called and *arrested the father*, says the report, *for what they termed failure to take care of the child. They then inspected the body and discovered that several parts were missing, but suggested to the family not to mention this to the public because the family did not have money to conduct an autopsy on the body. Therefore, they should forget about the case. The body was later buried at Clara Town.* The newspaper published a photo.

No, but Tubman was not so smart. In his day Liberia was hugely dependent on America, and that open-door policy meant big investments but even bigger loans, loans which never got paid off, despite the profits from iron ore and rubber. And although women and up-country people were granted the vote, and although Tubman was the first President of Liberia not to come from Monrovia (he came from Harper), the gap between town and country persisted. And Tubman became jealous of his power; he had a nasty side. When he suspected one of his ministers of plotting a coup, he not only had him shot but had the body left in the centre of Monrovia to rot as a warning. Tubman: the passage of time has definitely made him a nicer person.

As we leave the museum something catches my eye. It is a boot, hanging by a bootlace from a nail. An army boot with an identity label sewn on the side of it. Brigadier General Prince Johnson INPFL. The man who fell out with Charles Taylor and formed a breakaway faction. A label says: *This right foot boot was found in the ruins of the Caldwell Base, formerly occupied by breakaway faction of the NPFL, the INPFL led by Brigadier General Johnson. According to an Armed Forces of Liberia soldier who found the boot, the boot belongs to Prince Johnson. General Johnson assisted greatly in the landing of the West African peacekeeping force at the free port of Monrovia on 24 August 1990.*

How did he lose his boot? I wonder. Was it giving him gyp because it was the wrong size, so he took it off? Did he pass out, or fall asleep, so allowing someone to remove it? Did he pack carelessly when he left the base? It's an intimate object, a boot, and invites speculation of a personal nature.

'Do you think he misses his boot?' I ask Sorsor's friend, the security guard.

He gives a little embarrassed laugh: 'Well, I don't knows. He may not if he hasn't got . . .' His sentence trails off into another laugh.

On 9 September, the label continues, *forces loyal to General Johnson captured former President Samuel Kanyon Doe and subsequently killed him on 10 September 1990*. A few days previously I had read a book about Doe, in which there was the chapter on his death; at first I skipped it. Then I could not resist the desire to look cruelty in the face. I read with pounding heart how they tied his arms, they broke his legs. All this was supervised by Prince Johnson, the owner of the boot. 'I'm a humanitarian,' he says at one point, 'cut off his ear.' Doe's speech becomes both agonized and courteous: 'Gentlemen, I am in considerable pain – I beg you, loosen my arms and I will tell you what you want to know.' His last hours were captured on video. But wasn't Doe the man who supervised the disembowelment of President Tolbert, followed by the parade of ministers in underpants to the beach where they were summarily executed? I expect that seemed a long time ago to Doe as his life's blood slipped away. And Prince Johnson has yet to meet his nemesis. He lives in Nigeria and has no doubt long forgotten his boot.

RUNAWAY TRAIN

The next day I am taken out for lunch at a Lebanese restaurant. After lunch my plan is to go shopping, to a Lebanese supermarket called Stop 'n' Shop. It takes delivery of regular consignments of Tesco's own branded goods. I am becoming a grand little expatriate after only four days. We take our seats in the restaurant near the window. The station manager nudges me as a bigwig enters with a glamorous ladyfriend. Two paces behind them walks his servant carrying his walkie-talkie. Here powerful Liberians, and all Europeans, have walkie-talkies. The Europeans usually carry their own. I greedily guzzle my chickpea and chicken snack and drink my nice cold Coca-Cola. Some children run past the restaurant. The city is full of them; many are former child soldiers who were given drugs to prime them for killing, and they are still addicted. They beg aggressively and have bad tempers if people don't give them enough, I am told. I avoid their eyes and give nothing, and so far they give me no trouble. Some more children, larger ones, now run past the restaurant window, down the road. The manager strides across the floor and looks out. He frowns. A walkie-talkie crackles, and just as it is tended to, another crackles into life – it's at our table.

'OK. There's a problem. Let's move.'

The American administrator of the station looks stressed – but I don't care, I want to finish my yummy snack. I look at the street through the dusty restaurant windows. There are people running.

'Let's get the car out of here before they go for that,' says the administrator.

Go for what? Oh dear, what is happening?

'Um . . . what's happening?'

'Little hiccup,' says the station manager, smiling vaguely.

The restaurant owner starts to close the shutters. We leave the restaurant and get in the car. It seems quieter now. We drive down the road. And then a crowd of people run across our path – like antelope leaping from an invisible enemy.

Women in smart dresses, men in suits, boys in shorts. They don't see us in our car, peering through the windscreen; their faces are contorted with anxiety.

'Go right,' says the American administrator.

The road is solid with people coming up the hill, we can't move.

'OK, keep going straight ahead.'

The car nudges on. The driver is calm and concentrated. I am very quiet. If I keep quiet and don't breathe too deeply I am sure it will be all right. But all this is making me feel very small – about four years old actually. I am in the garden, walking on the flagstones towards the rockery, which is a good place to play. You can pretend it's a mountain. Suddenly I can hear the big train puffing away behind me. What's the train doing in the garden? Trains go on the railway line. Oh no! The train's come off the tracks, and now it's in the garden. It can do what it likes now because it's off the tracks, and I know it's going to chase me. I start to run. But you can't escape from a runaway train. It's too fast and too big. I run as quickly as I can to the back of the house, past the wisteria, past the weedy patch by the vegetable garden – ouch, I've bashed my head on the dining-room window – past the smelly drain, across the backyard, and yes, there's the back door. I throw myself at the back door. It's shut. It's got a handle, but I'm too small to turn it. I bang the door. I kick the door, I howl horribly, 'Mama, Mama, Mama.'

The gates of the radio station swing open and in we drive. All the security men look lively, their walkie-talkies crackling away like mad. Up the stairs we go to the flat at the top of the building, two at a time. Through the gate and up another two floors and we're home.

'Cup of tea, anybody?' asks the station manager kindly as we walk into the flat.

'Yes, please.'

'It's those guys at the Barclays Training Centre. They want their money,' says the administrator.

The explanation is simple – the old national army (Armed Forced of Liberia), now no more than another faction, has not yet been paid off. They will continue a life in uniform until they are given the pension promised them.

'But why did everyone rush around like that?'

'To get out the way. Those guys can cause trouble. And to begin with nobody could tell what was going on. All they know is there could be another round of looting and killing.'

'But they didn't even look where they were going . . .'

'They were running to get their children from school and lock up their houses. People lost each other for months, years, even, during the war. Your shopping will have to wait until tomorrow, I'm afraid,' says the station manager.

Yes, I think, Stop 'n' Shop will have to wait until tomorrow, or else it might be Stop 'n' Get Shot. I keep this feeble joke to myself and enjoy it secretly. Out on the balcony the station manager says he can hear the distant sound of gunfire. I can't hear it from the back of the room. But if I stand up I can see the sea is rolling in and the clouds thickening. It's very hot, and I bitterly wish I was at home, sitting at the piano, playing the Londonderry air, trying to keep up with my girl on her violin, just the two of us bickering mildly about the tempo and tunefulness of our playing. Over the next few days the papers report the damage: four dead and two warehouses looted. Had the ECOMOG tanks not rolled in, it could have spread, so say the locals. But we are now safe as houses.

THE MEASURE OF THE MAN

The ten-day exorcism of evil spirits at the President's Executive Mansion has finally come to an end. I am too busy training to go to the press conference. But I heard it on the radio, and listened carefully. Under the tireless supervision of Bishop Reeves and his Soul Cleansing Clinic, the wickedness which had been unleashed by the civil war and before had, we were told, finally been banished. Bishop Reeves gives a thunderous description of a giant black cat leaping from one corner of the room on to the chest of one of his ministers. There's more: several bolts of lightning are drawn out by the exorcism – an ancient sign of mischief, and one traditionally attributed to women. After Bishop Reeves comes the big man. Charles Taylor's voice is mellifluous but distinct – his accent, a very Americanized version of Liberian English. He has total control over his words, using pauses and emphasis with precision to draw your attention, make you listen. 'I know some of you don't like me, oh yes, I know some of you hate me. But what you must remember is that I have been appointed by God.'

So there you have the measure of the man. Appointed by God. Well, that's pretty non-negotiable. In the past he has denied causing the war, describing it as an act of God so that Liberians might atone for their sins. Like Lenin and Hitler, Taylor is fond of the great imperative. It allows him to disassociate himself from what he has done. He has made it clear he no longer wishes to be referred to as a former warlord. He talks shamelessly of reconstructing the country which he tore up; he has charmed Jimmy Carter, the first and only American President ever to visit Liberia back in 1978 and now a regular visitor in the 1990s.

Taylor is a voracious money-maker, and is busy either running various commercial concessions or selling them off for tidy sums. 'Don't knock him,' says a journalist friend. 'Sure, he's ruthless, a terrific go-getter, but they say that the government procurement department was never as efficiently run as when he was in charge.'

But is he really in charge in the country? He owes the peace of Monrovia to ECOMOG soldiers from Ghana and Nigeria, and resents this deeply; he suspects they'd like to push him out if they had a chance. But ECOMOG's presence is a precondition of American aid and, as the unpaid soldiers incident showed, ECOMOG is effective. The agreement for their continued presence is being renegotiated during my stay, and the President wants to get his point of view across. When he talks, it is as if he's stalking his listeners like a lion stalking a herd of gazelles.

'That assistance from ECOMOG will mean that there must be a certain com-por-tation . . .' (*He slows down menacingly on the archaic word.*) '. . . on the part of those who are meant to assist us. Comportation will mean respect . . .'

(*He hits the 'P' of respect hard.*) '. . .for the government, respect for our laws . . .' (*Hang on – what laws? Didn't the Chief of Police have the head of human rights flogged last week?*)

'. . . we cannot have parallel authority in Liberia. There are rumours that we want ECOMOG out. No! We want a disciplined, retrained ECOMOG to (*pause*) assist (*pause*) the government of Liberia (*pause*) to build its capacity.'

(*His voice has become extra stealthy and spooky.*)

'We don't need a force to keep the peace, and referee between the government and the execution of our laws . . .'

(*I'm losing him here – ECOMOG has never sought to intervene in the country's legal process as far as I know.*)

'This is the fine line.'

(*He's closing in for the kill now. The English becomes literary, the tone more insolent, the pace teasingly slow, the proposition more outrageous.*)

'I need, instead of maybe several battalions of armoured units, I may need a battalion of school teachers from West Africa. I may need a battalion of doctors . . .' (*And with a flourish,*) '. . . send me some doctors.'

Taylor as blues singer J. J. Cale: 'Somebody call for a doctor, I think I'm sick – ain't had no medicine in over a week.'

But no shady lady is going to take Taylor's bread or ravish his body – he's too smart for that. He's more than smart: he's Mr Bigstuff, which means he always gets his way.

He frightens me. Me and the rest of Liberia, too. There are plenty of rumours about him: about what he did during the war, how he relaxes, how he treats his children, what he did to the college drinking supply when he was a student. But despite all this, the swagger still fascinates. I can imagine him in another life appearing on Oprah Winfrey, or the Rikki Lake show, to boos and catcalls from the audience, the villain of some domestic drama but enjoying every minute of his villainy. 'Now, Charles Taylor. What do you have to say to this lovely lady, Liberia? She says you beat her, you stole from her, you burnt her home, you murdered her children, and here she is on the show – so what you got to say to her?' Then Charles Taylor would drop his patrician pronunciation, along with most of his consonants: 'I ain' sayin' nothin'. She ma lady. She love me . . . if I trea' her ba', she love me. If I trea' her goo', she love me. She ma lady.' At this point I imagine the audience starts to cheer at his audacity. Watch out, US State Department for Foreign Affairs: this tiger's not for taming.

Actually Charles Taylor is married. He married Jewel Howard on 28 January 1997 in an up-country wedding in his old fighting HQ, Gbanga. She is deputy governor of the National Bank of Liberia and mother of his teenage son. Ofeibea Quist-Arcton was at the wedding for the BBC and took photos: there's one of the bride and groom looking extravagant but glum. Another of their wedding cake, a surreal affair consisting of two cakes one on top of the other – the whole balanced on four perspex pillars; above the two cakes is perched a sort of gazebo under which are two miniature figures representing the bride and groom. Leading down to the right and left are two perspex stairways. To the right, miniature men are descending; to the left, miniature women. Each staircase ends in another cake. It's a sort of frozen, sugar-frosted Busby Berkeley routine.

By May 1998 Charles Taylor's eye is roving, but only in the name of national unity, you understand. Says the *Independent Eye*: 'President Charles Ghankay Taylor has declared that just as men of the Mandingo ethnic group are getting married to women of their tribes, he as the father of Liberian national will also take a Mandingo tribal woman as his darling wife.' And there's a photo of him with a brooding expression on his face, looking into a multi-ethnic future.

FINDING A GIRL

It's a long time since Charles Taylor had a problem finding a girl. But for others it's not so easy; without a logging concession, a few diamond mines and the aid brigade at your bidding . . . well, you're less of a catch.

Sorsor and I sit in a pleasant suburb. It's lovely and quiet because it's too poor for generators; but there's a bustling small-town prosperity to the place. Some nicely dressed children watch us over a white picket fence and giggle; they don't skulk menacingly waiting for dollars to come their way. Sorsor considers my question carefully – how does one find a partner?

'If you have money, a job, you will always have women around you.'

'Are Liberians more, or less, romantic than they used to be?'

'I would say less, because everyone is trying to work hard to earn a living. Nobody paying much attention to . . .'

'. . . falling in love?' I jump the gun.

'No . . . that's hard to answer. People fall in love but I don't think it is as before, when we had no war.' He bows his head and looks at the dashboard.

'Do you have a girlfriend?'

'Yeah, I got a girlfriend.'

'Do you think you'll marry?'

'I appreciate her a lot, but I'm not actually ready to marry, to get a kid.'

Finding a boy

I ask Ellen-May, a newspaper journalist. She is twenty-three, fine boned, well dressed. But romance is a theme that makes her smile ruefully.

'It's very difficult now. As you know, we've had seven years of crisis. And most of the time you don't know who is who. Most of them were fighters, or should I say ex-combatants. And now you're trying to get someone that will benefit you in the future.'

'So you don't want to hang around with anyone who's fought, who has a gun?'

'Definitely, that is a problem. These boys are so harsh. The minute you say something out of the way, they are on you. A few of my colleagues have been killed because of that – just a common argument.'

'With a boyfriend?'

'Yes. They will have a gun or a knife and strike you and you are dead.'

'So how do you get the low-down on a new guy in your life?'

'Well, their friends won't want to give you the bad news about them. So you have to see for yourself.'

'And what about marriage?'

She laughs. 'You find a boy then you marry. Quickly. Then three months later it's over. The girl discovers things she did not know and it's over.'

'Do you have a boyfriend, Ellen-May?'

'Definitely I do.'

'So you feel you are a lucky woman.'

'Well, I am in the sense that I have a good man now but . . .' she pauses to lift her eyebrows quizzically, '. . . who knows what the future will bring.'

I feel sad. Ellen-May is pretty and deserves more certainty than that.

WAITING FOR BEAUTY

Looking good is important in Liberia, so everyone is looking forward to the Miss University of Liberia Beauty Pageant. 'You'll like it,' says the station manager. Oh really? Women parading on stage in swimsuits to male approval? Not quite my cup of palm wine. But on the other hand . . . I could do with cheering up. Against a backdrop of mutinous soldiers and giant black cats, the glitter and glamour of a beauty pageant is hard to resist.

The location is the Unity building, constructed at great expense by the Tolbert government to house the OAU conference of 1979. The economy was taking a slow nose-dive, the days of the True Whig Party numbered.

We take our seats after a sweaty three-hour wait outside. The hall is packed out; we have patron's tickets which entitle us to sit in the sumptuous executive-style swivel seats in front of the stage. 'You could be sitting where the Ethiopian delegate once sat,' remarks my English host. And so I could. A great expanse of desk is in front of me. It's reminiscent of some very grand school. What kind of pupils were these OAU delegates? Did they pass messages to each other, fall asleep, gossip? Or were they a bunch of goody-goodies, sitting bolt upright, taking notes? The woodwork and uphol-stery are unmarked. There's no graffiti, no 'J. Nyerere woz ere.' This is one of the few buildings in Liberia not to have been looted. Levels of cleanliness and maintenance are hard to ascertain because we are sitting in a strange sort of twilight. Mains electricity is scarcely functioning in Liberia. The organizers have hired too small a generator; it seems capable of powering only three small strip-lights, and they have the effect of silhouetting rather than illuminating anyone on stage.

The shadowy figure of the compere appears; it's just possible to make out he's wearing a zoot suit and sporting an American marine haircut. Then the camera crews of Dove TV, President Charles Taylor's TV station, save the day with their powerful halogen lamps. 'Please put your hands together for the first of our five beautiful ladies.' We put our hands together. But nothing happens. 'Come on now,' says the compere. We try again. Clapping may have kept Tinker-bell alive for Peter Pan, unfortunately it does not bring out the girls. The judges are smiling stiff, polite smiles. One of them is an American businessman, trying his luck at selling optic fibres. He thought judging Miss University of Liberia would be a pleasant way of passing a couple of hours in the evening. Foolish fellow. He's trapped now for the duration. Playing for time, the compere rockets the pageant in a wider context. 'The time for killing your brother is over.' His strategy works – the lethargic audience now springs to life with cheers of approval, but there's nothing to sustain them. The Don Bosco Band strikes up with a languid number, rather killing the excitement of the audience. Some are starting to snooze – after all, it is quarter to two in the morning.

Then there's movement from the wings. We, the audience, can see who is coming but the compere is startled. It's the first contestant in African evening wear. She is Miss Dekhontee Outland. Her favourite star is Whitney Houston and her philosophy is 'Life is what you make it'. She weighs 120 lbs and is a member of the Monrovia Community Mass Choir. She and the other contestants answer simple questions and try to keep their dignity to the whoops and whistles of the audience.

Lucinda, the station receptionist, who is herself very glamorous, digs me sharply in the ribs. 'Should be disqualified – it's no' proper Africa' wear. Headdress no' African.'

'But it's awfully pretty,' I venture.

Lucinda shakes her head, unimpressed. 'Should be disqualified.'

African wear is followed by swimwear as day follows night, and then it's time for the dramatic sequences. As it is now four a.m. we could all do with a bit of drama.

And we are rewarded by Miss Nepce A. C. Nepe appearing in a dowdy housecoat clutching a broom. 'Lord, why me?' she calls out. A few wags in the back row offer suggestions as to why her. The spirit of temptation then appears. 'What are you saying? Me sell myself?' 'Yes,' cry some, 'No,' cry others. She weeps a little. Then she gets up and delivers her tour de force – the housecoat is slipped off to reveal a glamorous little black dress. 'Can I do it?' she asks, this time with a gleam in her eye. 'Of course, of course,' a rowdy group call out, and their incitement catches on with the rest of the audience. She turns her back to us. There is a time lapse. Miss Nepe addresses the audience with a serious face now. 'I started to sell myself; the longer I did, the less I valued my body. I realize the error of my ways.' The crowd now bellows its approval. Miss Nepe has been to hell and back – temptation makes way for redemption. The crowd has followed her every move.

It's now five a.m. and I am too tired to stay. I leave the judges still smiling stiffly. Last year's Miss University of Liberia is asleep, curled up in her cloak, her crown askew. The curfew has just ended.

'Will we be safe?' I ask the driver.

'Only the taxi drivers are vulnerable,' he replies in his clear English, 'because they are carrying their takings – we'll be OK.'

And we are.

THIRTEEN

Recording the Moment

～～～

I am sitting in a house by the sea outside Monrovia. In front of me on the table, a photo album. And there on one page is a photo of my host, Joseph. He's sitting, or rather snoozing, in a chair identical to the one I was snoozing in last week at the beauty contest – the same sandy-coloured, executive-style swivel chair. On the carpet is the same map of Africa pattern. It's the same place all right – Unity Conference Centre, Virginia – but it's eight years ago, March 1990. Joseph gives a chuckle at the snap of his slumbering form: 'We were waiting for the delegates of the Pan-African Telecommunications Union to arrive.' Joseph then worked in the Ministry of Information. He's now a news editor at the radio station. March 1990, Taylor is already slipping backwards and forwards across the border causing mayhem up-country, but he hasn't reached Monrovia yet. Give him another four months. Then Liberia will drop off the list of suitable venues for Pan-African events. And it will stay off the list.

Joseph and Jemima have let me look at their photo album. That it exists still is something of a miracle. 'Just before the house was looted in August 1990 – we'd already gone, but a cousin dropped by and spotted the album. He rescued it for us.'

283

Joseph and Jemima's house is on the campus of the radio station ELWA – Eternal Love Winning Africa. There's the transmitter. ELWA has broadcast its Christian message on and off for over thirty years. In July 1990 Taylor got a hold of it, and with his flair for showmanship broadcast his defiance to President Samuel Doe. Maddened, Doe sent a missile across the bay to shut him up. It's hard to imagine that now; here it's peaceful and a little wild. The house looks out to sea. There are other houses, similar in shape, bunga- lows, but there's plenty of space between them. They once had all the amenities you could want: nice big windows, water, electricity, telephone. Joseph had a car. But that all went when the looting began: everything was either stolen or smashed. Joseph shows me where the ceiling was smashed by looters looking for concealed treasures.

The house is tied to Jemima's job. She is a nurse at the hospital on the campus. As Joseph shows me round, his two sons and their friends dance and jump about, sometimes singing snatches of little hymns: 'I'm marching with the Lor', marching with the Lor' . . .' Every time I turn to look at them they shriek with laughter.

THE WEDDING PHOTO

Joseph and Jemima met through mutual friends. It was a long and determined courtship on the part of Joseph. Jemima was a single parent with a daughter of five. 'She didn't believe I could be serious about her because she had a child,' says Joseph, lifting his eyebrows slightly, smiling and looking down. He's a big comforting sort of man, who takes his time to get where he needs to get.

'Love at first sight, Jemima?'

'For him. Not me.' She looks tough and then laughs.

In her wedding photo Jemima is dressed in white – in a

sort of grand glazed cotton gown. Across her chest is a triangle of gold cloth. The dress is decorated with pearls and lace. Joseph is dressed in a suit. They look serious and calm.

Jemima turns another page of the album.

THE FATHER-IN-LAW

Here is a photo of Joseph's father-in-law. He looks stern in gown and mortarboard, newly graduated.

'Did he approve of Joseph?' I ask.

'No. My father wasn't happy at all.' She pauses. 'We have something in Liberia called tribe,' the tone is delicate, tinged with irony, 'and Joseph and I were not of the same tribe.'

So how did Joseph overcome this thing called tribe, when a large part of the population had been sacrificed on its altar? Joseph looks down, smiles and coughs very gently.

'By showing myself who I am. You see, he had a misconception of the tribe I came from. He was angry with his daughter for coming around me. But he began to see I was not the way he was thinking. And I think the best testimony will be when he was sick and had to be hospitalized here. The way we take care of him changed his whole mind.'

'He now calls Joseph son,' adds Jemima, 'not even son-in-law.'

THE NURSE

Here is a photo of Jemima in nurse's uniform. She is in the dispensary and is momentarily distracted by the photographer from taking drugs out of the cupboard.

'The worst time was in the children's ward. I was newly graduated and one night the children were so bad. First one baby died, then another, a third was dying. The doctor came. I said, "I can't make it. The children are dying. The children are dying." ' Her voice rises with the memory of the moment, then falls back. 'He told me to go home. I had been there too many hours. I used to cry when the babies died. Now I'm more grown up. I don't cry. No, I don't cry any more.' She gives a sad little laugh.

THE BROTHERS

Here's a photo of Jemima's three brothers. It's captioned 'The Three Up to Date Ones'. They are wearing thin jackets over tight shirts, and flared trousers; one of them has his hair in an Afro. The photo is in black and white with a hint of sepia which makes it seem as though it were taken a very long time ago. But it was only the mid-1980s.

'That one is attending the university,' says Jemima. 'He's studying . . .'

'Biology,' Joseph prompts.

'This one is dead.'

'How did he die?' My voice goes low; I am unhappy asking the question.

'He was killed when he was trying to escape, to get to Nimba Country, because he was Gio – the Krahn soldiers killed him.'

She moves on to the third brother with only a fraction of pause. 'This one is in the United States.' We turn a few pages and there he is again in an American children's playground pushing his two children on the swings; they are wearing thick jackets and woolly hats. And here's a photo of his wife, walking down the path from a neat modern house, carrying shopping. She's smiling. Jemima studies it carefully.

'I miss my brother, I miss his children and I miss his wife.'

'She's pretty,' I venture.

'She's pretty, and a very lovely lady.'

And here's a photo of Jemima taken just two weeks ago.

'I just felt like having this photo taken. I would like to show my husband that I'm still pretty and young. So I had the tailor make me this suit. And then had the photo taken.'

'What do you think, Joseph, still pretty and young?'

He takes the photo, studies it and smiles gently. 'She reminds me in this photo of when I first met her; very nice looking, and my memories go back . . .'

It is now perfectly dark outside. Inside the candle is struggling to light our faces. We are all tired. Too tired to talk much now. The roar of the Atlantic and the pulse of crickets take over; then a third sound insinuates itself – the throb of an impatient car engine. The driver has come to take me away.

Epilogue

❧

It's a cold wet day in Muswell Hill. But what do I care? I've just taken delivery of a little bundle from Supasnaps. I can't wait to get home. I'll just have a little peep now as I walk along the pavement. Yes, there are four children, gazing solemnly at the camera. Ah but in this print that lovely light that comes with the gloaming has been reduced to a dull grey.

Here are the two little girls on their own. In this photo they look cold in their cotton dresses. But I remember it was warm that late afternoon. And I remember how exquisite their faces were in repose. Here they are pulling grotesque expressions at the camera, which retaliates by rendering them underexposed.

And here are Joseph and Jemima. Technically, this photo is even worse: very pale and grainy. But you can see they are looking at each other lovingly; she trades serious eyes for his smiling lips. Behind them, what should be the rich green of the grass at the edge of the beach has come out dark and matted; only in places does the camera allow the light to catch it. In the far distance, caught in a haze, high on the promontory, is a lovely cluster of houses nestling among trees – impossible to say if they are sound or derelict, lived in or deserted. And then, of course, there's the steely Atlantic sea, barely ruffled, but coming in fast. A thick grey sky hangs above, waiting.

Acknowledgements

❧

Within and without the continent I have been helped, advised and inspired by many people, among them: John Collins, Kuldip Sondhi, Bode Sowande, George Bennett, Sola Odunfa, Jerusha Arothe-Vaughn, Liz Blunt, Sousa Jamba, Catherine Cole, Charles Mulekwa, Nazli George, Frederick Philander, Adam Lusekelo, Mike Popham, Laura Harwood-Smith, Deborah Lee, Dan Macmillan, Jeillo Edwards, Nnamdi Moweta, Gabriel Gbadamosi, Gcina Mhlope, and Zenga Longmore.

Also thanks to all friends and colleagues in the African Service of the BBC World Service for the discussions, and arguments, and shared pursuit of new ways to entertain and inform the listeners, among them: K. B. Mensah, the late Dorothy Grenfell-Williams, Robin White, Veronique Edwards, Neil Curry, Florence Akst, Neville Harms, Akwe Amosu, Max Bankole-Jarrett, Mary Harper, João van Dunem, Penny Boreham, and Israel Wamala.

I should also like to point out that this book came to life thanks largely to the deft midwifery skills of my agent, Christopher Sinclair-Stevenson, and editor, Mary Mount.